EARLY BUDDHISM: A NEW APPROACH

CURZON CRITICAL STUDIES IN BUDDHISM

General Editors:

Charles S. Prebish and Damien Keown

The **Curzon Critical Studies in Buddhism Series** explores the complex and extensive Buddhist tradition from a variety of perspectives, using a range of different methodologies. The Series is diverse in its focus, including historical studies, textual translations and commentaries, sociological investigations, bibliographic studies, and considerations of religious practice as an expression of Buddhism's integral religiosity. It also presents materials on modern intellectual historical studies, including the role of Buddhist thought and scholarship in a contemporary, critical context and in the light of current social issues.

THE REFLEXIVE NATURE OF AWARENESS
Paul Williams

BUDDHISM AND HUMAN RIGHTS
Edited by Damien Keown, Charles Prebish, Wayne Husted

ALTRUISM AND REALITY
Paul Williams

WOMEN IN THE FOOTSTEPS OF THE BUDDHA
Kathryn R. Blackstone

THE RESONANCE OF EMPTINESS
Gay Watson

IMAGING WISDOM
Jacob N. Kinnard

AMERICAN BUDDHISM
Edited by Duncan Ryuken Williams and Christopher Queen

PAIN AND ITS ENDING
Carol S. Anderson

THE SOUND OF LIBERATING TRUTH
Edited by Sallie B. King and Paul O. Ingram

BUDDHIST THEOLOGY
Edited by Roger R. Jackson and John J. Makransky

EMPTINESS APPRAISED
David F. Burton

THE GLORIOUS DEEDS OF PŪRṆA
Joel Tatelman

CONTEMPORARY BUDDHIST ETHICS
Edited by Damien Keown

EARLY BUDDHISM: A NEW APPROACH
Sue Hamilton

EARLY BUDDHISM: A NEW APPROACH

The I of the Beholder

Sue Hamilton

CURZON

First Published in 2000
by Curzon Press
Richmond, Surrey
http://www.curzonpress.co.uk

Typeset in Sabon by LaserScript Ltd, Mitcham, Surrey
Printed and bound in Great Britain by
TJ International, Padstow, Cornwall

British Library Cataloguing in Publication Data
A catalogue record of this book is available from the British Library

Library of Congress Cataloguing in Publication Data
A catalogue record for this book has been requested

ISBN 0-7007-1280-1 (Hbk)
ISBN 0-7007-1357-3 (Pbk)

To Richard and Catherine, with love

Contents

Acknowledgements

I am grateful to the many people, family, friends, colleagues and students, who have contributed, directly and indirectly, to the completion of this book.

More particularly, my profound thanks are extended to Muriel Anderson, Bryan Appleyard, Tyrrell Burgess, Damien Keown and Anthony Storr for their comments on various draft stages of the book. Their generosity in giving up their time to offer invaluable constructive criticism is greatly appreciated. I accept full responsibility for the final version.

To Richard and Catherine Sarson, whose support was at times a *sine qua non*, thanks always.

Abbreviations

AN	*Aṅguttara Nikāya*
Bṛ. Up.	*Bṛhadāraṇyaka Upaniṣad*
Ch. Up.	*Chāndogya Upaniṣad*
DA	*Dīgha Nikāya Aṭṭhakathā*
DN	*Dīgha Nikāya*
J	*Jātaka*
MN	*Majjhima Nikāya*
PED	Pali-English Dictionary, PTS edition
PTS	Pali Text Society
Ṛv	*Ṛg Veda*
Śat. Br.	*Śatapatha Brāhmaṇa*
SN	*Saṃyutta Nikāya*
Thag.	*Theragāthā*
Vin	*Vinaya*

INTRODUCTION

Sources, Methods and Caveats

This book is an attempt to draw out the ideas about and understanding of human experience in early Buddhism. With particular reference to central doctrinal teachings relating to the issue and nature of selfhood, continuity, and the operating of subjective cognitive processes, it seeks to present such teachings as coherent in themselves and as collectively contributing to a coherent overall picture of the early Buddhist view of the experiential world in its entirety. I also hope to show that apparent anomalies, inconsistencies and, indeed, incoherencies in previous scholarly and traditional interpretations of certain key issues such as the *anattā*, not-self, doctrine are unnecessary, and that a close reading of the relevant texts suggests that an alternative interpretation is both more appropriate and more informative in the context of the teachings as a whole.

I am drawing primarily on a group of texts known as the *Nikāyas* of the Pali canon. The Pali canon is comprised of a large collection of texts, written in Pali, belonging to the Theravāda school of Buddhism. The canon has three sections (called *piṭakas* – baskets), and the *Nikāyas* comprise most of what is called the *Sutta Piṭaka*, the section on doctrinal teachings. So when I use the expression 'early Buddhism', it is to what is contained in the Pali *Sutta Piṭaka* that I am referring. These texts are only one of the sources of early Buddhism known to us. Other sources, in languages other than Pali (notably Sanskrit and Chinese), and belonging to schools of Buddhism other than Theravāda, also represent a very early period in the history of Buddhism. In using the term early Buddhism about what is to be found in the *Nikāyas*, I am not seeking to imply that the Theravāda sources are the earliest, or that what they say is more truly representative of early Buddhist teachings. Nor am I seeking to establish an identifiable period in the history of Buddhism that might universally be labelled 'the early period'.[1] I am, rather, using it for simplicity of expression to refer to what is to be found in some of the early texts.

In focussing on this specific collection of texts, I am not seeking to make claims about the teachings, textual interpretations, beliefs or practices of Theravāda Buddhism as a whole. Such an exercise would require one to consult a far wider corpus of canonical, commentarial and other Theravāda textual material than just the *Nikāyas*.[2] Theravāda Buddhism is a living tradition that has grown and spread from its beginnings in the Indian sub-continent over a period of nearly two and a half millennia. It would be extraordinary if one relatively small section of its texts precisely represented all of its understanding of Buddhist teachings. It would also be unlikely that such a thing as 'the Theravāda view' would be arrived at. Because it has grown and become as diversified as it has, it would be surprising if different Theravāda communities within the tradition did not emphasise or concentrate on different parts of their textual corpus, ranging as it does from monastic disciplinary rules to story literature, doctrinal treatises to technical scholarly definitions, *Heilsgeschichte*-type chronicles to meditation manuals. There is evidence that different sections of the canonical parts of this material were originally preserved by different specialising groups.[3] It would therefore be very much within the tradition if different communities were to regard different aspects of the teachings as a whole as central to their understanding and practice of the religion, or to relate certain aspects of the teachings to their particular situations. Because the *Nikāyas* are part of the canon of the Theravāda tradition, though, and because what they contain is about doctrine, it is quite possible that some of what I write will correspond to a Theravāda understanding of the material. But I am not trying to establish that it does or, in offering alternatives to traditional interpretations, that it should.

Furthermore, in presenting what seems to me to be a coherent and fairly comprehensive account of human experience as suggested by the *Nikāyas*, it is not my aim to establish that this, definitively, is 'what the Buddha taught'. It may be that it was: but we cannot know that it was. This uncertainty is because the early teachings recorded in the *Sutta Piṭaka* of the Pali canon, and the early monastic community rules of discipline contained in the

Vinaya Piṭaka, were for many years (more than three centuries) preserved orally. At some stage during the latter part of this period, the earlier sections of *abhidhamma* material, the more scholarly and technical interpretations of the teachings, began to be added (perhaps incrementally), eventually becoming the third section of the canon (the *Abhidhamma Piṭaka*). The canonical material as a whole first began to be written down in Sri Lanka towards the end of the first century BCE.[4] But the extant versions of these texts date from the fifth century CE, when Buddhaghosa compiled the final version of the canon at the same time as writing and/or translating the commentaries on the canonical texts into Pali.[5] Recent scholarship has pointed out[6] that care is therefore needed both in separating out what is called the canon and in ascertaining its status since all of the material derives from within a developed tradition. And it follows that any claim to have arrived at a core teaching coming directly from the Buddha would be difficult if not impossible to substantiate.

That having been said, I believe that familiarising oneself with the texts over a period of years renders one hard put to deny that there are aspects of the *Sutta* and *Vinaya Piṭakas* of the canon that are significantly different in content and style both from the *Abhidhamma Piṭaka*, which comprises scholarly technicalities and explanations of what it itself says are earlier texts, and from the commentaries. If one were to proceed as if the compiler of the canon did not preserve the earlier material he inherited separately from its commentaries, as has been suggested,[7] this would not, in my view, be doing him justice. Furthermore, it is in these very canonical texts that evidence can be found of their oral preservation from the very early stages of the Buddhist tradition. There is considerable evidence that conscious efforts were made to ensure accuracy in such preservation, and that accuracy continued to be a factor when teachings began to be written down.[8] The prime reason why accuracy was desired was to preserve the teachings for as long as possible. The specialising groups who undertook this would have taken their task extremely seriously, not merely for the sake of taking pride in their accuracy but because the survival of the Buddha's teachings, the *Dhamma*, depended on it. As key figures from the early stages of the developing tradition, I think it reasonable to assume that such work would have been highly respected by later successors. And in my view the retention of the evidence of organised oral preservation in the canonical texts suggests that the compiler and commentary-writer(s) were actually seeking accurately to preserve the earlier material independently from the commentaries themselves rather than simply to produce a body of material representing the Theravāda point of view in the fifth century CE.

Another feature of the *Sutta* (and *Vinaya*) *Piṭaka* that has been included by the compiler also suggests a faithful preservation of at least some of the earlier material in its original form. This is the wealth of references, direct or allusory, to the thought and teachings of others who lived contemporaneously with the Buddha during the fifth century BCE. It is such references that have helped scholars to build a comprehensive picture of the context in which the teachings were first given.[9] I therefore do not accept that it is futile to imagine that anything found in the canon is earlier than the commentaries just because "the same tradition, at the same time and in the same place, has simultaneously preserved for us both the canon as we have it and the commentaries."[10] Rather, I take it that it is highly likely that the early reciters of different parts of the canonical corpus originally memorised the texts specifically to ensure accurate oral transmission until they were written down, and that their work continued to be safeguarded and recorded.

Following on from these points, and notwithstanding any further problems and limitations there may be to understanding what is and what is not 'a canon',[11] I think much can be gained rather than lost by adopting a common-sensical approach to the material. Some parts of the canonical material, large chunks of the *Sutta Piṭaka* particularly, are pre-supposed by other parts of the Pali material as a whole, including the *Abhidhamma* and the commentaries. It seems reasonable, therefore, to use the books that incorporate those seemingly earlier sections as one's starting point. The *Nikāyas* of the *Sutta Piṭaka* constitute no small body of material (some twenty-five books) and provide us with so rich a resource in their own right that it is my opinion that one need make no apology for choosing them as the focus of one's study. One can, I think, regard them as representing what is found in the doctrinal treatises of early Pali Buddhism which the writers of the *Abhidhamma* and the commentators used as their own foundational material. Though this approach does treat the *Nikāyas* generally as earlier than or prior to the rest of the Pali canonical and non-canonical texts as stated,[12] it makes no claims as to their actual origin or date. And though it may not in fact represent 'what the Buddha taught', it seems reasonable to think that it is the nearest one can come to it.

One other aspect of choosing the *Nikāyas* as my main source material and in treating them as a source of ideas which I then present as coherent may be open to criticism. This is what has been called 'synchronic essentialism'.[13] In effect, this is synchronically analysing a large, ancient, and undatable collection of texts without taking into account how they in all probability changed over a period of time. While one can thus come up with what seem to be the 'essentials' of what they say, it may be that because the material developed incrementally there was never a time when the tradition itself viewed it in quite that way. I do not see a way around this problem and accept any criticism that may be due. Having said that, given the way the Pali Buddhist texts were preserved and compiled I do not see how anyone could treat the *Sutta Piṭaka* other than broadly synchronically. Any attempt to take into account a diachronic perspective would immediately render one vulnerable to far more serious criticism from those who suggest one should take the *entire* Pali canonical corpus as being 'simultaneously preserved'. I would also restate that I am not seeking to establish how Theravāda Buddhism itself might understand, or have at any time in the past understood, the texts. Rather, I am seeking to draw out some of the ideas as stated or implied in the texts themselves.

In taking this approach, what I hope to arrive at is a comprehensive picture of the worldview which provides the theoretical basis of teachings that were originally given solely for the purpose of putting them into practice. Over and over again it is stated in the texts that the Buddha taught only what would help people to achieve the goal of nirvana. And the style in which the early teachings are given notably shies away from theoretical underpinnings. Indeed, there are strong suggestions that theoretical speculations – especially those to do with metaphysics – are both pointless and potentially misleading in the quest for nirvana. In spite of this, and notwithstanding my profound respect for this last point (which I hope will be apparent as I write), all systems of practice *are* based on theoretical underpinnings whether the latter are explicit or not. At the very least, there are *reasons why* the systems of practice are thought to be efficacious in achieving their aim, and reasons why *that* is their aim. If in the early texts these largely remain unexplicated, this does not mean they are not there at all. This view is supported by later Buddhists who presented the teachings in a completely different, even abstract, way. Nāgārjuna, for example, a great Buddhist thinker who lived during the first century of the Common Era, has become known to Westerners interested in Buddhism as 'a philosopher' (in the sense of theoretician), and 'Buddhist philosophy' is thought to start with him. His style of writing is such that it is sometimes asked of his seminal work, the *Madhyamaka Kārikā*, whether it is 'just a philosophical treatise' or whether it was intended to form the basis of a system of practice. But Nāgārjuna himself stated he was merely drawing out the implications of what the Buddha had taught. And this is further reflected both in the fact that the word *madhyamaka* means 'the middle way', which is an expression used about the early Buddhist teachings from the beginning, and also in the fact that Nāgārjuna makes frequent reference in the *Kārikā* to the Pali texts. He takes it as axiomatic that there is no point to theory without practice. Theory and practice are understood as complementary, two sides of the same coin. Furthermore, in the early material, there are suggestions to the effect that clarity of understanding of the teachings can be helped by testing their meaning. Leaving aside whether or not one chooses to put it into practice, the aim to draw out the theoretical basis of early Buddhist teachings – what I have called the ideas contained in the texts – is therefore neither an entirely non-Buddhist nor a wholly anachronistic exercise.

This aim has been arrived at via two routes. First, it builds on aspects of my previous work. This has focused on central areas of Buddhist doctrinal teachings, notably those concerned with the structure of the human being, including the notion of identity and how this relates to personal experience (and vice versa – how personal experience relates to identity). Indeed, it has come to seem to me that the Buddhist teachings found in the *Sutta Piṭaka* emphasise above all else the centrality of personal experience. It is this that has drawn me to continue this area of research because the having of personal experience is the foundational aspect of common-human-being-ness between all people. This is not to suggest that we all have the same experiences, but, rather, that what we have most in common is that we all do have experience – and, most fundamentally, the experience of being a human being on earth. Moreover, we all experience the notion of identity, of being human being A and not human being B. Along with countless others in the fields not only of Buddhism and other religions but also of philosophy, psychology, the social sciences, and even physics, as well as those whose interest is existential rather than professional, I find this a very interesting and relevant area for research. I therefore hope that this book will contribute not just to Buddhist Studies but to broader discussions about issues such as epistemology, identity, and the nature of experience.

Second, I have over the years found myself perplexed by some of the Buddhist teachings, at least by how they are often traditionally or superficially presented or described. Though not a Buddhist myself, I shared with many others an immediate interest in them. But aside from the attractiveness and profundity of their ethical teachings, I found aspects of them, or at least the way they were put, either meaningless or apparently internally incoherent. So I found myself either unable to grasp the point of one of the teachings taken in the context of the others, or, if taken on its own face value alone, unable to see how it could fit in with the rest of them. And for teachings that seemed to centre on the human being, much of what they apparently said seemed counter-experiential, at least to this human being. My feeling of perplexity was intensified because one of the cardinal factors about Buddhism is that one is not expected to make leaps of faith about the teachings: one is meant to be able to check them for oneself.

Much of this, Buddhists would say, is to be done in and through meditation; but there are also several indications in the *Nikāyas* themselves that, at least initially, Buddhists would also say that it is not an illegitimate exercise to attempt to find some more obvious level of coherence. In particular, in the early stages of the tradition it was the task of the disciples of the Buddha to decide whether or not individual teachings were to be included in the growing corpus of legitimate material on what was the *Dhamma* (the true teachings), sometimes referred to as the teacher's (i.e. Buddha's) doctrine (*satthu sāsanaṃ*).[14] In an environment where different teachings or parts of teachings were being preserved orally by a variety of people, it is not difficult to imagine the problems associated with such decisions. One of the principal criteria for making such a decision was whether or not the material in question was compatible with the teachings as a whole: if someone claimed to have 'heard' (*sutaṃ*) or 'received' (*paṭiggahītaṃ*) from himself, the community, a group of monks or a single monk, that something is the teacher's doctrine, it could be so regarded if it was compatible with the other teachings.[15] Another passage suggests that an even more subjective assessment is permissable (if difficult to put into practice): "You may understand as the teacher's doctrine those things (or teachings – *dhammā*) which you know lead to ... the goal (*nibbāna*)."[16]

The suggestion embodied in such criteria is that what one should seek to understand is the spirit rather than the letter of the teachings: and it follows from this that overall coherence was always meant to be of central importance. That it was the spirit rather than the letter of them that mattered is further supported by the style in which the central doctrinal teachings have been preserved in the *Nikāyas*: they are nearly all given cryptically, open to various interpretations but with no one definitive interpretation attached. It is, indeed, this cryptic equivocal style that has allowed there to be confusion and disagreement about what the teachings mean at all, both within the world of Buddhist scholarship and, more importantly, within Buddhist tradition itself. The later Theravāda Buddhist *Abhidhamma* scholars, for example, pronounced the style of the early material to be just 'a way of putting things' (*pariyāya*). And though they then interpreted and explained the teachings in definitively 'put' terms (*nippariyāyena*) in their own texts, the early ambiguity accords with the further point that it has always been a characteristic of Buddhism that on hearing or coming across its teachings one should understand them not according to the teacher's rules or any intrinsic doctrinal criteria but according to one's own abilities. This is not at all an excuse to deconstruct or relativise in the interests of bending the material according to fashionable academic methodological criteria.[17] Rather, it is a check against the unquestioning acceptance of a teaching as gospel that in fact does not make sense to one. This is different from how most of the religious traditions with which Westerners are familiar believe their teachings should be understood, but in the context in which the Buddhist teachings were first given the contrast was with the way the Brahmin priests insisted that literal precision and accuracy (the letter and not the spirit) were more important criteria in their religion than meaning and understanding. So important was it considered by the Buddha that one arrived at one's own understanding of the teachings, that it is recorded in the texts that when asked who would succeed him as teacher when he died his reply was that we should be "lamps for ourselves and use the *Dhamma* as a lamp".[18] Similarly, it is stated that clarity of understanding of the *Dhamma* can be aided by investigating it for oneself.[19]

In the light of all this, and given my own confusion, I felt that it might be legitimately productive to try to draw out some of the ideas from the teachings as given in the *Sutta Piṭaka* and see if they might be understood coherently and if one might suggest what they mean in terms that make sense. In so doing, I also hoped that the place of early Buddhist thought in the history of ideas might more readily be apparent.

The nature of the material I am working with, however, is such that in certain contexts drawing out the ideas has involved a certain amount of speculation as to implications, connections between points, the way things fit together. In many cases key aspects of the teachings are not explicitly explained but are only suggested by the material. In some such cases no interpretation has previously been suggested, either by scholars or Buddhists. Indeed, the material is so abundant that there is a great deal of it that has not been written about in any detail. And in common with other religious traditions, Theravāda Buddhism has long since accepted certain key features of their textual material as representative of all of it without continuing to question whether this is justified. In other cases, the way I draw out particular suggestions from certain passages is only appropriate in the light of previous suggestions and interpretations I have made. In other words, one might say that what I am doing is building up a specific hermeneutic: if one starts in a certain way, one can build up from there and various interpretations of the material follow. So in some contexts my interpretation of what is suggested by the material might not be the only possible one. In such cases my guidelines have been consistency, plausibility, and coherence – none of which preclude the possibility that other interpretations might be equally legitimate, and might, indeed, fit happily alongside mine.

I write in a climate in which an aim empathetically to draw out ideas from primary source material in this way might be considered unfashionable, at least in certain quarters. There seems to be an increasing tendency to give priority to methodological theories, pedantic detail, excessively long footnotes listing countless cross-references of secondary as well as primary sources, feminist or environmental approaches, and even computer skills. Such priorities mean that books and articles spend as long discussing and agreeing with or refuting other scholars' methodologies for studying or writing about the subject as they spend on the subject itself; that whole books and articles are written pedantically analysing linguistic variations, paying no regard to the fact that language is an instrument whose practical usage rarely takes such things into account and whose communicative meaning is almost never understood in such a way; that in reading such books and articles it is almost impossible to follow the thread of what is being said as one is diverted to the interminable minutiae of the notations; that primary sources are anachronistically viewed through the spectacles of late twentieth century modish concerns; and that technology that should be a tool has become a toy to some and a tyranny to others.

A great deal of the work produced in such ways is interesting and/or useful, and, indeed, in some cases superbly scholarly. But I believe that any work that seeks to draw out and discuss ideas from, and make interpretations of, primary material is better served by giving priority to a genuinely empathetic approach to one's subject area – though it goes without saying that this must be coupled with appropriate scholarly care. Empathy goes a very long way towards ensuring that one does the material justice. While precluding apologetics, it ensures that one is not reductionist (in any sense) about what one finds; while seeking to understand, it requires that one be faithful to the conceptual framework underpinning the content of the material; while struggling to balance apparent inconsistencies in the material, it prefers to take into account that the abundance and nature of the sources are much more likely to have resulted in the preservation of different ways of saying the same thing than to make academically rigorous but unenlightening lists of different words; and while ensuring that one does not distort the material merely for one's own intellectual satisfaction, it seeks to express what one finds in terms that can have meaning in today's world – not in some modernising sense but so that the material itself may be better understood.

This latter point (that is, seeking to express what one finds in terms that can have meaning in today's world) is one about which I have come to feel strongly – though in itself it presents at least one major problem, which I will come to. A very great deal is written in the field of Buddhist studies about what terms (originally written in Pali, Sanskrit, Chinese, Tibetan and so on) mean and how they should be translated and defined. I have written in such vein myself. But there is very little consensus about the translations and/or definitions of any term, and more scholarly time is then spent explaining either why one is in agreement with others' translations and definitions, or why one disagrees and wishes to suggest alternatives. One problem is that one often finds that in being faithful to the literal meaning of a particular term, the way in which one defines or translates it itself needs further explaining. And if one is not to go on explaining indefinitely one tends to settle for definitions or translations that are unsatisfactory because they do not convey what one is saying to the reader in terms s/he can readily understand. Another is that one finds that a perfectly ordinary word one wants to use is no longer permitted to have its perfectly ordinary meaning because it has been appropriated for some technical usage in any one of a number of disciplines that a reader might then accuse one of not knowing about. And such accusations seem almost intended to indicate the intellectual superiority of the reader rather than to question the appropriateness of the use of the word in the work one has written. Furthermore, it is this situation as a whole that exacerbates any tendency subsequent authors may have to pedantry.

I cannot believe that others do not also find it extraordinarily frustrating to find that the central thesis of a piece of work is sidelined because of a disagreement over a translation of terms, even though the thesis is not thereby put in question. Conversely, I cannot believe that others do not also find it frustrating to read otherwise excellent scholarly work about which one keeps wondering what the writer means by the unusual English words (or combinations of words) s/he is using in defining or translating non-English terms. And I cannot believe that others do not also feel that pedantry serves more to obscure than to reveal the meaning of anything more conceptual than a grammatical rule.

In short, I do not think it should be an aim of Buddhist scholarship that translations from original languages should be so literal or technically faithful that English readers cannot any more readily understand what the translations mean than what the original means. I do not think it should be considered a virtue either to refrain from using ordinary words for clarity or to criticise others for using them. And provided one is faithful, indeed rigorous, in applying empathy and care in one's attempt to understand the ideas in one's material, I do not think pedantry should have any place in the exercise.[20] Rather, I think the aim of the writer should be clarity of communication to one's reader of what one wants to say. And then that if what one is saying is important to one's thesis, it should not be the words one uses that are the criterion by which the reader judges the thesis.[21]

The main problem that arises from the aim to use meaningful English is that many fields of study, including Buddhist studies, require one to use material that is not just in a different language but that originates in a different time, place, and conceptual framework from our own. Even when one can ascertain most of the contextual factors, general and specific, that need to be taken into account in understanding the material (and there is already available some foundational work for early Buddhism in this respect[22]), there remains the deep problem of transposing expressions across millennia and cultural worldviews. Even if one believes one is justified merely in attempting to do this, for whatever reason, some of the terms one comes across in Pali texts, many of which are key or commonly used terms, are simply untransposable into any English that makes meaningful sense. Tathāgata, for example, which is a frequently used epithet of the Buddha, translates as 'thus-gone-one' if one is being literal. Even when one explains that it refers to someone who has achieved a state of having left behind any notion of independent individuality,[23] it is still virtually impossible to find a comfortable conceptual place for this within our own cultural worldview. The more so in this case as the term refers to a living human being (the Buddha) who still appears to be, and is certainly functioning as, an individual. For other key terms, the problem lies in the danger of a translation resulting in misinterpretation. The term *dukkha*, used in the first of the Four Noble Truths taught by the Buddha, is perhaps the classic in this respect. Until recent years, *dukkha* was usually translated as 'suffering', with 'pain' or 'ill' being common alternatives; now 'unsatisfactory' is more usually used. The term describes the intrinsic characteristic of human existence, and its meaning refers to the fact that all aspects of human existence prior to achieving the goal of nirvana are impermanent, and hence ultimately unsatisfactory or imperfect. In the context in which the first Noble Truth was given, the prevailing concern of religious seekers was to find permanence (in the sense of immortality): this was considered to be perfection. So in the Buddha's teaching the point was being made that it was not to be found within cyclical human experience. But it is important for proper understanding of what *dukkha* means to realise that it is being used to make a truth statement and not a value judgement. It therefore has no more intrinsic value attached to it than does the statement 'it is raining'. So even though words such as unsatisfactory or imperfect may in principle be used to describe a state of affairs factually, the negative connotations that they have in normal usage are potentially misleading if the way in which the term *dukkha* is used is not understood. In particular, it is not stating that all human experience is unpleasant.

I think the way to handle the tension between the aim for clarity and the untransposability of some terms is again to apply commonsense. The main criterion for this is in fact obvious: can this be said simply and clearly in English without distorting its original meaning? If it can, then so well and good. If not, then it seems both unnecessary and undesirable to make do with a problematic or misleading English expression in place of a Pali one. English-speaking scholars working with Greek, Latin, German, French (and so on) have long since arrived at this conclusion and expect their readers to work at understanding untranslated words in their contextual terms. Indeed, almost all disciplines require one to assimilate certain of their key terms: and I see no reason why Buddhism should be different. Though one usually learns a relatively superficial application of a given term at first, and, indeed, may have to keep reminding oneself of this, one is then gradually able to build up one's understanding of its usage and the extent of its reference. Sometimes a full understanding requires imagination on the part of a reader more than anything else: imagining the conceptual context in which the word applies so that one can understand it without its being transposed into English.

In this book I have adopted the criterion as described above as my yardstick in deciding how to handle terms. As I have said, my aim has been to draw out some of the ideas found in the *Sutta Piṭaka* concerning human experience and to express these in a way that has meaning in today's world, whether or not the reader has any expertise in Buddhist studies. Wherever possible I have, therefore, used simple English in translating from the Pali, with qualifications where necessary. In some places, where translations from the Pali also required clear communication of the conceptual point being made, I have used considerable licence in making the point in English. If, however, it seems that a term cannot helpfully be transposed into English then I have left it in Pali. Sometimes this applies to key terms relating to major topics of the book, and in such cases I hope that their reference will eventually become clear to the extent that the terms themselves do not matter. I would in any case ask any non-specialist readers to give priority to understanding the reference in favour of the word itself: that is to say – and in a Buddhist context this could not be more profoundly relevant – the spirit rather than the letter.

I stated above that the subject of this book builds on aspects of my previous work, and I will start, in Chapter One, by setting the scene in this respect. In Chapter Two, I shall give some contextualising background, both historical and conceptual, for the study as a whole. This will be my version of what Richard Gombrich was the first to call "Gotama Buddha's problem situation".[24] Though I hope to provide sufficient information for a proper understanding of the context in which Buddhism started, because this is not specifically a history of the period the interested reader who would like more detail may have to consult other sources. I will go on in Chapter Three to establish more fully than hitherto that the central focus of the teachings of early Buddhism is the understanding of human experience. This will necessarily involve some rehearsal of the teachings of the Buddha that a scholar of Buddhism might find tedious. But I would ask such a reader to bear with me. I include the rehearsal not just for other readers but also because it is only if one considers the teachings as a package, so to speak, that one can see certain features that might otherwise be easy to overlook. And I also believe that understanding of the package of teachings is facilitated by the slightly unusual angle from which I present them. In Chapter Four, I will draw out and discuss the implications of the doctine of dependent origination as it relates to ourselves as experiencing subjects and the world that we have experience of. In the course of this I shall refer to the way Buddhist cosmology has been referred to as a spacial metaphor for the spiritual path.[25] I will discuss this metaphor further in the light of the experiential focus of the teachings, and contextualise the use of this particular metaphor by discussing other common and relevant metaphors found in the early texts. In Chapters Five and Six I will attempt to draw out from the foregoing some further implications about the nature of subjectivity and objectivity respectively. And in Chapter Seven I will suggest a way one might understand the nature of the world by means of a specific ontological model. Finally, in Chapter Eight I will discuss the extent and importance of the Buddha's use of metaphor, including references to Māra, variously a tempter figure, the supervisor of hellish realms, and a representative of death (*māra* means death), and the way these relate to ignorance. I shall also discuss how one might best understand dependent origination as it applies to karma (that actions have consequences). And in tandem with this I will consider the Buddha's concept of personal responsibility, the promise of being able to change and improve one's experience, and the possibility of freedom from rebirth.

I should perhaps make a brief preliminary comment about my focus on the human being to the exclusion of other sentient beings. For Buddhists, and Indians generally, the cosmos is a highly complex, multi-levelled place in which many types of beings live in a wide variety of states and conditions – whether or not we are aware of them.[26] So as well as human beings, and all the other sentient beings of which we are all aware, there may be both lesser and greater beings which exist in ways or places we do not, or cannot, see. Buddhists (and again Indians generally) believe that *all* beings – 'gods', humans, animals, demons, and so on – greater or lesser, seen or unseen, are subject to cyclic existence and in the long term may aspire to the same goal of liberation. Though in order to avoid repetition I will not keep referring to all these other beings, none of what I write is intended to suggest that they are not thought of in this way. Rather, I focus on the human being because it is at that level of existence that the teachings are given and to be practised: the Buddha was a human being addressing other human beings.

As to my use of predominantly masculine pronouns, I have written elsewhere[27] about the inappropriateness of sex discrimination in the light of what Buddhist doctrinal teachings mean. But however inappropriate it may be it is nevertheless difficult (though perhaps only women also find it emotionally difficult) for writers who wish to do so to accommodate equality without awkwardnesses of expression. I decided to use masculine pronouns throughout simply because it is in keeping with the greater part (though not all) of the early Buddhist texts. I believe that anyone who understands the full implications of Buddhist doctrinal teachings will not question that they refer to man *qua* human being, not man *qua* male of the species. I hope in particular that females of the species will agree and either understand or forgive my decision.

Last but not least, I make no apology for my enthusiasm for my subject. As my work has progressed, my fascination has deepened.

Particularly with regard to thinking about and drawing out certain implications, I have found the process to be an absorbing, stimulating, and profoundly enriching experience. But then, it is the extra-ordinariness of the ordinary that this book is all about.

Notes

1 Steven Collins (1990, and in his introduction to Wijayaratne, 1990) has suggested three periods: early (pre-Aśokan), middle or traditional (post Aśokan) and modern.

2 This point is made in Hallisey, 1996, p. 42.

3 See, for example, Adikaram, 1953, pp. 24–32.

4 Collins, 1998 (pp. xxff), sets out an uncomplicated but comprehensive textual chronology of the Pali corpus of material, canonical and post-canonical. On the preservation and compilation of the Pali canon see Frauwallner, 1956; Zürcher, 1962; Norman, 1983; Cousins, 1983; Lamotte, 1988; and Collins 1990 and 1992.

5 Traditionally, this huge task is attributed to Buddhaghosa, though he may well have had assistants. Norman (1983) gives perhaps the best account of the compilation of the material.

6 Collins, 1990, for example.

7 Ibid, p. 111, note 29 in particular.

8 See, for example, Adikaram 1953; Norman, 1983; and Collins, 1992.

9 See, for example, Gombrich, 1984, 1988, 1992b, 1996a and b; and Collins, 1990.

10 Collins, 1990, p. 111, note 29.

11 cf. Gorak, 1991 and Collins, 1990, in particular; and Hoffman, 1996, for some further notes and suggestions.

12 Leaving aside the *Vinaya*, which traditionally originated from the beginning of the Buddhist period along with the *Sutta Piṭaka* as mentioned above.

13 Said, 1979, p. 240.

14 Buddhist teachings are believed to be about the Truth of the nature of Reality. Thus *Dhamma* can accurately be rendered either as teachings or as Truth, and Buddhists would accept either of these as valid.

15 DN II 123f, AN II 167f. These passages are discussed by MacQueen, 1981 (p. 314f), and Collins, 1990 (p. 109, n.18 – where AN II 167 is mistakenly given as AN I 167).

16 AN IV 143 (also discussed at the references given in note 15). *Nibbāna* is the Pali form of the Sanskrit word *nirvāṇa*. Except in the context of translating from Pali, when I will italicise it as *nibbāna*, I shall use the Anglicised form nirvana.

17 See Gombrich's comments on this point in his 1996b, p. 7, where he also refers to Ruegg, 1989, p. 31f, n.40: "In Buddhist hermeneutics as traditionally practised, there can be no question of radically relativizing the intended purport of a canonical utterance or text (so-called semantic autonomy) and banishing the idea of authorial intention (so-called authorial irrelevance) in favour of an interpretation, or 'reading', gained against the background of the reader's or (listener's) prejudgement or preknowledge."

18 DN II 100.
19 MN I 134.
20 Walpola Rahula's model of clarity *What the Buddha Taught* is appropriately introduced by Paul Demiéville as 'free from all pedantry' (p. x).
21 This, together with a strong denial of the need for definitions, is a feature of the philosophy of Karl Popper (see Popper, 1984, Vol.II, pp. 9–21, Popper's own words in Magee (ed.), 1971, p. 79, or a summary in Magee, 1982, pp. 49–51). I am indebted to Bryan Magee for specifically drawing my attention to this point. See also Richard Gombrich's recent remarks on the redundancy of definitions (1996, p. 1f.), also referring to the writings of Karl Popper.
22 Notably Collins, 1982, Part I.1; Gombrich, 1988, chapters 2 and 3, and 1996b; and see also Hamilton, 1996, Introduction; and Reat, 1990.
23 *Ananuvejja*, untraceable, is the Pali used at, for example, MN I 140.
24 This is the title of chapter 2 of Richard Gombrich's book *Theravāda Buddhism* (1988).
25 cf. Gombrich, 1975, p. 134 and Hamilton, 1996, p. 150f.
26 See, for example, Gombrich, 1975.
27 Hamilton, 1996b.

CHAPTER ONE

Setting the Scene: We have no self but we are comprised of five aggregates

"To be, or not to be, that is the question."
Hamlet, Act 3, Scene 1.

The subject of this book builds on several aspects of my previous work. In particular it continues two interrelated themes which comprise the central theses of an article entitled "*Anattā*: A Different Approach" and my book *Identity and Experience*.[1] The first of the two themes arises from an attempt to understand what is meant by the important Buddhist teaching known as *anattā*. *Attā* means 'self' and *an-* is a negative prefix, and the Buddhist teaching states that *all* things, of whatever nature and including human beings, are *anattā*. The second theme arises from a study of what is meant by a related and equally important teaching that is usually explained as stating that human beings are comprised of five constituent parts. Referred to as *khandhas* (and collectively 'the five *khandhas*'), these five are one's body, sensations, apperceptions, volitions and consciousness.[2] Prior to my research into the subject of *anattā*, I had found (and I suspect I was not alone in this) that except at the most superficial and theoretical of levels, any attempt to understand the way it was usually interpreted ran aground: perhaps especially because it seemed to be inconsistent when brought into context with the other teachings. And little seemed to have been written on the subject of the *khandhas*. Indeed, little had been written about how, according to early Buddhist texts, the human being might properly be understood in any positive sense: focussing on the negative prefix attached to *attā*, self, the major part of previous scholarship had been concerned with what the human being is not. For preliminary background and scene setting purposes the following fully summarises my previous work on the *anattā* doctrine. Additional relevant and compatible comments will also be made in later chapters. With regard to the *khandhas*, however, their significance, and the implications of that significance, are central topics of later parts of this book which constitute new research in this area. So on them the scene setting here will be only minimal.

First, then, *anattā*: how is this to be understood? In a great many, one might almost say most, secondary sources on Buddhism this aspect of the teachings has regularly been singled out as being the heart or core of what Buddhism is all about. But though it holds an undeniably significant place in the teachings, what is often not so regularly discussed is that the way it should be understood is not actually explained in the primary texts. The doctrine itself is given in a simple formulaic statement: 'all things are *anattā*', and this is described as having generic application in that it is referring to 'the fact that things are a certain way' and 'the fact that there is a regularity of things'.[3] But the most frequent application of the doctrine is more narrowly focused: that a, b or c is *anattā* – where a, b and c refer, almost always, to something to do with the human being – usually one or other of the five *khandhas*. In these latter instances, having the necessary contextual information concerning what sort of self is being denied allows one to deduce what a, b and c are not. But what is actually being established or implied by the doctrine as a whole remains open to different interpretations. And these can then be used to accord different kinds of emphasis to the doctrine of *anattā* in the context of the teachings as a whole.

Traditionally, the *anattā* doctrine has been interpreted in such a way as to give it a specific and dominant place alongside an interpretation of what is involved in realising nirvana. This is the goal of the Buddhist path and is understood to bring liberation from the cycle of rebirth to which one is otherwise bound. Until quite recently nirvana was understood to be achieved by, or to involve, the extinguishing of your self. The word nirvana means 'blowing out', and it was thought that it referred to the blowing out of the self. In fact this interpretation, which represents the view of people called annihilationists (the self is annihilated at liberation), is strongly denied in the early Buddhist texts and was clearly wrong. Buddhists and scholars alike were thus able successfully to refute this error, correctly pointing out that what nirvana refers to is the blowing out not of one's self but of what fuels one's continuity.[4] The corrected interpretation they offered, widely accepted to this day, still associated *anattā* with nirvana. What it means, it was now stated, is that in order to achieve liberation you need to understand that you are not, and nor do you have, and nor have you ever been or had, an abiding self.[5]

This interpretation draws out the fact that the teaching was in direct contrast with other prominent religious ideas being taught at the time of early Buddhism, notably those of the early *Upaniṣads*, which stated that in fact the essence of a human being, one's Real Self,[6] is identical with the immortal and unchanging essence of the universe. This is famously expressed in the *Upaniṣadic* formula '*ātman* is Brahman'. *Ātman* is the Sanskrit form of the Pali word *attā*, meaning self, and Brahman refers to the universal Absolute. Another well-known *Upaniṣadic* way of putting this is 'you are [all] that' (*tat tvam asi*).[7] So the *Upaniṣadic* teaching, given within what is called the Brahmanical religion of India, was that if one realised, in the sense of existentially experiencing, this micro- and macrocosmic identity, then one achieved liberation (called *mokṣa*, release, by the brahmins) from the cycle of lives on earth in which all human beings otherwise continue. The Buddhist teachings culminated in a similarly experiential goal, but, it was suggested, it was the experience not of what your self is, but that you do not have one: ultimately, you *are not*.

This interpretation of *anattā* is taken in tandem with the teaching that one should understand oneself in terms of the five *khandhas*. Traditionally, the link between *anattā* and the *khandhas* is established by way of an analogy found in the texts which states: "When all constituent parts are there, the word 'cart' is used; in just the same way, where there are five *khandhas*, there is the convention of a 'living being'."[8] This suggests that we are made up of five separate parts which, when together, constitute our functioning self; but there is (and never has been and never will be) in fact no essential self other than that temporary combination.

It is as thus understood that I found the doctrine of *anattā* at best seriously problematic and at worst incoherent in the context of the way other key Buddhist teachings are collectively characterised. Even a relatively casual acquaintance with them, especially if one looks at how they are given in the texts and not in secondary sources, impresses on one that the focus of the teachings is primarily not just on the personal experience of cyclical lives but on personal responsibility: understanding that through the knock-on effect(s) of one's desires and volitions, one has created one's own present and will create one's own future (and can therefore change it); that it is because those desires and volitions originate in a matrix of ignorance that we keep having them and thus keep fuelling our continuity (this is the fuel that needs to be blown out); that it is the qualitative state of one's own mind that determines the qualitative context of one's rebirths. Perhaps above all the teachings are about knowing how and why one is continuing as one is, and about knowing that one can, and how one can and eventually does, attain liberation. There is a strong emphasis on knowing: the aim of the teachings is described not at all as a trancelike state but is, on the contrary, a state of Enlightenment – of the cessation of ignorance. Indeed, after achieving nirvana, the Buddha, referred to as the Enlightened One, continued to live and teach for forty-five years. How might this combination of understanding one's experience, accepting personal responsibility, attending to one's state of mind, and progressing from ignorance to acquiring some profound insight with which one can continue to live, accommodate a *goal* of experiencing that one has no self?

Several scholarly studies have drawn together extensive textual evidence suggesting that early Buddhist texts do in fact allow for a conventional everyday self, and it was at this conventional level that the teachings applied.[9] But they did not satisfactorily explain what to me was the more fundamental problem: how *can* one experience that one is or has no self? With the best will in the world, I could not but think that in any context outside of a madhouse the very idea of it is incoherent. In offering alternative interpretations, some scholars went so far as to suggest that the point of the *anattā* teaching was that one should not confuse any conventional notion of self with one's eternal and real transcendental self.[10] But eternalists are coupled with annihilationists in the texts and get equally short shrift. I felt one needed to try another approach.

I did this by looking at the way all of the other main doctrinal teachings found in the Pali *Nikāyas* are structured. What I found was that they have one significant feature in common. And I suggested that interpreting the *anattā* doctrine in the same way not only overcomes the problem with that doctrine but in fact shows that it fits together with the other teachings very well. The point of commonality of the teachings is that they are all concerned with how something works: none of them is concerned with what something is, or, indeed, with what it is not. Most crucially, they are focused on how all the factors of human existence in the cycle of lives are dependent on other factors. This is stated in perhaps the most elementary of ways in the Buddha's very first teaching, known as the Four Noble Truths. I shall be discussing this teaching at length in later chapters, but here it will suffice if I explain that its structure is to state that x is the case because of y and can and will cease if y ceases, where x is intrinsic to cyclical human existence. Drawing out the implication of this is the teaching that it is the dependent nature of all of our actions (karma[11]) that explains the mechanics both of how one is responsible for one's own experiences, now and in the future, and also of how one can achieve liberation: in understanding how this process works in fuelling the continuity of the cycle of lives one can do something about changing it. The *raison d'être* of the teachings as a whole is, indeed, the giving of information that will enable individuals to achieve this.

More generically, the focus on how things work is exemplified in the metaphysical doctrine that everything is dependently originated (the doctrine known as *paṭiccasamuppāda*). And whatever is dependently originated is also described as conditioned (*saṃkhata*). In the entirety of the experience that comprises one's cycle of lives nothing, of whatever nature, exists or occurs independently of conditioning factors. All such things, therefore, are conditioned things. In contrast to the more overtly soteriological – one might say subject-focused – teachings, it is important to grasp the generic relevance of this: that it applies both subjectively *and* objectively. Not only is the state of any individual human being (who for explanatory purposes and not in a technical sense I take to be a subject) at any given moment dependent on conditioning factors, but so are chairs, trees, stars, the air we breathe, toenails, musical notes, ideas and thoughts (all of which I take to be objective in relation to the subject), and so on.

Here lies the link to an alternative understanding of the *anattā* doctrine. If all things are dependently originated, then it follows that nothing has independent self-hood. The way human beings occur is therefore not as independent selves. As such, any self-hood one may have, of whatever kind, cannot be permanent and unchanging as independence would be a pre-requisite of such qualities. Accordingly, it is clear that early Buddhist teachings *are* in direct contrast to the *Upaniṣadic* teaching that the essence of one's self is immortal and unchanging: identical with the essence of the universal absolute. According to the Buddha we do not have *that* sort of selfhood. But though the contrast is clear, it does not necessarily follow that the teaching is concerned to establish that there is *no* self. As mentioned above, the doctrine of *anattā* is itself described as referring to the fact that things are a certain way, and the fact that there is a regularity of things. Like dependent origination, it applies generically: not just subjectively, but also to all of the objective factors of our experience, including the examples given above. As such, its relevance lies not in the question of whether or not a (human) self exists but in how *whatever* there is exists. And, further, taken together with the other teachings of early Buddhism it is stating that in seeking to know what you *are*, or even whether or not you *are*, you are missing the solution to the problem of cyclic continuity. The solution lies in understanding the mechanics of your situation. *That* you are is neither *the* question nor *in* question: you need to forget even the issue of self-hood and understand instead how you work in a dependently originated world of experience.

At the time the Buddha was embarking on his search to understand how to achieve liberation from the cycle of lives, many others were doing the same. And most of them, including the brahmins, thought that the answer lay, one way or the other, in knowing what you are, or whether you are or are not. Hence the above-mentioned references to annihilationists and eternalists, amongst others. So strong was this orientation that the line of questioning in this respect by the spiritual seekers of the day was extraordinarily pervading and persistent. And there are many references in the *Sutta Piṭaka* to the Buddha having denied that this that or the other part of what makes up a human being, particularly one of the five *khandhas*, is actually one's 'self'.[12] It is such references that constitute what I described above as the most frequent application of the doctrine of *anattā*. And it is the frequency with which such questions are clearly denied that has greatly contributed to the view that the early Buddhist doctrine of *anattā* teaches that there is no self, and that realising this is the goal of the path to liberation. But in fact the denials are not inconsistent with the alternative interpretation of *anattā* I have suggested and described here. Being dependently originated, all the things within the scope of human experience in the cycle of lives, including the *khandhas*, are impermanent and subject to change. As I have said above, it follows that the way such things occur is not as independent abiding 'selves'. Any question asking if any particular thing is in fact one's permanent 'self' would, therefore, be denied. But the repeated denials should be construed as a response both to the persistence of the line of questioning, and also to the assumption on the part of the questioners that the self they are seeking is independent and permanent,[13] rather than as the focus of the Buddhist teaching in a more positive sense. That focus is, as described above, centred not at all on what one is or is not but on how things operate.[14]

An analogy will perhaps explain more clearly. I acquire an object that I am told is a computer. The salesman tells me that though it will perform a range of functions it is at the moment programmed for just one. I realise that it is not the function I want it to perform, so it is important that I learn how to change the programme. But I am fascinated to the point of obsession by the whole idea of 'a computer', and I persistently and repeatedly ask what exactly it is about it that constitutes the fact that it is a computer, referring to part after part asking 'what is this bit?' and 'is this bit the computer?'. The salesman keeps trying to explain how to change the programme, and every time I ask 'what is this bit?' and 'is this bit the computer?' he just says 'no it's not the computer', and 'you need to understand this programming section'. At the end of the day, I have heard from him countless times the expression 'that bit is not the computer'. Given my fascination, I am very puzzled about this, and though I continue to speculate as to exactly what the computer *is*, I also have the very distinct impression from what the salesman kept saying that there is really no such thing at all. It takes me a while to realise that what the computer was not *was not what the salesman was trying to tell me.* Rather, he understood that what I needed to know was how to change the programme and so all he was trying to tell me was how the computer *worked*. It was only my perpetual questions that forced him to answer as he did. Furthermore, none of his denials was spoken with the intention of informing me that there is no computer at all. Rather, he did not intend to tell me anything whatsoever about it in those terms because what the computer *is* is simply not relevant to me: for the solving of my programming problem it is neither *the* question to ask nor is its existence *in* question. It may be that there is some part or collection of parts that *is* the computer in the sense that I am seeking, and it may be that there is not: I do not need to know either way, and so the salesman did not tell me, either directly or indirectly.

A well-known analogy found in the Buddhist texts can also be drawn on here.[15] Though the context in which it is given is slightly different, it is nevertheless not irrelevant to the point I am making. A man is shot with a poisoned arrow and his glaring need is to have it removed so that he will not die. But he says he will not let it be removed until he knows the class of the person who shot him, what his name and family are, whether he is tall, short, dark, fair, where he lives, what the arrow is made of, what feathers are used on it, and so on and so on. The point of the analogy in the texts is to indicate that these questions are so completely irrelevant to the solving of the man's problem that he will die while they are being answered. He should therefore allow the person who comes to his assistance to leave them unanswered and to address instead the pressing problem of the removal of the arrow. This refers to the fact that the Buddha did not answer certain questions which others were interested in but that he considered irrelevant to achieving liberation from rebirth. Classically, these are called the Unanswered Questions, and I shall refer to them again later in this book. But, and this is where the analogy can be extended to support my point about *anattā*, in diverting attention to the removal of the arrow nothing is actually being said about the content of the unanswered questions *except* that they are irrelevant. In either of the two analogies I have given one can, especially if one has other information to hand from elsewhere, draw out for other reasons implications about the points that are irrelevant in the narrow context of the analogy alone. One might, for example, be able to answer what a computer part is made of or what feathers are on the arrow. But this is a separate matter and not specifically what the analogies are seeking to indicate.

Understanding the doctrine of *anattā* as I have suggested, by means of the metaphysics of dependent origination that the Buddha taught, does several things. First, it removes the profound incoherence of the idea of aiming to know that one is not. Second, it allows one more readily to focus on the fact that the dependent way of existing it refers to – *anattā*-ness, so to speak – is applicable generically, to *all* things, and not just to human selves. That is, it is about the nature of all of the factors of one's existence as a whole, rather than the nature of one's self alone. In the later form of Buddhism known as Mahāyāna this point is much more obviously stated in that the term 'emptiness' (*śūnyatā* – sometimes called 'voidness') is used. This refers to the fact that all things are 'empty' of the inherent existence (*svabhāva* – literally 'own being') that independence would require. The neutrality of the term emptiness does not lend itself to what one might call subjective appropriation in the way the term *anattā*, not self, does. And third, it allows one to see more clearly how intimately connected are the metaphysics and soteriology of the early Buddhist teachings: it is because everything is dependently originated that one can, in understanding how the process of individual continuity works, then reverse it. And this is what the Buddha's teachings were given for. My point is supported by passages in the texts which state not just that thinking "this is mine, I am this, this is my self" is not helpful,[16] but also that when one understands dependent origination one *will no longer ask* (my italics) questions such as: "Am I, or am I not? What am I? Why am I? This 'being' that is 'I', where has it come from, where will it go?".[17] Such passages should not be construed in the sense that thinking 'this is mine' (and so on) is not helpful because actually there *is* no such thing. Rather, that such a person has views about 'neither self nor not-self'[18]: for the solving of the problem of continuity, these are all, quite simply, irrelevant questions.

Further, though the distinction I am suggesting may in some respects be subtle, it is important in that it shifts the emphasis and place given to *anattā* in the Buddha's teachings as a whole. Not only does focussing on the notion that *anattā* means 'there is no self' misleadingly suggest a solely subjective reference for the term, and wrongly emphasise it as a denial of being instead of the way what we think of as self-hood occurs. But it also, in sticking out like a conceptual sore thumb, allows such wrong emphasis to draw attention away from the harmony of *anattā* with the all important focus of the rest of the teachings. In the more or less perennial context of deep interest in the nature of selfhood, both at the existential level and at the level of scholarship in a multitude of disciplines, the idea that this issue not only lies at the centre of Buddhism but also that it does so in a radically negative form has been seductively attention grabbing. But attention – as the Buddha himself indicated, and as I shall be discussing in later chapters – should be directed elsewhere.

Turning now more specifically to the *khandhas*, perhaps the first thing to state is that as with *anattā*, little is clearly said or explained about them in the texts.[19] We read that the Buddha was consistent in referring to the *khandhas* as the focus of what one should understand about oneself. Throughout the *Khandha-Saṃyutta* they are taught as the correct focus of one's attention. In several other places they are equated with *dukkha*, the content of the first Noble Truth, traditionally the first teaching given by the Buddha.[20] But in spite of this, there is very little clear account either of why this is the case or of how each or all of the *khandhas* should be understood. Traditionally, however, they have been understood as follows.

The Pali terms for the five *khandhas* – *rūpa*, *vedanā*, *saññā*, *saṃkhārā* and *viññāṇa* – are typically translated matter, sensations, perceptions, mental formations and consciousness.[21] The doctrinal context in which they are traditionally understood is explained in terms of the analogy referred to above: in just the same way that a cart is made up of various bits and pieces that, when assembled, we *call* a cart, but there is no separate independent thing that *is* the cart, so each human being is an assembly of these five *khandhas* which gives rise to the convention of a living being, but there is no separate independent thing that is the self of that person.[22] The *khandhas* are thus most often described as being aggregates: a human being consists of a group of five aggregate parts, none of which, individually or collectively, is one's self. "What we call a 'being', or an 'individual', or 'I', is only a convenient name or a label given to the combination of these five", states Rahula, for example.[23] Furthermore, it is because we erroneously think of ourselves as being or having a separate self that we experience the unsatisfactoriness (*dukkha*) which is stated in the first Noble Truth to be the intrinsic characteristic of cyclical human existence. We fail to recognise that there is no self, and so, acting in this state of ignorance, we perpetuate unsatisfactoriness. If we realise we are merely a temporary collection of parts we will cease acting in this way and our unsatisfactoriness will cease.

According to Theravāda tradition, the five aggregates should properly be regarded as representing one physical (*rūpa*) and four mental (*arūpa*) aggregates, or, collectively, mind and matter. This is how nominal Theravāda descriptions of what each is are offered:[24] we are, and should realise ourselves to be, a coming together of one physical and four mental aggregates. That the traditional descriptions are only nominal perhaps reflects the fact that little is clearly said about what they are in the texts. Indeed, the vast majority of references to them are reiterating that none of the *khandhas* should itself be thought of as the permanent self which was the object of the spiritual quest at the time of the Buddha, as mentioned above.[25] From a Theravāda point of view, this is taken as no more than making the point that if one is attempting to understand that rather than having a separate permanent self one is a collection of parts, then one must not fall into the trap of thinking that any one of those parts is so to speak a substitute self. Perhaps because of this, it is traditionally less important to understand what each *khandha* is than that we have no self. Put differently, Theravāda Buddhists understand the cart analogy as offering sufficient explanation of the point of the *khandha* teaching.

From this can be seen the extent to which the traditional interpretation of the teaching on the *khandhas* is associated with the traditional interpretation of the doctrine of *anattā*. Further, the subordinating of the relevance of the *khandhas* to their interpretation of *anattā* effectively diverts attention from the possible relevance and place of the *khandha* teaching in any other or more positively illuminating sense. So it follows from this that a different understanding of the meaning and place of *anattā*, such as I have described above, has ramifications for how the *khandhas* might be understood: and as their position in the texts is rendered far from obvious the opportunity arises for further investigation.

In the light of my understanding of *anattā*, I began to wonder what the suggestion that one should think of oneself in terms of five *khandhas* was about. Why would a body of teachings concerned with the dependent originatedness of all things describe the human being in terms of these five clearly delineated constituents? How did this fit in with the structure of the rest of the teachings? And if gaining liberation was neither about knowing what one's self is or that one has no self, then in what way was understanding oneself as being comprised of a temporary combination of five *khandhas* helpful to gaining liberation? Furthermore, though perhaps less obviously incoherent than the idea of experiencing that one has no self, the notion of the *khandhas* perplexed me for the additional reason that I found the idea that we are so comprised counter-experiential. Not only superficially but even on deep reflection I found such an analysis at best simplistic: several more meaningful and readily recognisable alternative ways of analysing oneself could be arrived at without too much difficulty. None of these questions or issues is addressed by the way the *khandhas* are traditionally understood. And all of such questions and issued led me to wonder Why the *khandhas*?

I shall later be drawing at some length on the research involved in my previous attempts to answer this question, but what we need to know here for scene-setting purposes is that what emerged from that study was that the *khandhas* are not a comprehensive analysis of what a human being is comprised of: that is what – indeed, all – we *are*. Rather, they are the factors of human experience (or, better, the experiencing factors) that one needs to understand in order to achieve the goal of Buddhist teachings. In other words, closer study showed that in line with all the other teachings, they are about how the human being operates.

The first suggestion of this emerged from my study of the *rūpa-kkhandha*.[26] This is traditionally, by Buddhists and scholars alike, referred to as the physical *khandha*, or just as matter.[27] But it became clear that what is being referred to here is the body as a living organism and not just the body *qua material* body. It certainly includes matter, or solidity is a better way of putting it. But it also includes mobility, temperature and fluidity. These four – solidity, mobility, temperature and fluidity – are the four elements, earth, air, fire and water, put abstractly. In the Pali texts the term *rūpa* is used to refer both to the *khandha* and to what we think of as the external world. Both these two aspects of *rūpa*, what are called internal and external *rūpa* respectively, are characterised by one or more of the four elements. In the context of the *rūpa-kkhandha*, though the nominal Theravāda explanation of it does refer to the four elements, the implications of this are not drawn out.[28] What the elements correspond to are the physical aspect of the body in terms of its solidity and extension; its mobility, both in the sense of movements of air that are our breathing, the intestinal movements of food, and so on, and in the sense of one's ability to walk and move about, and so on; its temperature regulating, decaying (our cells are decaying all the time) and digestive systems; and blood, water and other fluid systems of the body.[29] And what this is all referring to must be the living body rather than simply its flesh.

The relevance of the fact that the *rūpa-kkhandha* refers to the living body becomes clear if one puts it in context by relating it to the problem situation the Buddha was seeking a solution to. Put briefly, he saw his problem as human existence in the cycle of lives: why it is how it is, why it continues in the way that it does. He wanted to solve the problem by finding how to change it and, ideally, bringing about a cessation of its continuity. Linked to the problem in this way it is highly unlikely that *rūpa* qua matter would be so important as to be mentioned as one of only five aspects of the human being. It would give lumps of flesh literally *qua* flesh a virtually incredible order of importance given the context. But as the living, breathing, functioning body it is immediately more relevant both as the locus of the problematic situation for each individual and in terms of the operating processes it provides.

Further research along such lines showed that the central operating process in which all the *khandhas* are involved is how human cognition operates. Perhaps the most important single indication of this is a passage which states: "Seeing occurs when there is contact between an eye and [visible] forms, accompanied by consciousness; this gives rise to sensations, which are then identified; and what is thus identified one reflects on and makes manifold."[30] Involved in this are the *khandhas* of the body (*rūpa*), providing both the living locus of subjectivity and, more specifically, the sense organs – in this case the eye; sensations (*vedanā*), in the sense of the initial feeling of awareness of seeing; apperception (*saññā*), in the sense of being the process of identifying what that initial feeling of awareness is; and consciousness (*viññāṇa*), the fact that the process is one of knowing that one is (in this example) seeing something. The significance of the reference to an occurrence of seeing giving rise to reflection and making manifold lies in the metaphysics of dependent origination. If all things are dependently originated, then the fact that we normally see them as independent and separate, as we do, is itself dependent on what happens in the process of cognition: it is that process that 'makes manifold'.

So the answer to the question 'why the *khandhas*?' is that it is not the *khandhas qua khandhas* that is being referred to, but that what they represent is the process by which one is having one's experience. And it is this process that one needs to understand. The two themes from my previous work on which I am now building, then, are, first, that the central orientation of all of the teachings of early Buddhism is the need to understand how personal continuity operates (so that one can achieve liberation from that continuity), and that it is not focused on what one is or is not; and, second, that the starting place for such an enterprise is one's own cognitive process. It is these two themes that underpin my attempt here to draw out from early Buddhist texts their ideas about and understanding of human experience. And, further, it is the fact that my previous work seemed to show ways in which two central but highly problematic and obscure teachings of early Buddhism might be understood coherently that has led me to continue the search for a coherent understanding of them within the wider frame of reference of the theoretical foundation of the early Buddhist teachings as a whole. Before continuing, though, the next chapter will provide some contextualising background.

Notes

1 Hamilton, 1995 and 1996a.

2 These are my translations of the Pali terms for the five *khandhas*, not the traditional translations. If English words are needed, I believe these most appropriately represent what the Pali terms refer to.

3 *Sabbe dhammā anattā; dhammaṭṭhitatā; dhammaniyāmatā*: AN I 286. The formula is also found at *Dhammapada* 5–7; 277–9; and cf. also MN I 336; DN II 157.

4 This is most clearly stated in Rahula, 1985, and Gombrich, 1988.

5 Rahula (1985, chapter 6) is the *locus classicus* for a description of this.

6 The language of the *Upaniṣads*, Sanskrit, has no capital letters. I am using them here only to highlight the essential nature of what is being referred to. Sometimes in English the word soul is used to make this point. And in this respect the terms Self and soul tend to be used interchangeably to refer to essential identity. In following this practice myself, I am not, however, making any suggestions as to what exactly that is or might be. In the context of the Buddha's time the key characteristic of what was meant by it was that it was a permanent and unchanging entity of some sort.

7 Ch. Up. 6.8ff. cf. also Ch. Up. 3.14 and Bṛ. Up. 2.4.6, 2.5, 4.4.13. Though the monism implicit in these references was not formally drawn out until the later Vedānta tradition, it is nevertheless clear from the way in which the Buddha's teachings are given that it is to these key *Upaniṣadic* passages, as taught by the brahmins of the day, that he is referring.

8 SN I 135.

9 See, for example, Collins, 1982, and Harvey, 1995b, for two very different (both in style and in interpretation) studies in this vein.

10 cf., for example, Pérez-Remón, 1980.

11 The Sanskrit *karman*, Pali *kamma*, is given in English as karma. Literally, it means action.

12 cf. in particular the *Alagaddūpamasutta*, MN I 130ff; and throughout the *Khandha Saṃyutta*.

13 cf. Norman, 1991, p. 202 on this point.

14 In previously published work, I have not commented on the *Alagaddūpamasutta* (MN I 130ff), where the word *asati* is found in connection with the self (p. 136).

This means 'is not', and can be used in the substantialist sense that something does not exist. But it might also mean, and in my view does mean, that what is being referred to is not the case. And what is being referred to is that the *khandhas* and whatever comes within one's sensory/mental experience are not one's self. So, the text states, perceiving that this is not the case, one will not be concerned about it. My interpretation is compatible with the commentator's view that *asati* means *avijjamāne*, being untrue – arising from ignorance. And it also means that this *sutta* ties in with other similar references and is not the single context in which it is explicitly stated that there is no self.

15 MN I 428ff.

16 For example, MN I 232f: *etam mama, eso 'ham asmi, eso me attā ti*. This expression is also frequently found in the *Khandha Saṃyutta*, SN volume III.

17 For example at MN I 8; SN II 27: ... *ahaṃ nu kho smi, na nu kho smi; kiṃ nu kho smi; kathaṃ nu kho smi; ahaṃ nu kho satto kuto āgato so kuhiṃgāmī bhavissatī ti.*

18 *Sutta Nipāta* 787: *attaṃ nirattaṃ na hi tassa atthi.*

19 The key Pali text on the *khandhas* is the *Khandha Saṃyutta* (*Saṃyutta Nikāya* volume III).

20 cf. Vin I 9f. cf also: *Saṃkhittena pañc' upādānakkhandhā dukkhā*: e.g. SN V 421; MN I 48; AN I 177; SN III 158: *Katamañ ca bhikkhave dukkham? Pañc' upādānakkhandhā ti 'ssa vacanīyaṃ*; and *Dhammapada* 202: *N'atthi khandhādisā dukkhā*. On the significance of *upādāna* in association with *khandhā*, cf. *Identity and Experience*, p. 9, and Gethin, 1986, p. 41.

21 These are the translations used by Rahula in his classic book on Theravāda Buddhism, *What the Buddha Taught*. This book also gives the traditional interpretation of the *khandhas*.

22 SN I 135.

23 Rahula, 1985, p. 25.

24 See ibid. p. 20f.

25 This is repeatedly stated throughout the *Khandha Saṃyutta*.

26 See chapter 1 of *Identity and Experience*.

27 See, for example, Rahula, 1985, p. 20, and Boisvert, 1995, p. 31f.

28 See, for example, Rahula, 1985, p. 20.

29 See MN I 185–188. External *rūpa* is also referred to in this *sutta*.

30 This is a free translation, in order to draw out the meaning, of MN I 111f: *cakkhuñ c'āvuso paṭicca rūpe ca uppajjati cakkhuviññāṇaṃ, tiṇṇaṃ saṅgati phasso, phassapa.*

CHAPTER TWO

The Indian Context

"And ye shall know the Truth, and the Truth shall make you free."
St. John, Ch.8, v.32.

We need to go back some two and a half thousand years in time: from the modern to the archaic. And we need to cross into not just another continent but another cultural worldview: from the occident to the orient. These might seem daunting obstacles in the path of arriving at some sort of understanding of the socio-religious context in which the Buddha lived. But if we are clearly to comprehend what the teachings of early Buddhism mean we need to be aware of the extent to which and ways in which their presentation was determined by their context.

As it happens, the time to which we are returning marks a crucial chapter in the history of religious thought. Some have referred to it as the Axis Age because great and influential figures in world history such as Pythagoras, the Buddha, Zoroaster, Mahāvira, the Old Testament prophets, Confucius and Lao Tze were all more or less contemporaries. But a more specific aspect of what was crucial about it, and of more relevance for us, is that it is the period during which religious practice in India developed several new features. Not only are these new features relevant to the understanding of Buddhism, but they also went on to take such a strong hold of Indian thought in general that it is they that characterise the conceptual framework of India's worldview. And it is these same characteristics that represent the most fundamental differences between oriental and occidental (or, more specifically, between Indian and Western) worldviews. It is the period during which a transition was made from religious practices that were predominantly exoteric to religious practices that were predominantly esoteric; from religious concerns that were world-centred to religious concerns that were person-centred. And it was the particular ways in which this person-centredness was understood that were so very different from anything that happened in the religion and developing worldview of the West. As this is the case, it is by homing in on these points that I shall begin our overview before going on to include other relevant aspects of the contextual background. We will thus in the first instance have before us a clear picture of the main principles of the conceptual framework with which any interpretation of Buddhist teachings needs to be familiar and of which one's attempt at understanding needs to take account, as well as the key differentiating features of the worldview which we are visiting compared with our own.

The predominantly exoteric and world-centred religious concerns of the religion of India prior to the transition were part of the Vedic sacrificial religion. This was the religion of the brahmin priests, brought in to North West India from central Eurasia by the Aryans. Though the Brahmanical religion had not spread over the whole of India by the beginning of the fifth century BCE, as it went on to do, it was already gaining both religious and social hegemony in the North of the sub-continent. And it was this geographical area that provided the crucible from which emerged the changing Brahmanical ideas, and the new Buddhist, Jain and other religious traditions. In the Vedic religion, sacrifices were offered by men to a pantheon of deities or *devas*, which included quasi-deified aspects of the natural realm, such as sun, wind, lightning, earth, as well as similarly deified abstractions such as the principles of contract, vow, alliance, right and wrong.

Underpinning the sacrificial religion was the rationale that the ritual actions, performed as prescribed in the Vedic ritual manuals, would have specific consequences: if correctly addressed through ritual, the *devas* would in consequence respond by performing their cosmic functions in an optimally beneficial manner. The actions of the sacrifice are understood to be both the physical movements and also the sounds of the priests in the course of the ritual: spoken formulas, mutterings, chants, and so on. The correctness with which they were performed would determine whether or not the right consequence occurred. The need to perform many of the sacrifices – the obligatory rituals – was self-validating: those who were enjoined to do them did so because they were so enjoined, and the enjoining was enforced because they had to be done. Others – desiderative rituals – were performed for a variety of reasons, some more clearly stated than others. But at the risk of oversimplifying a complex situation, their overall purpose can perhaps be summed up as representing the maintaining of the world (in its cosmic sense) at its optimum level of status quo. And, optimally, this is a comprehensively ordered cosmos. Cosmic orderliness, at this period known as *Ṛta* and later being referred to by the term *Dharma*, has remained ever since a central feature of the Brahmanical religion. It was, and still is by many, believed that the injunctions of the Vedic texts are minutely correlated to this cosmic order. And that the Brahmanical religion's injunctions to perform one's religious duties in specific ways were designed to maintain Order/*Ṛta*/*Dharma* was one of the reasons why they carried such weight and were able to become normative: to gainsay such norms was to threaten cosmic order itself. During the Vedic period there was also considerable and profound speculation about the nature of the world (in the cosmic sense) – its origin, unifying substance, co-ordinating power, and so on. (None of the *devas* was considered to be all-powerful in the sense associated with monotheism: not only was the power of each of them limited to their specific function, but ultimately they too were this-worldly. Moreover, they were in effect manipulable by man through the sacrifice.) This cosmic speculation is readily apparent from many of the *Vedic* hymns (a famous creation hymn, the *Puruṣa Sūkta*, is referred to below). But the central point at this period was that sacrificial rituals should be performed. And the key object of human knowledge was how to perform those rituals correctly, such knowledge being the prerogative of only a small hereditary minority, the brahmin priests.

The fundamental shift from this world-centred religious focus to a profoundly person-centred focus had begun to take place just prior to the time of the Buddha. In place of activities for the well-being, and speculation about the nature, of the world, it began to be believed that the key concern of the religious quest should be the nature of the human being – its origin, substance, destination, and so on. In contrast to needing to know how to perform rituals, religious practice could be summed up in terms of 'know thyself'. In fact it took centuries for this to become a pan-Indian religious phenomenon, and the Brahmanical religion never left behind the need to perform sacrificial rituals as well. But by the time of the

Buddha, the new focus had become widespread enough among the actively religious for it to encompass not just the Brahmanical religion but also others of different religious backgrounds, some of whom grouped around a leader and some of whom were solitary wanderers. The result of this was that how to know thyself, and what thyself was, was interpreted in many different ways. Early Buddhist and other texts record that the Buddha became familiar with many different versions, Brahmanical and otherwise. But it was to the early stages of its formulation within the dominant Brahmanical religion, as recorded in the early *Upaniṣads*, that his own teachings mainly responded, and it was in the light of the terminology they used that his were phrased. And it was the way the Brahmanical religion developed its formulations of this person-centredness that was to become so indelibly a part of the Indian worldview as a whole.

The new religious teachings recorded in the early *Upaniṣads* can be summarised as follows. In the same way that the ritual actions of the sacrifice were believed to have consequences, so the actions (karma) performed by each and every human being in their daily lives (whether or not they were entitled to perform sacrifices) would have consequences for them in the future. This was not understood as a moral law: as in the sacrifice, these consequences were thought to correspond to how correctly one performed one's actions, in this case in the light of one's duty according to the brahmins' socio-religious ideology. Thus the criterion for determining good actions, with beneficial, desirable consequences, was correctness: and for bad actions, with disadvantageous, undesirable consequences, incorrectness. Reinforcing the point that the contribution of each was essential to the maintenance of the whole, conceived of in terms of cosmic Order or *Dharma*, this individual duty came to be referred to as one's 'own *dharma*'. And the future during which consequences might be experienced could extend beyond one's present life because each human being was repeatedly reborn in a cycle of lives on earth, the cycle being called *saṃsāra*, 'going round'. The reason why one continues being cyclically reborn is that one is ignorant of the true nature of one's self. Conversely, one can attain liberation (in the *Upaniṣads*, and since then in Hinduism generally, called *mokṣa*) from the cycle by gaining knowledge of that true nature. The truth, and it is a metaphysical Truth, that one needs to know is that the essence of one's self, *ātman*, is in fact identical with the essence of the universal absolute, called Brahman. I mentioned this early *Upaniṣadic* ontological equation earlier.

These notions of karma, *saṃsāra*, and *mokṣa* are usually singled out in descriptions of the Indian worldview as the three principal features of its conceptual framework, and indeed they are. The notions that one's actions have consequences for oneself in the future, that one is reborn in a cycle of lives according to those actions, and that the possibility of achieving liberation from that cycle of lives is the goal to which one might aspire, all first introduced during the period of transition to which we are returning, have become the bedrock of many different traditions of Indian thought. But however much these differ from the principal features of the conceptual framework of the Western worldview, the most radical difference between the two worldviews in fact lies in another feature of the new religion of that transition period: the practical methodology that accompanies these three teachings as the way to achieve liberating knowledge. This practical methodology is not explained in the early *Upaniṣads* themselves, but it is clear from other sources that for most people, including those in the Brahmanical tradition, it was thought that what was needed was meditation, or the practising of mental disciplinary exercises which were later given the generic name yoga.

What is radical about this is the combination of the object and the nature of yogic knowledge. As I have just stated, the object of knowledge is metaphysical Truth; and the nature of the knowledge of it that is given primacy – that indeed is essential to the efficacy of the practice – is experiential knowledge: it is only this that brings liberation. In its own context, this is what makes this a period of transition from exoteric to esoteric: the focus of knowledge has shifted from the minutiae of sacrificial ritual to gaining metaphysical insight. And gaining such metaphysical insight in order to achieve liberation from rebirth is the rationale that underpins the practice of yoga. Since yoga was first introduced, it has been factually accepted that the Truth is something that can not only be known *about* but can also be known *by experience*. It is the point of yogic practices that they enable one to achieve this. More importantly, the teachings given in the *Upaniṣads* were arrived at by this method, and it is this very factor that gives those teachings the status of 'insights': the Truth they record had been experientially *seen* by sages who were called 'seers' (*ṛṣis*/rishis). This is quite unlike the nature of revelation in Western religions because it can, in principle, be seen by anyone.[1] Later, this latter point was philosophically formalised by certain *Upaniṣadic* exegetes in that they recognised the *Upaniṣadic* accounts as having (at least) the same epistemological validity as one's own perception.

The aspect of the Indian worldview that needs to be drawn out here is that it does not presuppose realism. Rather, it presupposes that what we call normal everyday perceptions are appearances that do not correspond to Reality. And it is accepted as a given that by the (sometimes extensive) practising of mental disciplinary exercises one can so reorganise one's mental faculties that one is able to penetrate through the level of ordinary perception and experience the Truth of what there really is. Because this *does* involve the reorganising of one's mental faculties, and because Reality is *not* what we normally see, experience of the Truth is radically different from any other experience – indeed one might accurately say from any conceivable experience.

From the perspective of the Western worldview, different sorts of knowledge are not a problem: we do not need to refer to the formal distinctions of philosophers to recognise the difference between, for example, factually knowing that childbirth is painful and knowing this experientially. But what is not normally accepted from the Western perspective is the possibility that human beings might have experiential knowledge of metaphysical Truth. We live at a time when twentieth century scientific discoveries mean that it is no longer tenable that any thinking person should presuppose that things are what they seem to us to be in ordinary everyday experience. But it nevertheless remains the case that most Westerners are no nearer now than they were two and a half millennia ago to accepting as a given that one's mental faculties might be reorganisable to such a degree that one might be able to see Reality for oneself. So notwithstanding the other major conceptual innovations mentioned above, perhaps the greatest of the distinguishing characteristics of our period of religious thought in India is that it recorded the beginning of the view that the human mind can develop super-normal capacities which enable it to penetrate the appearance of how things seem to be. Since that time it has been axiomatic in India that any theory about the Truth is pointless unless it is the theoretical basis of a more practical aim. Indeed, that practical aim is seen as the very culmination of human aspiration. And since that time the Indian mind has taken this so much for granted, and the Western mind has not, that it is this that has ever since been the greatest gulf between Indian and Western worldviews: while Westerners – virtually always without trying it – regard this Indian belief as derisory, Indians regard Westerners as profoundly in error for accepting such a self-imposed limitation.

So the main principles of the conceptual framework in which Buddhist teachings were given can be summed up in terms of karma: one's actions have consequences; *saṃsāra*: each person lives a series of lives; *mokṣa*: one can aspire to achieve liberation from that series of lives[2]; and that liberation is brought about by means of experiential knowledge of metaphysical Truth. And from this summary, we can also clearly see the key differentiating features of the worldview to which we are returning compared with our own. Relevantly for us, we can also note in passing that the most strongly developing religious trend of the time was the focus on personal experience.

I mentioned above that during our period the actively religious included not just members of the Brahmanical religion but also others of different religious backgrounds. Though some of these others grouped around leaders and some of them were solitary, they were collectively characterised by the fact that they were peripatetic. Reflecting this, they were called wanderers (*śramaṇa*), and reflecting the fact that this involved the giving up of family life they were also called renouncers (*saṃnyāsin*). Family life had long been the central social pin of the Brahmanical religion, and it was from this religion that the prevailing social norms of the day had evolved. Though the world maintained by sacrificial rituals was cosmic in its extent, it was at the social level that human beings lived their lives and performed the sacrifices. If the entire edifice was to continue, men must marry and have sons. A detailed structure had developed according to which a man's specific inherited contribution to the maintaining of the socio-cosmic order both had to be performed by him and also assured of continuity through his sons. So important was this continuity that what marked the point from which a man was personally responsible for performing his sacrificial duties was his marriage: religious adulthood was associated with what was called the life of the householder. One had no choice in this: because the wellbeing of society was dependent on the continuing performance of sacrificial rituals, marriage was seen in terms neither of emotional fulfilment nor of social nicety but as a religious duty, an aspect of each person's 'own-*dharma*'. And because everyone had their contribution to make to the continuity of the socio-religious order as a whole, it was the duty of *all* people to marry and produce sons, whether one's task was central to the actual performing of sacrifices or merely a supporting role.

Social continuity being an intrinsic part of the religion, and the social structure therefore being determined by the religious leaders, it comes as no surprise that those religious leaders, the brahmins, were placed at the top of the socio-religious hierarchy. The hierarchy was (and still is) based on the concept of ritual purity. The brahmin priests, alone permitted to perform the vital sacrifices and preserve the relevant sacred texts, were ritually purest and had religious power. Next was the ruling class, the kings and warriors, who wielded temporal power and whose duty it was to employ the priests to perform the rituals. Below them were the mass of economic producers: in the predominantly agricultural communities of the time these were mainly workers of the land, but later included those involved in trade and commerce as the economy developed. These, too, were meant to employ priests to sacrifice on their behalf. Lower still were the servants, whose task it was to perform services for those above them. At the bottom, and technically outside the four-class hierarchy above them, was a group later known as 'outcastes' or 'untouchables', whose sole *raison d'être* was the performing of the necessary but dirtiest of social tasks, such as laundry, the tanning of animal skins, the removal of waste, cremation of dead bodies, and so on.[3] Because the servants and untouchables had nothing directly to do with the sacrifices as such, those above them in the hierarchy were thus enabled to retain their optimum level of purity. In fact the members of each class, and sub-class within it, rigorously maintained (and still do maintain) their level of ritual purity by keeping themselves to themselves as much as possible, and when not possible by undergoing ritual purifications.

The earliest reference to the fourfold class system is in a book of the *Ṛg Veda*, one of the sacred sacrificial ritual books. Hymn X.90 of the *Ṛg Veda* is called the *Puruṣa Sūkta*, the Hymn of the Cosmic Man. It describes a primordial sacrifice by which the universe is created, the cosmic man becoming the cosmos as a whole. The four classes of society derive from his mouth, arms, thighs and feet respectively. The notion that the resulting society is ordered according to a hierarchy of purity is implicit because the mouth, from which come the brahmins, is pure through its association with the sacred sounds uttered at the sacrifice, and, at the other end of the scale, the feet, from which come the servants, are the supporters of the rest of the body and at the same time unclean. When the new teachings of personal karma and the cycle of lives were introduced in the *Upaniṣads*, the structure was if anything reinforced as it was asserted that the situation into which a person is born in any given life is determined by their actions in previous lives.

Not only was this Brahmanical social ideology the only one to be developed to any great extent in India, but its origin in sacred texts legitimated it in the most powerful way possible. It endures to this day, in a way comparable to the entitlement Jews feel they have to the state of Israel. It developed, adapted, and became more rigid over time, so that in the later Brahmanical texts known as the Law Books (*Dharma Sūtras* and *Śāstras*) the duties or 'own-*dharma*' of each person were codified in great detail and with the injunction that it was better to do one's own-*dharma* badly than another's well.[4] And until India gained independence in the twentieth century, it was these Law Books that formed the basis of the secular legislative system.[5] Though less minutely articulated, it is clear that by the fifth century BCE there was already a clear stratification of society along the lines described above, and that every member of society was expected to do their inherited duty and to expect only inherited rights. This system not only meant that all must embark on marriage as described above, but also that each person's religious activities were minutely prescribed both as to what each *must* do and as to what each *could* do. So important was it that sacrificial rituals were always performed that there was no room for innovation in a personal or ad hoc sense, and as the religion developed any new feature was ascribed its precise place. Thus at the time of the transition in religious focus to the new teachings of the *Upaniṣads*, the practice of yoga was accommodated by prescribing it for a stage of life when one's sacrificial, productive and reproductive duties had been fulfilled: it became, as it were, the ritual to be performed after the crucial householder stage of life. One could thus maintain the cosmos for one's descendents *and* seek to maximise one's own chances of liberation from the cycle of lives.[6]

Notwithstanding the twin underlying rationales of the Brahmanical social structure that this was how society and the cosmos as a whole could best be maintained, and that if each did their duty then all would be reciprocally provided for, many found its injunctions and restrictions oppressive. And whether born into the system or not (there were still a significant number of geographically isolated tribal clans which were not part of the brahmanical system as such), it was such people, who renounced – either by opting out of or rejecting in principle – the family-centred social norms and the religious restrictions of the Brahmanical religion, who were the wandering religious that made up the second important religious group at the time of the Buddha. As mentioned above, renouncers either joined groups, some with a leader, or remained solitary. But they were all peripatetic mendicants, and for this reason are usually referred to collectively just as Wanderers (*śramaṇas*), in contrast to practising members of the Brahmanical religion who are referred to as Householders.

As implied by their rejection of the religion of the brahmins, Wanderers saw no merit in sacrificial rituals, no need for marriage, and no authority in the priests. Rather than accepting that the complex socio-cosmic structure should be maintained, they rejected the givenness of the structure as a whole and went back to square one seeking answers to fundamental questions about the nature of the world and the human being in it. And underpinning their search was the hope that the answers to their questions would bring liberation from the cycle of lives. To achieve this most performed some sort of yoga, mental disciplinary exercises believed to be efficacious in bringing insight of the Truth, as described above. Having rejected marriage, virtually all were celibate. Their prime concern was to achieve unencumbered mental concentration with which sexual activity was not thought to be compatible. Indeed, all sensory pleasures were considered to be distractions best renounced and at least controlled. Many took this view to its extreme, denying themselves even clothing and regular shelter, and many also practised horrific self-mortifications such as starvation, having nothing to drink, sitting in the sun all day, pulling out all their hair, sleeping on beds of thorny branches, and so on, believing such practices would better enable them to attain the insight they sought. Because of such practices, Wanderers came to be associated with asceticism.

Though there were other religious views and practices at the time, including, for example, the socio-religious concerns of the tribal/clan communities (many of which survive and are often now referred to as the 'folk' elements of Hinduism as it is today), the

Wanderers and the Householders together represented the majority. And it is within these two that one can see the central contrasting polarities of the religious activities of the time. It is largely in reference to these two that Buddhist teachings are, and were from the beginning, referred to as the Middle Way. This expression has several implications, organisational, practical and metaphysical, the relevance of all of which is best understood contextually. We shall come to its metaphysical relevance below. Organisationally, the Middle Way is intended to place the structure of the early Buddhist community (called the *Saṅgha*) so to speak between the social structure of the Householders and the total absence of structure of the Wanderers. The way each of the early Buddhist communities was set up provided a base for its members which was both separate from living in a household alongside other householders, but also acted as a centre from which interaction with the laity could take place by means of a reciprocal relationship: the giving of Buddhist teachings was exchanged for food and other necessities. Though members of these Buddhist communities gave up the social and reproductive activities associated with the life of the Householders, they did not renounce society in the extreme way that the Wanderers did. In terms of practice, for Buddhists the Middle Way lies between the extremes of sensual indulgence, in particular the sexual life and other domestic comforts of the Householders, and of asceticism, in particular the self-mortification of the Wanderers. Members of the Buddhist community are provided for to the extent that their bodily needs are met (food, clothing, shelter, medicine, and so on). Though they have to overcome their sexual desires, and other sensual desires for anything beyond basic necessities, the practice of the Middle Way is intended to facilitate concentration on mental exercises by ensuring that bodily needs are not a constant distraction.[7]

Other than their common search for liberation from the cycle of lives by means of achieving insight of the Truth, and their contrasting ascetic practices, the main feature of the religion of the Wanderers that impinged on early Buddhist teachings was the plethora of speculative questions they formed as they went about their search. Though the new Brahmanical teaching, recorded in the *Upaniṣads*, clearly stated the Truth to be that the essence of one's self (*ātman*) was identical with the essence of the Absolute (Brahman), and that it was by experiencing this fact that liberation was achieved, those who did not accept the validity of the

Brahmanical religion continued to speculate as part of their search, and many alternatives were put forward. The focus of the speculations was, as mentioned above, the nature of the world and, more importantly, the nature of the human being in it: the point being that it was thought that human liberation was associated with 'knowing thyself'. The most clearly identifiable, and clearly contrasting, views on the nature of the human being were those of the eternalists and the annihilationists, mentioned in Chapter One. Eternalists (and a variation of these would have been the *Upaniṣadic* teachers) believed that everyone has an eternal Self/soul, which existed before birth and will continue to exist after death, being reborn again and again. Annihilationists believed that though one has a soul during life, it is annihilated at death and never comes to be again.[8]

Several passages in the early Buddhist texts record a large number of other views which collectively correspond to the different ways in which certain key speculative questions might be answered.[9] And the questions themselves are subsumed into four, expressed as follows: Whether or not the universe is eternal; whether or not the universe is finite; whether or not the vital principle of a person (*jīva* – in effect, soul) is separate from the body; and whether or not a liberated person exists after death, whether s/he exists and does not exist, or whether s/he neither exists nor does not exist.[10] The questions, to which I shall be referring again, are known in Buddhism as the classical Unanswered Questions as it is reported that the Buddha pointedly remained silent in response to all of them. But it is in the context of their formulation reflecting the widespread concern with whether or not certain things, usually the world and/or the soul, exist that the metaphysical implication of the Middle Way of the Buddhist teachings lies. Though the full meaning of this may perhaps not become apparent till later chapters of this book, in brief the point is that the Buddhist teaching that everything is dependently originated indicates that the ontological status of all things is neither that of existence nor that of non existence, but of a middle way between such extremes. More specifically, the Buddhist teaching on metaphysics takes the Middle Way between all of the contemporary metaphysical views held by Householders or Wanderers.

As might be expected, central to the Vedic sacrificial ritual was the use of fire. Sacrifice has perhaps been the one constant factor through all the various stages of the Brahmanical religion, and there had been major developments in its practice even before the century with which we are concerned. By our period, the sacrifice had become much more elaborate than it had earlier been, requiring not just many more priests, longer and more complicated rituals, more implements and materials, and richer patrons to pay for it all, but even common sacrificial rituals required three fires rather than one. One might say that what had originally been a simple hospitality rite between lone sacrificer and deity over a single fire had become, via various stages, a complex ritual celebration orchestrated by the priests. Though it has to a large extent since been re-simplified (partly because of the need to accommodate new concerns within the religion), it is clear that one of the main features of the sacrificial life of the Householders of our period, or at least the orthodox among them, was that they were each responsible for the maintaining of three sacrificial fires for the performing of their own ritual duties. From marriage, the three fires would have become, in effect, associated with their household hearth, one actually being used as such. (It is still the case for an orthodox member of the Brahmanical religion that his ritual fire is his household hearth but there is now only one fire involved. Larger public sacrifices still use three fires.) And because it was so important that each individual householder should keep making his own small contribution to the sacrificial maintenance of the universe, it was the responsibility of each to keep these fires alight throughout his lifetime. The centrality of the sacrificial fire as mediator between the sacred and the profane was symbolised by the elevation of fire to the status of *deva*. And constant accessibility to this mediating deity was ensured because the household fires of each sacrificing householder came to symbolise the householder's own identity. Thus from the time of his marriage until his death the continual burning of the three fires was of as much concern to him as was his own continuity.

It is important to note that a sacrificer is in fact a sacrificial patron and not an officiant. According to the rationale of each making their own contribution to the order of the whole, and the whole thus functioning reciprocally, only the priests were officiants. As mentioned when explaining the Brahmanical social structure, it is the duty of members of the two classes below the brahmins to employ the priests to be officiants at sacrificial rituals on their behalf. No sacrifice could be performed without the presence of at least one priest because only they were permitted to learn and perform the physical and verbal rituals. The language of all the ritual instruction manuals, and the language of the verbal rituals themselves, Sanskrit,[11] was also closely guarded by the brahmin priests. This was because it was, and still is, believed that the language of Sanskrit is intrinsically correlated to the structure of cosmic Order. Thus it was that the Sanskrit sounds uttered at the sacrifice had the consequence of maintaining, in the sense of continually re-creating, that cosmos.[12] The power that this represented had to be safeguarded from any who might tamper with it. But such safeguarding also preserved the powerful position of the priests in the socio-religious hierarchy. Priesthood was as much of an hereditary occupation as any other, and it was the task of priestly families to preserve specific ritual details for successive generations. The nature of the rituals was such that what their preservation required above all else was memorisation: it was the action *qua* action that brought the consequence, so what mattered was that each movement or verbalised word or sound had to be accurate. Beyond believing that correctly performed rituals brought corresponding results, *meaning* was neither required nor sought.

As the Brahmanical religion underwent its transition from being sacrificially cosmos-centred to being yogically person-centred, and as it absorbed the new soteriological teachings of the early *Upaniṣads*, so the priests extended their remit from sacrificial rituals to include the teaching of yogic practices. There is evidence, especially in the early *Upaniṣads* themselves, that the yogic teachings originated outside the brahmin class. But the transition has also been described in terms of sacrificial mysticism, or the internalising of the sacrifice, and as such one might expect the priests to be interested in it. And by extending their remit they were also able to retain religious control as their religion evolved. What this meant was that though the new yogic path was essentially about personal experience, within the Brahmanical religion it was taught by priests whether they had themselves experienced it or not. So used were they to the exoteric and repetitive requirements of the sacrifice, which they were able to preserve and practise so meticulously, that the necessity for experiential insight seemed to be beyond many of them.

During a considerable period of his own search, the Buddha is reported to have encountered many other seekers of the Truth and, indeed, to have practised some of the methods they taught for attaining insight. Though he eventually stated that none of them was entirely efficacious, his most vociferous criticism was aimed at the Brahmin priests who were teaching something of which they had no personal experience.[13] Many would like the Buddha to have denounced the notion of the socio-religious hierarchy as instigated by the Brahmanical religion. But he did not. What he did do, at least so far as we can tell from the texts, was to redefine what it meant to be a brahmin, someone who had spiritual authority and was reputed to be at the purest end of the spiritual spectrum. What made a true brahmin, he said, was nothing to do either with the family lineage into which you were born or with learning from the *Vedic* texts. Rather, the *sine qua non* of a true brahmin was that he must himself have experienced insight into the Truth. No-one, the Buddha said, had any authoritative right to teach anything of which they had no experience. And rather than being a status acquired at birth, to be preserved by strenuously avoiding polluting people and substances, the purity of any given individual was determined by their state of mind.[14] We shall see in the next chapter how this fits in with the rest of his teachings.

This, then, is an overview of the socio-religious milieu at the time of the Buddha and in which the Buddhist teachings were first given, at least sufficient for our purposes. According to the early Buddhist texts, the Buddha himself was born in the town of Kapilavatthu, just inside what is now Nepal, into a clan called the Sākyas, hence his title Sākyamuni – sage of the Sākyas. His given name was Siddhartha, his family name Gotama, and Buddha is the title he acquired on Enlightenment: Buddha means 'awakened'. Common epithets found in the texts, both terms of respect for his status as Buddha, include Tathāgata, which I mentioned in the Introduction, and Bhagavan – Lord. His family's position seems to have been one of material privilege in a community that was flourishing with newly developing trade and commerce. There is no evidence in support of the common claim of later Buddhists that the Buddha's family was of the second of the classes of the Brahmanical hierarchy, the ruling class, and it is more likely that his community had not yet been absorbed into the Brahmanical system at all. It appears from the texts that it was not until he had embarked on his spiritual search that he became familiar with the dominant religious teachings of his time through meeting others with a similar quest and through debating with brahmin teachers. And his decision to make the search seems to have been prompted not by any specifically religious encounter or reaction but by an existential concern with the human lot. The texts state that it was in particular his observation that everyone becomes ill, everyone ages, and everyone eventually dies, that set him wondering about the meaning of life. And we are told that he decided to leave his home environment and travel in search of anyone or anything that might bring him to understand why life is as it is.

We are told that the Buddha's search lasted for six years, and during that time he was to all intents and purposes no different from any other Wanderer of the day. As mentioned above, as he met others on his travels he tried the practices advocated by many of them. These included different sorts of meditative disciplines as well as extremes of asceticism. Eventually, we are told, he realised that none of them was bringing him certainty about the answer to his question. Accordingly, having taken food and drink to make his body healthy after a period of fasting, he retired on his own and went into a deep contemplative state to ponder on things. It was during this deep contemplation that he had the experience which is called his Enlightenment. And it is from this point that we shall start Chapter Three.

Notes

1 In the context of numerous lives, there is no element of elitism either: gaining insight is dependent only on making spiritual progress and limited only by one's own actions (karma).

2 One sometimes reads of the 'endless' cycle of lives. This is wrong: the whole *point* is that rebirth can be ended.

3 Many untouchables have become extremely rich through providing such necessary services but this in no way alters their ritually impure status: this is not a hierarchy determined or affected by wealth.

4 *Manu* 10.97.

5 The failure of independence fully to overcome this is graphically explicated in Freeman's *Untouchable: An Indian Life History* (1979), perhaps especially on pp. 96–7: an untouchable has been legally wronged by a brahmin. In a court of law the brahmin challenges the untouchable to touch him if he is telling the truth. The untouchable cannot bring himself to touch a brahmin, and loses the case.

6 Only men from the three highest classes had religious rights and opportunities: servants, untouchables, and women from all classes, had to hope that if they did their duty well they would be reborn as a high class man in a future life.

7 For a fuller account of Buddhist community life see Wijayaratna, 1990. Bechert and Gombrich (1984) chapter 2, part 1, "The Evolution of the Sangha", also gives an account of the way the community started and developed. I have necessarily generalised the situation here.

8 Among the annihilationists, interpreting the nature of the human being in their own way which did not include an acceptance of karma or the cycle of lives, or of a soul of any kind, was a prominent group of materialists. They did, however, add their materialistic views on the nature of the human being, no less speculative than the views of others, to the debates of the day. On this group see Basham, 1951.

9 cf. in particular the *Brahmajāla Sutta* (DN I, *sutta* 1); the *Pāsādika Suttanta* (DN III, *sutta* 29); and the *Sabbāsava Sutta* (MN I *sutta* 2).

10 MN I 157. (I have taken the Pali *tathāgata* in question 4 to imply any liberated person.) cf. also the *Cūḷa-Māluṅkya Sutta* (MN I 426ff), the *Avyākata Saṃyutta* (SN IV 374ff) and the *Aggi-Vacchagotta Sutta* (MN I 483ff) (much of the last two are phrased as a series of questions and answers). Because of the 'whether or not' structure of these questions, and the fourfold composition of the fourth question, they are sometimes numbered as twelve.

11 Some of the sounds of the sacrifice are not words as such. But the structure of those sounds is analysed by the tradition according to the rules and symbols of Sanskrit, and it is not inaccurate to think of Sanskrit as being the language of the sacrifice.

12 In the word Sanskrit can be seen the same verbal root, *kṛ*, from which the word karma – action – derives, thus highlighting the active, that is to say creative, aspect of the sound of the language.

13 The classic passages are the *Tevijja Sutta* (DN I, sutta 13) and the *Brāhmaṇavagga* of the *Dhammapada* (chapter 26). As we shall see, the whole gist of the Buddhist teachings also emphasises self-sufficiency in a way that renders the priests utterly redundant.

14 There are many passages in the *Sutta Nipāta* to this effect, but perhaps the most obvious is the *Āmagandha Sutta* (vv. 239ff.), translated by K.R. Norman as 'Tainted Fare'. Elsewhere (SN IV 180f.) the point is made graphically by referring to anyone – of whatever class status – who behaves immorally, with evil deeds and lustfully, as 'rotting within', a 'rubbish heap of impurity'.

CHAPTER THREE

The Focus on Experience

"Just as the ocean has only one taste, the taste of salt, so the Buddhist doctrine and discipline have only one taste, the taste of liberation."
AN IV 203; Vin II 238; *Udāna* 56.

The significance of the Buddha's Enlightenment experience is that it was the occasion when he realised that he was no longer going to continue being reborn in the cycle of lives: he had achieved liberation from that. I have come to think that it is by starting with an attempt to understand what the experience of Enlightenment involved, and what it meant, that one can best understand what he subsequently taught. This is partly because it was not until after he had had the experience that he taught anything at all, and partly because he himself said that everything he taught was intended to help others have the same experience, and *only* that. The *locus classicus* for this point is the passage which contains the analogy of the man shot by the arrow to which I referred in Chapter One.[1] The point is that just as the shot man needs to have the arrow taken out rather than be given a lot of unhelpful information about its provenance, so nothing is taught by the Buddha that does not contribute to the purpose of achieving liberation.

The intimate association between the Enlightenment experience of the Buddha and his teachings is acknowledged by the way they both relate to what in early Buddhism is called *Dhamma*, the Pali form of the Sanskrit word *Dharma*. I have mentioned that the Brahmanical religion was profoundly concerned with maintaining cosmic orderliness, and that optimal Order abstractly understood was and is known as *Dharma*. By extension from its association with Order in this sense, *Dharma* represented the eternal Truth as expressed in the Vedic texts. Each individual contributed to its maintenance by the performing of his or her duty, or own-*dharma*. *Dharma* was thus understood both descriptively and prescriptively. As the Brahmanical religion underwent the transition of incorporating into itself the soteriological teaching of the *Upaniṣads*, so too the concept of *Dharma* underwent a transition. In addition to its descriptive and prescriptive dimensions, both of which remained, it became associated with the experience of the eternal Truth that was sought by the seeker of liberation from the cycle of lives: it was not just to be maintained but also known or seen by the individual. *Dharma*, then, was Truth abstractly understood, the experiential goal of a man's spiritual life, and the injunctions by which he lived his life until the goal was reached.

Illustrating the way the Buddha phrased his teachings in the terminology of the Brahmanical religion, the same term refers in Buddhism both to the Truth one is aiming to experience for oneself as the Buddha did at his Enlightenment, and also to the Buddhist teachings one is practising in order to achieve that aim. As the Truth one is aiming to experience, *Dhamma* is the implicit object of the common, and very important, early Buddhist expression that one's goal is to 'know and see things as they really are', usually abbreviated to 'seeing things as they really are'.[2] The notion of *Dhamma* as teachings has a place of central importance for the Buddhist tradition as a whole because it is one of what are called the Three Jewels of Buddhism. The other two are the Buddha himself, and the *Saṅgha*, or Buddhist community. The relationship between these three is symbolically explained as that of the physician who diagnoses the disease (the Buddha), the cure for the disease (the *Dhamma*), and the nurse that administers the cure (the *Saṅgha*). And as this symbolism clearly suggests, it is both relevant and helpful in attempting to understand Buddhism to interpret its structure in the sense of the curing of a disease. In more modern terms, this corresponds to the solving of a problem.

The Enlightenment experience of the Buddha can, then, be best understood as the occasion on which he solved his problem, and the solution was the Truth he had been seeking. And as mentioned at the end of Chapter Two, his problem derived from an existential concern with the human lot. From simple observation he could see that it involved a great deal that was manifestly unsatisfactory: for any of a number of reasons one loses things and people one is fond of, pleasurable experiences do not last, people become ill, they age, and they all eventually die. The Buddha wanted to know why this was the case, and whether it was possible for a human being to experience something better: in particular to achieve liberation from bondage to continuity of such a state. So one might say that he set up his problem in this way: why is human experience as it is, and how can one do something about it? In this chapter it is this specific focus on human experience, and the way it pervades both the Buddha's Enlightenment and his subsequent teachings, that I want to establish and draw out. I believe that it is primarily in understanding the implications of this focus that we can better understand the teachings as a whole.

As we already know, there were many seekers of the Truth at the time of the Buddha. And in a manifestly changing and uncertain world, most were concerned to find something unchanging and permanent, or in other words something that was immortal: this, they thought, was the ultimately desirable discovery. Recognising the specificity and relative transience of the *devas* associated with the sacrifice, even the ancient Vedic hymn-writers were concerned to find the unifying substance or power, called by them the One, behind the changing multiplicity of the cosmos as they conceived of it. For them this question was answered by the *Upaniṣadic* teaching that everything is Brahman, the universal Absolute.[3] The more famous teaching that the essence of one's self (*ātman*) is identical with Brahman, mentioned previously, is in fact implicit if everything is Brahman: one could not be anything else. The point for us here is that within the Brahmanical religion, what they thought they had found was the permanent and unchanging unity behind apparent change and multiplicity.

Those among the seekers of the Truth who did not accept the Brahmanical teachings were nevertheless also concerned with the issue of finitude in this substantialist sense. For them the Truth was not understanding human experience itself, but finding some permanent thing beyond the limitations of human experience. Where the *Upaniṣadic* teaching had established the eternality of both soul and world (ultimately not two things but one), others likewise formulated their questions and putative answers in a number of variations on the theme of the permanence or otherwise of one's soul and of the world. Such people began their search for Truth with the view that finding it would involve no more and no less than the answers to such questions: the framework of their search had the same format as that of the *Upaniṣadic* teachers. The questions and putative answers, to which I referred in Chapter Two, are given in several different formulations in the early Buddhist texts. One textual source gives the following: "Did I exist in the past? Did I not exist in the past? What was I in the past? How was I in the past? Having been what, what did I become in the past? Shall I exist in the future? Shall I not exist in the future? What shall I be in the future? How shall I be in the future? Having been what, what shall I become in the future? Am I now? Am I not, now? What am I? How am I? Where has this being come from? Where will this being go?" It goes on to give the following putative conclusions: "I have a self. I have no self. I perceive [my] self by means of [my] self. I perceive no self by means of [my] self. I perceive [my] self by means of no self. This self of mine which speaks and feels, that experiences the consequences of good and bad actions now here and now there, this self is permanent, stable, eternal, unchanging, the same always."[4] In several places, all the questions are subsumed into the fourfold formula mentioned earlier and collectively referred to within the Buddhist tradition as the classical unanswered questions. Classical refers to the fact that the questions reflect the central concerns of most seekers of the truth, and indeed most religious traditions, and unanswered indicates that in spite of such centrality and the frequency with which he heard the questions, the Buddha himself never answered them. It is their unanswered status that is noteworthy in Buddhism. The questions, in their formula form, were: Is the world eternal or not? Is the world finite or not? Is the soul different from the body or not? Does an Enlightened person, after his death, exist or not, exist and not exist, neither exist nor not exist?[5] The logic-defying combinations of the last two parts of question four are undoubtedly intended to ensure that all possible permutations of forming questions along these lines are covered. And all of these should be understood in the context of seeking something permanent.

According to textual descriptions, the Buddha appears to have started his search somewhat differently in that he began with no frame of reference other than observable and common features of human experience. If he had any assumptions about the nature of the insights he hoped for then they are not recorded in the texts. It is quite possible, if his life prior to the start of his spiritual quest was primarily concerned with secular issues, that he did not become acquainted with any of the religious concerns of others until after he had set out and began encountering and discoursing with those other people. If this was the case, it would have meant that he had the great advantage of setting out with open-mindedness. If it was not the case, then the way in which he was able to extend his frame of reference away from those of his contemporaries is all the more remarkable.

It is not only the canonical descriptions of the beginning of his search, the formulating of his problem, as it were, that indicate the nature of the Buddha's particular existential observations. Descriptions of his Enlightenment experience, the solving of the problem, are also phrased in a way that shows its focus to be significantly different from the concerns of his contemporaries. There is no reference whatsoever to issues of an ultimate nature relating to the finitude or eternality of the soul and the world, or, indeed, with what the human being *is*, or with whether or not it is. Rather, Enlightenment is described in terms of insights relating to human experience and the mechanics of its continuity in the cycle of lives, with the nature of human experience and how it might be changed. In other words, they are concerned with questions of how and why something is the case, and not with what things are or are not. Three insights are described in the texts.[6] First, the Buddha is able to see his former lives: where and how and why he was reborn as he was. Second, he is able to see other beings being born and reborn in different conditions and *why* they are so reborn. In effect, what this means is that he could see the mechanics of the law of karma – how actions have consequences, and that what happens is qualitatively conditioned by what occurred previously: this is both the how and the why of any given individual history over a series of lives. Third, he is able to see, and know how to uproot, the very deepest of what I shall call the continuity tendencies, in Pali the *āsavas*, that bind one to continued rebirth. What this means, in effect, is that in understanding the mechanics of continuity, he is able to do something about liberating himself from bondage to that continuity. The deepest continuity tendencies are given as sensual desire, the desire for continued becoming, ignorance, and, in one account, the holding of 'views', broadly speaking in the sense of holding to specific and fixed dogmatic opinions or theories.[7] Little reflection is required in order to see how deep-seated are these continuity tendencies, and why getting rid of them might constitute the final stages of the path. Immediately prior to turning his mind to the uprooting of these tendencies, the texts state that the Buddha 'understood human experience as it really is, its cause, that it can cease, and how to bring about its cessation'. And immediately after he had uprooted them he realised 'I am liberated, I am no longer subject to rebirth, I have done what I had to do'.

Before drawing out other implications of this description of the Buddha's Enlightenment, it is worth making a point concerning what is to all intents and purposes the pan-Indian belief that human beings are reborn again and again in a series of lives. I mentioned in the last chapter that this is one of the key features of the conceptual framework of the Indian worldview, introduced into the Brahmanical tradition at the time of the early *Upaniṣads* and also taught by many of the Wanderers. The point to note here is that descriptions of the Buddha's Enlightenment given in the early Buddhist texts suggest that he did not include rebirth in his teachings because it was a given aspect of the prevailing worldview. Rather, his own experiential insight revealed or confirmed its truth to him.

The same observation applies to the reference to karma in the descriptions of the Buddha's Enlightenment. We are told that the Buddha's second insight was that he could see *why* other beings were being born and reborn in different conditions: the way in which their actions in previous lives had had the consequence of qualitatively conditioning subsequent lives. This, as far as he was concerned, was a confirmation that one's actions have consequences for one's future in tandem with the fact that one will experience rebirths. For the Buddha, both of these were part of the Truth, or *Dhamma*, as he had seen it and not just culturally accepted norms.

Having made these two similar observations, the main implication to be drawn from the *structure* of the description of the Buddha's Enlightenment is, as stated above, that it relates to human experience and its continuity in the cycle of lives, and with how human experience might be changed to the extent that it is no longer bound to such continuity. It is the Truth of *this* as it really is that the Buddha gains insight of, and it is to this that the expression 'seeing things as they really are' refers. With regard to the *content* of the Enlightenment, the most significant implication to be drawn out is that what needs to be attended to in order to achieve liberation from the cycle of lives is focused in the individual person's state of mind. The description of the third insight relates to the uprooting of sensual desire, desire for continued becoming, ignorance, and holding 'views'. If one were to attempt to objectify or universalise such things one would arrive only at abstractions. But in terms of experiential insight, each can be related only to oneself as an individual human being: each person can only have access, and effect changes, to their *own* desires, ignorance and opinions.

According to the Buddha, the Truth, *Dhamma*, that one needs insight of lies here, then: in the way one's own mind is instrumental in perpetuating experience as we know it. It is not knowing the Truth in the sense of becoming omniscient, nor in the sense of knowing about what is or is not immortal. This is one reason why all the various questions formulated by other seekers after Truth are stated to be irrelevant: as none of them is focused on the workings of one's mind, so absolutely none is relevantly formulated. It is clearly stated that the main reason he never answered them was because they are not conducive to "good . . . to insight, Enlightenment, *nibbāna*."[8] Occasionally he adds to this that such questions cannot meaningfully be answered: they have to be understood through insight,[9] and I shall return to this aspect of his silence in later chapters. The point to note here is that the Buddha consistently confined himself to the solving of his problem and saw no point in encouraging one's attention to be diverted away from that.

The specific focus on one's own state of mind is reinforced by the way the Buddha explained how karma operates, the workings of which were the subject of the second of his Enlightenment insights. The consequence-producing aspect of any action, whether it be effected physically, verbally or mentally (by body, word or thought is how it is put), is, the Buddha said, the intention behind it.[10] With this teaching alone the Buddha rendered the Brahmanical priests redundant.[11] Though in the Brahmanical religion it was the duty of each qualified householder to undertake certain rituals, he could not actually do much of this on his own: he had to have a priest to perform sacrifices, and administer other aspects of the religion, on his behalf. Even the social duties he had to fulfil in order to ensure a favourable rebirth were enumerated for him by the priests. Insofar as he was personally involved in any actions, all he had to do was to act correctly according to criteria laid down by the priests: he had no personal responsibility other than to do his duty as he was told it. The priests in their turn were also bound by the injunctions of the ritual manuals as preserved by their ancestors. Beyond the developments that take place over time in any tradition, each of which may be almost imperceptible on its own, there was little if any room for spontaneity or improvisation. In contrast to all of this, one can only intend for oneself, and one's intentions, unlike one's visible actions, do not conform to injunctions.

There is a further contrast between the Buddha's explanation of karma and the Brahmanical teachings on this subject. The Brahmanical ritual religion, in requiring accuracy and precision in conforming to the ritual injunctions, both for the sacrificial rituals and for the performing of one's own-*dharma* in the social hierarchy, held that it was ours to do very precisely but not to reason why. The Buddha's teaching, in suggesting that what was required was a comprehensive understanding of one's state of mind, insisted that reasoning why was precisely what we had to do. One had to understand that the psycho-cognitive matrix underpinning all states of mind prior to the Enlightenment insights is one of *not* 'seeing things as they really are': one is ignorant of the Truth that will solve one's problem. This is why, in enduring right to the end of the path, when one *does* see things as they really are ignorance is seen to be one of the deepest binding continuity tendencies. And as we have seen above, its rooting out is achieved only by gaining insight into 'human experience as it really is, its cause, that it can cease, and how to bring about its cessation'. The cessation of human experience as we know it is co-terminous with the cessation of ignorance. In Buddhism this is understood supremely positively: one is not aiming for extermination, but to attain the highest insight it is possible for a human being to attain so that one is not subject to the *bondage* of continuity. Enlightenment is thus the summation of human life: what ceases when one attains the highest insight is what is restricting one to continuing in the same old way. In short, one is free. So though the terminology used refers to cessation, the point is that it is what has been negative that ceases, not that the cessation is in itself a negative event.

That it is one's intention that is the consequence-producing aspect of any action is relevant to the way purity is understood in the early Buddhist texts. I mentioned in Chapter Two that according to the Buddha purity was not to do with hereditary status, as it was for the brahmins. Rather, it is metaphorically interpreted in terms of the extent to which one has both understood that it is from negative states of one's own mind, such as anger, hatred, greed, and so on, that negative intentions arise and have corresponding consequences, and then proceeded to clear one's mind of those negativities. Many Buddhist meditative exercises are concerned with examining one's state of mind at any given moment, and in ensuring that one 'purifies' it.[12] The reason for this is so that eventually one's mind is clear enough – 'pure' in *this* sense – to allow one to 'see things as they really are'. As seeings things as they really are is also the cessation of ignorance, it follows that all the negative aspects of one's state of mind, in the affective, or appetitive, sense, prior to the Enlightenment insight, arise from, or are part and parcel of, some degree of ignorance in the cognitive sense. Purity, then, is both affective and cognitive. Achieving this can take lifetimes, but it is why the Buddhist path to liberation is also sometimes referred to as a path of purification. It is also why the Buddha criticised the brahmins for their concern to avoid contact with polluting people and substances. Purity comes from within, not from without, he stated.[13] And he also parodied their insistence on keeping alight the three sacrificial fires by parallelling them metaphorically with greed, hatred and ignorance as the three most important fires one is associated with, and stating that rather than keeping them alight what one needs to do is to put them out. Negative states of mind, all of which can be subsumed into this threefold metaphor,[14] constitute the fuel that keeps one continuing in the cycle of lives as they give rise to consequence-producing intentions. And collectively they are the fuel that needs to be blown out – it is to this that nirvana, which means 'blowing out', refers.

The fact that ignorance is so closely linked with desire in the descriptions of the Buddha's Enlightenment, and that both cognitive and affective aspects of one's state of mind are included in the continuity tendencies that are uprooted on that occasion, in my view clearly suggests that in early Buddhism the terms Enlightenment and nirvana refer to the same occasion. Though in some later forms of Buddhism they become separated, largely because what is said to be involved in Enlightenment is changed, in early Buddhism Enlightenment is the insight which effects the blowing out of the fuel. The association of insight with the uprooting of the continuity tendencies is both explicitly stated and is also conceptually coherent in a way other understandings of nirvana are not. This seems so obviously the case that in my view one should not permit muddled references in the texts to what nirvana is to allow confusion to arise concerning the central point of it. I refer in particular to the references to nirvana being something one experiences occasionally, and the confusion that the term *parinibbāna*, usually explained as something like 'final nirvana', gives rise to.[15] In my opinion one needs to consider such things in the light of the nature of the textual material in which they are found. First, one can imagine that over a period of decades many questions might have been asked of what nirvana is, at times and places far removed from the occasion of the Buddha's Enlightenment, and many different ways of referring to it might have been given by different people. And second, it is highly likely that records preserved orally from the beginning, in an environment in which communities were both dispersed and lacked anything like a kind of formal communication system, of a teaching that was novel, radical, and difficult to grasp, should include anomalies, variations, slightly distorted repetitions, and any number of oddities of various sorts. It would, I think, be surprising if they did not. I think one should discount as unimportant the bulk of these, and interpret *parinibbāna* in the obvious and uncomplicated sense that it simply refers to the occasion on which one who has previously attained nirvana subsequently dies.[16]

The need to clarify one's mind so that one can get rid of ignorance and 'see things as they really are' highlights what in my view is perhaps the most central feature of what Buddhist teachings are about. Quite apart from the fact that the need as stated establishes the centre of activity, in the sense of where one needs to direct one's spiritual energy, in the workings of one's own mind, it also immediately suggests the importance of perception. This is not just perception in the sense of visually seeing with one's eyes – looking. Rather, it extends the notion of seeing to one's cognitive eye, seeing in the sense of knowing. A simple exercise of imagining the way in which one frequently thinks or states 'I see' in the sense of 'I understand' demonstrates what I mean by perception here: and this correlates with the full Pali expression of 'knowing and seeing' things as they really are. But as well as operating on individual occasions of understanding, one's perception acts as the cognitive lens through which we in fact have our experience in its entirety: none of us can have experience in any other way. Apart from homing in on the fact that we all have this cognitive lens, the need for clarity of perception also focuses on the fact that for each of us our experience is as it were led by our *personal* cognitive lens. In the same way that we are each ignorant (in every sense) in our own particular way and degree, so we each have our own perception and understanding of the world.

This is not at all to suggest that we all live in *entirely* different, randomly subjective, worlds. In my view only a mad person would deny that unless we are damaged or ill in some way – such as exemplified in Oliver Sacks' graphically entitled book *The Man Who Mistook His Wife For a Hat* – we all see the same chairs and tables, trees and sunsets, cats and dogs, and so on (or that at least we can in principle do so if we are looking at and paying attention to the same thing), that we can all feel the same variety of textures, hear the same variety of sounds, and so on, and that broadly speaking we share an understanding of what they literally are. Further, it is cardinal to the Buddha's teaching that the problem and its solution is common to each of us. But though we do all so to speak share the fundamentals, we also all see (and feel and hear, and so on), understand, interpret our experience of those fundamentals in our own way. Though we all might see the same chairs and tables, to take a visual example (and similar examples could easily be found with regard to each of the senses), we may well differ as to our reactions to their design, colour, degree of comfort, and so on. What person A sees as a masterpiece of modern chair design might even appear so absurd to person B for him to think 'that is not what I call a chair'. Similarly, seeing the same tree or sunset may represent and conjure up entirely different connotations and responses in different people: the tree may be a wonderful example of ancient English oak, a symbol of tradition, reliability, courage and patriotism to one person, and an obstacle to a motorway route to another. And if each were to comment 'Gosh, look at that tree', the expression would be loaded with very different meaning – to the extent that they would in effect each be having different cognitive experiences. Person C might be so indifferent to the chair design and the tree that his registering of their presence is next to non-existent. This might just be that he cannot later say anything about them at all: they leave no impression on his experiential memory; indeed we all routinely respond like this to a vast number of the objects around us all the time. But it might also be that not even the injunction 'Gosh, look at that tree' has any effect: not even looking at the tree penetrates his cognitive indifference. This is described in the texts as occasions when one's eye and the visible object are present but there is not the appropriate concentration (*samannāhāra*) for visual consciousness to occur.[17] So though we each *literally* see the same objects, our experience is so coloured by our subjective responses that we may well describe the objects themselves quite differently. What we literally see with our eyes is processed through our cognitive eye subjectively.

All this emphasises my point that the focus of Enlightenment is entirely subjective and not about objective universals. Just as it was the Buddha's own perception that changed when he gained the insights of his Enlightenment, so the focus of the Buddha's teachings is the perception of each and every one of us, so that we can gain similar insights for ourselves. Whether or not one accepts that one can attain those insights, it is because the focus of the teachings is on so indisputable a feature of human existence – that we all have our own perception of the world of experience, or, more simply, our own experience – that I feel there is a more reasonable chance that one might come to a meaningful understanding of it than our chronological and cultural disadvantages might suggest: neither time nor place affects the fact that we are common experiencing human beings.

Having made this last point, it is important to emphasise that it is with one's pre-Enlightenment perception that the teachings are concerned. This qualification is an important one: as I have stated, Enlightenment is not cessation of perception *per se*; rather, it is a change from one way of perceiving to another. But the perception of and post Enlightenment is of a different order of perception from anything prior to it: it is the yogic perception to which I have already referred. The very term Buddha, which, as I have explained, means awakened, implies that the difference between one's perception pre-Enlightenment compared with the insight one gains at Enlightenment is analogous to our first being asleep and then waking up: two states that are so different that we give them different names. A similar but more powerful analogy is that of a person blind from birth gaining sight. This is more powerfully explanatory because of the radical difference between the perception, in the sense of one's cognitive lens, of a blind person and that of a sighted person. It is so radical that though a blind person can know, factually, *that* he is blind, because he does not know what seeing is he cannot actually know what his blindness *is*.[18] Further, it would, in theory, be possible for him genuinely to think the very notion of sightedness, of having the use of a cognitive faculty wholly outside what to him is normal experience, absurd.[19]

Therefore perception *as we know it* is a pre-Enlightenment experience. And in using the term perception it is to this that I refer. For Enlightenment I shall use the term insight.

According to the early texts, after his Enlightenment the Buddha gave what is referred to as his first sermon.[20] The content of this sermon is a formula called the Four Noble Truths, and these refer back to what he himself had understood, during his Enlightenment, before he attended to the uprooting of his continuity tendencies. I have twice above mentioned that he is described as having 'understood human experience as it really is, its cause, that it can cease, and how to bring about its cessation', and these words are my paraphrase of what he subsequently teaches as the Four Noble Truths. In the first sermon the fourfold formula is given as follows: the fact of *dukkha*; *dukkha* arises because of cravings; cessation of *dukkha* can be attained; the Noble Eightfold Path is the way to attain such cessation.

Leaving aside for a moment any reference to, or discussion of, the way I have paraphrased this formula, what is immediately obvious from the Pali is the central place given in the formula to *dukkha*. And it is clear both that one's understanding of the formula would be profoundly affected by one's understanding of *dukkha*, and, conversely, that without a proper understanding of *dukkha* one would not be able to arrive at a proper understanding of the formula. I think this is a crucial point, and I shall be suggesting that in order to arrive at a full understanding of the formula – and thus perhaps the most foundational of the teachings of Buddhism – one needs to understand that *dukkha* has a more extended frame of reference than it is usually stated to have. This is not to suggest that the way it is usually understood is incorrect, but that it fails to go far enough in recognising its complexity, and the resulting implications of that. I shall come to my suggested extension of the frame of reference, which will pick up on the paraphrase I have already given, shortly. But because a discussion of this will lead us to other relevant areas, I will first explain the way it is usually understood.

The way *dukkha* is usually explained follows most of what is given in the very brief explanation of it given in the textual account of the first sermon. We read: "Birth, decay, illness and death are *dukkha*, as are all sorts of unhappiness; to be separated from what one likes, and not to have what one wants, are also *dukkha*".[21] In the context of the concern of seekers of the Truth to find permanence, unchangingness, immortality, this Truth arises from the fact that there is nothing about human experience that is any of those things: rather, everything changes, and is therefore impermanent. And because it is impermanent, it is unsatisfactory. The generality of this is also found in another teaching, a formula called the 'three characteristics of existence'.[22] Here the first characteristic of everything in our cyclical experience is stated to be impermanence. And all such things, and this is the second characteristic given in the formula, are therefore unsatisfactory (*dukkha*). This applies not just to any obviously unhappy states: however good or pleasant anything might be for a while it is unsatisfactory because it does not last.[23] It is thus as 'unsatisfactoriness' that *dukkha* is nowadays usually translated.

The second Truth states that *dukkha* arises because of cravings: it is our cravings that collectively fuel the on-going unsatisfactoriness. The brief explanation given of this Truth in the textual account of the first sermon states that it is because we are always wanting things in one way or another, ranging from all sorts of sensual pleasures to the desire either to live for ever or not to live at all, that we are perpetuating the experience of unsatisfactoriness, because even if we get what we want it does not last and we have other wants. In this way is explained the mechanics of unsatisfactoriness. The second Truth corresponds to the Buddha's interpretation of karma, to which I have already referred. It is the intention behind all our actions, he said, whether they be effected mentally, verbally, or bodily, that is consequential. Though the two words cravings (*taṇhā*) and intentions (*cetanā*) do not on the face of it necessarily refer to the same things, it seems to me that if one understands what is being said here they must both have been used generically. One way of putting it is that one persists in the cycle of lives because one's intentions produce consequences for us, and another way of putting it is that unsatisfactoriness persists because of one's cravings. But because the cycle of lives is *characterised* by unsatisfactoriness it is the same thing that is being referred to here, not two sorts of cycles of lives. Intentions and cravings are simply different words used to point to the fact that the fuel of continuity as we know it arises from the affective matrix of one's state of mind. I do not think we need be surprised that these different words are used. First, there is no evidence that the specific explanation of karma and the four Noble Truths were expounded by the Buddha at the same time (far from it), and it is an extremely common feature of verbal communication that we vary the way we say things on different occasions. That this may have been what occurred in these instances is even more likely given the Buddha's general rejection of the brahmanical insistence on precision and correctness of terminology. Second, what is being referred to in either case – the second Noble Truth or the explanation of karma, both of which are given in very cryptic form – is so conceptually vast that one can easily imagine that any one of a number of words could be employed as an umbrella term to refer to the complex of mental states involved, even if in other contexts they might be referred to severally and differently. In the wider context of the Buddha's teachings as a whole, though, as I said in the Introduction, one needs to remember that they are all given in a way that explicitly and implicitly encourages one to seek their spirit and not to be distracted by the letters employed in the giving of them. And given this situation, it is my view that it makes little sense to think that the Buddha's teaching on karma is not reiterating the second Noble Truth using slightly different words. And I am more of the opinion that this is the case because it was immediately following his own Enlightenment experience, which involved his insight into how beings are reborn according to their karma, that the Noble Truths were taught by the Buddha: it is hard to think he would have taught something different at such a time.

The unsatisfactoriness that is intrinsic to the impermanence of everything in our experience, then, is perpetuated by our continually craving for things that do not last. Here we have *dukkha* understood as a descriptive truth about our experience, and the truth concerning the mechanics of *dukkha*. Taken together, these Truths clearly home in on the psychology of what we experience. On its own the first Truth so described is not a radical insight: and the Buddha himself started his search wanting to know why human experience is manifestly unsatisfactory. So what we are being told in these two Truths, according to this interpretation of *dukkha*, is that it is because we cannot accept the fact of impermanence that we go on wanting the things we desire to last. And it is because we cannot accept the value neutrality of impermanence that it is unsatisfactory to us.

In stating that the cessation of *dukkha* is also a factual possibility, the third Truth tells us that one can achieve a situation in which one no longer has the cravings that fuel its continuity. This suggests that, psychologically, one can achieve a state of mind when one *can* accept the fact and value neutrality of impermanence. And when one achieves such a state, in understanding the situation as it really is one will no longer have any cravings or desires: the mechanics of the continuity of unsatisfactoriness will cease. A word of caution is needed here. If one takes this at face value to be stating that the aim is to stop wanting anything *at all*, this raises the question of how one eats and functions normally after Enlightenment. The Buddha lived for forty-five years after his Enlightenment, so this is an important point. In my view the solution is simple: one must accept that it is only bindingly consequential cravings that are relevant here, and that when one sees how things really are one can function spontaneously without in any way having selfish wants that are affectively consequential. Such spontaneity does not preclude either being concerned for the welfare of others or normal living. The Buddhist emphasis on compassion clearly indicates actively involving oneself with caring about other beings not just while one is on the path but also post-Enlightenment, the latter perhaps classically suggested by the Buddha's desire to teach so that others can attain nirvana. In this respect, one needs to understand that the distinction between spontaneity and bondage lies in one's motive. Similarly, there is a difference, for example, between eating to live and being greedy for one's food; there is a difference between sleeping because one needs to and being lazy. There are any number of examples of such nature one might give from everyday life. Providing for the needs associated with normal functioning is part of keeping healthy rather than the affectively consequential causal nexus being involved here. In fact this point is made in the texts themselves, where moderation in eating, control of the senses, and composure of thoughts are associated with living a life of ease (*sukha*), the opposite of the dis-ease that is *dukkha*.[24] And where 'eating just what is necessary' is associated with the cessation of passion.[25] And the fact that members of the Buddhist monastic communities are provided with basic bodily needs makes the point in a more practical way.

The fourth Truth, to which I need refer here only briefly, relates to *dukkha* in the sense that it gives a path to follow, or a programme of what needs to be attended to, in order to achieve a situation of the cessation of unsatisfactoriness. Called the Noble Eightfold Path, it consists of eight aspects of one's life one needs to get 'right': understanding, thought, speech, action, livelihood, effort, mindfulness, and concentration. Given the magnitude of the goal it is intended one should reach by following it, it is hard to imagine a less precisely given teaching, and the Eightfold Path perhaps classically exemplifies the extent to which the Buddha did not wish to pin down anything he said in too precise or detailed a 'thou shalt' way. Over time, traditional interpretations of each of these 'rights' have become accepted, such as that lying and slander are incompatible with right speech, and that trading in arms is not a right livelihood.[26] But there remains room for each of the 'rights' to be effected differently in any one of a number of ways according to one's understanding, personal circumstances, options, and so on. This is not at all an excuse for gratuitous self-indulgence in the putting of the different aspects of the path into practice, and nor is it to be taken as the establishing of a theory of relativism in the philosophical sense. The former would be a travesty of the point of the teachings, and the latter would be simply to miss the point. The travesty would lie in overlooking the profoundly ethical implications in the metaphysics of dependent origination. If the manner in which all things, including human beings, occur is not as independent selves, then whatever is self-ish or self-centred – that is, based on the view that one is separate – is wholly rooted in the ignorance that following the Buddhist path is intended to dispel. In fact this is a supremely demanding and difficult ethic to aspire to as even the commonly sought feel-good factor associated with being a do-gooder, and particularly with wanting to be seen to be one, is exposed as self-centred congratulation-seeking. And if the consequence of any action is determined by the intention behind it by way of a naturally operating law, then no matter how much one may be able to fool others, or even oneself, ultimately the need for genuine integrity of motive is both inescapable and unfakeable. But, alongside the need for integrity, it does allow for genuinely problematic circumstances to be approached realistically. For example, though the ideal of right speech is speaking the truth, or, alternatively, remaining silent, there might be occasions when the only effect and purpose of telling a lie is that it avoids unnecessarily hurting someone. In such cases what would be crucial would be that one's motive is genuinely altruistic, not that one wanted by lying to achieve something advantageous for oneself. Given this proviso, the way the teachings are given suggests that the difficulty of ascertaining an overall picture of the ramifications of one's actions in any problem situation is recognised – no-one can become a paragon of wisdom and virtue even in the whole of one lifetime – and that what one should look to in practice are one's motives, in the knowledge that one's actions will have consequences.[27]

Missing the point would lie in overlooking the fact that the context in which the teaching was given was that of the detail and rigidity of the Brahmanical system's injunctions to do one's duty and nothing but one's duty. Not only was this system based on a specific view of the nature of the cosmos, but for it to function at all one needed to know precisely what one should do in any given circumstance. By contrast, the focus of the Buddha's teaching was one's own state of mind, and the Eightfold Path emphasised the Buddha's insistence on accepting personal responsibility for one's actions. The point of making choices and decisions for oneself, be they of a mundane occupational nature or more overtly ethical, and in accepting whatever may be their consequences for one's future, does not lie in understanding some underlying relativism but, rather, in not devolving responsibility. Though it draws attention to the areas of one's life that need seriously and genuinely to be addressed, the looseness of the phrasing of the Eightfold Path both realistically recognises the infinite variety of personal circumstances in which each of us finds ourselves and refrains from providing any comforting or convenient authoritative injunctions behind which one might hide.

The first aspect of the path is, if one renders the Pali into English literally, 'right view' (*sammā diṭṭhi*). Though it is the same word, *diṭṭhi*, that is used, this refers not to views as dogmatic opinions which need rooting out, but, rather, to view in the sense of understanding, which is why I have rendered simply as 'right understanding'.[28] As such, it can be seen as representing both the beginning and end of the following of the path in that deciding to embark on it requires, according to Buddhism, a 'right understanding' of the teachings and their aim and applicability, and the goal of the path is 'right understanding' (insight) of how things really are. This perhaps exemplifies the way the structure of the path is multi-dimensional and not linear: the different aspects of it are not separate stages to be achieved or worked on in sequence, but, rather, relate to the dynamic complexity of a learning, developing, and one might say evolving (in the sense of making progress on the path) individual.[29] Each of the eightfold aspects of the path continues to be relevant for so long as one is following the path, but the nature of their relevance at any given stage, and of course this would be over a series of many lives, might change quite considerably. This structure is simply and effectively indicated by the way the eight aspects of the path were from the earliest stages of the tradition divided according to three interrelating and continuously relevant focuses – ethics, concentration and insight.[30] Ethics covers the multitude of ethical aspects involved in how one lives one's life; concentration refers to the mental (meditative) disciplines one needs to practise in order to understand that one's state of mind is central to the continuity of unsatisfactoriness and how to control it; and insight refers to the gradual cultivating or developing of the liberating understanding one is seeking to attain.

To return to *dukkha*, then, we can see that this is usually understood as the unsatisfactoriness that is intrinsic to the impermanence of all the things within our experience. In now discussing how *dukkha* might be better understood to have a wider frame of reference, I will pick up on my paraphrase of the Four Noble Truths. And this discussion will also provide an opportunity to discuss further the analysis of the human being in terms of *khandhas*. This will in turn lead us to the central aspect of my interpretation of the teachings as a whole as the understanding of experience in the sense of how we use our cognitive lens.

The context in which I gave my paraphrase of the Truths was that it was having 'understood human experience (*dukkha*) as it really is, its cause, that it can cease, and how to bring about its cessation' that the Buddha attended to the uprooting of the continuity tendencies. So what I am doing here, quite simply, is referring to *dukkha* as 'experience' rather than the more usual 'unsatisfactoriness' *of* experience. My reasons for doing so are several, but begin with my view that this way of describing the Truths better draws out that *dukkha* is *intrinsic* to the experience of the cycle of lives. If one is to understand its meaning fully, one has first to grasp that *dukkha* is not descriptive in the sense of saying of driving in London that it is frustrating: not only is driving in London sometimes *not* frustrating, but what constitutes frustration to one person does not do so to another. In other words, frustration is a wholly contingent feature of driving in London. But *dukkha* is not contingent to experience. Rather, one cannot have experience that is not *dukkha*.

Note that what is being referred to here is pre-Enlightenment experience: the experience whose continuity is fuelled by cravings.

It is *this* experience one is aiming to bring to an end, and by contrast nirvana is referred to in terms that are the very converse of *dukkha*. Though Enlightenment, the occasion on which one knows one has achieved liberation, may also be described in terms of an experience, in Indian religions the specificity of the cyclically-bound period of experience is indicated by the single term *saṃsāra*, 'going round', mentioned earlier. It is, indeed, liberation from *saṃsāra* that one is seeking to attain, and that nirvana indicates one has achieved. In order to avoid asking the non-specialist reader to cope with another alien term, I would ask all readers to accept that in the same way that I use the word perception exclusively in a pre-Enlightenment context, so in using the word experience I am refering to pre-Enlightenment experience, *saṃsāra*. In referring to the transition from perception and experience that takes place at Enlightenment I shall in both instances use the term insight.

If one cannot have experience that is not *dukkha*, then what is being referred to in the First Noble Truth *is* simply one's experience: and it is this that one has to understand as it really is. And though from a psychological point of view it is with the unsatisfactoriness, as explained above, that one can perhaps most readily identify, I think the value neutrality of the Truth is better grasped if one recognises that it is about experience. I mentioned above that in the textual account of the first sermon each Truth is briefly explained, and related the explanation given about *dukkha* in the psychological terms of unsatisfactoriness. But there is a further line of the explanation that is easy to overlook, and which usually is overlooked – certainly in terms of what it might mean or imply – but which is the linchpin of my interpretation of everything that follows. The last line is: "In short, it is the five *khandhas* that are *dukkha*."[31] If one understands *dukkha* as straightforward unsatisfactoriness, then the first part of the description, given earlier, is self-evident, as I have already said. But in concluding by explaining *dukkha* as the five *khandhas*, the textual description is in my view suggesting that the distinction I am making here, however subtle it may be, is nevertheless of crucial importance to one's proper understanding of the formula.

So what I am suggesting is first that we take *dukkha* to be referring to experience, and then note that experience is further explained by the Buddha in terms of the five *khandhas*. What we need to discuss more fully now, then, so that we can better understand the nature of experience, and the way we should understand *dukkha* in the four Noble Truths, are the *khandhas*. In the context of the first sermon, when they are first mentioned, no explanation of any kind is given as to what the *khandhas* are, or what is being referred to in mentioning them. The term is not one used by any of the other religious teachers of the day, and they are hardly explained in any coherent way anywhere in the *Sutta Piṭaka*: there is no text which gives a full and clear account of what is being referred to by the term *khandha*. But the *khandhas* are frequently mentioned nevertheless, even if in a somewhat piecemeal way, and the impression one is given from the texts is that after giving his first short sermon the Buddha was subsequently questioned over and over again on this unexplained detail that is perhaps the least easy to understand aspect of the sermon.

In the vast majority of contexts in which the *khandhas* are discussed they are referred to individually: in English, body, sensations, apperception, volitional activities and consciousness.[32] It appears that they are being understood in terms of one's physical body and mental activities as a whole, but there is no indication of what might be meant by them in any further detail. As briefly explained earlier, the point being made in most of such contexts tends to be that it is a mistake to identify with any of the *khandhas*, to think that any one of them is one's essential self. Here we have again to recall the prevailing concern at the time to know what is or might be one's permanent, unchanging self or soul. Given that nothing the Buddha taught was explicitly about such a self, others appear frequently to have questioned him as to whether something he had referred to was in fact this in another guise. And as it was neither self-evident nor explained what the *khandhas*, important enough to have been referred to by the Buddha in his very first sermon, actually were, they must have been a prime case for speculation in this respect. We read that the Buddha denied in various ways that any one of the *khandhas* was one's soul. He pointed out that since one knows that one's body, sensations, apperceptions, volitional activities and consciousness are all changing and impermanent, so any tendency to identify with any one of them brings with it the psychological sense of unsatisfactoriness; if what one wants is to know what it is about oneself one can identify with as permanent, then thinking that it is any one of the *khandhas* will only constitute mental sickness: an altogether negative state of mind.[33] The Buddha makes the same point slightly differently when, in stating that each of the *khandhas* is impermanent, he adds that that which is impermanent is unsatisfactory, and that that which is unsatisfactory is (in fact tautologically) not the perfect, permanent self most were seeking.[34]

Discussions about the *khandhas* in this vein are numerous, and constitute by far the most common way in which all references to them are treated. I suspect it is for this reason, coupled with the seemingly obsessive search for the soul that was going on at the time, that they came to be associated with the analogy of the cart, which suggests they are an actual analysis of what the human being consists of. This analogy, to which I referred in Chapter One, states: "When all constituent parts are there, the word 'cart' is used; just so, where there are five *khandhas* there is the convention of 'a living being'."[35] And, as I also explained earlier, it is this analogy that the Theravāda Buddhist tradition has used for the purpose of illustrating their view that the Buddha was stating that human beings actually have no abiding Self or soul. According to this view, what we call human beings *are* in fact just the five *khandhas* operating together, and not only is none of the *khandhas* in itself one's soul but there is nothing other than the *khandhas* that is one's soul either. While it is clear that the Buddha did repeatedly deny that any of the *khandhas* was one's soul, as I stated in Chapter One, and explained by means of my computer analogy, I do not think this was the purpose of his referring to the *khandhas*. Rather, I think the repeated denials simply reflect quantitatively the extent of the questioning of him about whether one of the *khandhas* was one's soul. And I think the cart analogy arises from a misunderstanding that this was the case.[36]

So we know what the *khandhas* are not: they are not the self in any essentialist sense because they are all impermanent. But if, as I have suggested, *dukkha* is better understood as the fact of experience, in what way are the *khandhas* synonymous with that? What is meant when it is said of *dukkha* in the first Noble Truth that it is, in short, the *khandhas*? What the *khandhas* are was the question I set out to answer in my book *Identity and Experience*. I shall not rehearse here the detailed research that constitutes the main part of that book, but will, rather, draw on it in order to concentrate on what is of particular relevance to us in our present context. Buddhist scholars may consult the earlier research for further details if they so wish, where they will find separate chapters on each of the *khandhas*.

There are two aspects to understanding what is being referred to by the term *khandha*. First, what are they each individually? And second, what are they collectively? In his first sermon, when they are referred to for the first time, the Buddha uses the term collectively, and it is only in other contexts that the five *khandhas* are enumerated and referred to individually. So though one can come to some sort of understanding of each of them individually from a large number of textual contexts, I believe that it is important to remember that it is collectively that one most relevantly understands their function, and that it is also in understanding them collectively that one is most likely to grasp the point of the teaching in the first sermon. And as I have stated above, I believe this is particularly important not just because this teaching is called the first sermon of the Buddha, but because the four Noble Truths refer to the very same points the Buddha attended to at his Enlightenment.

The order of the *khandhas* is never explained, but they are almost invariably (the single exception being to accommodate the metre of a verse[37]) in the order given above; that is: body, sensations, apperception, volitional activities, consciousness.[38] The first important point to note about body is the one I have mentioned before: that what is being referred to here is the living body. It is not the matter of the body *qua* matter that is relevant, but that one's body is the physical locus of one's experience. As such it provides and is characterised by certain features that are collectively represented by what are called the four great elements: earth, water, fire and wind.[39] Each of these elements abstractly represents certain appropriately corresponding features or processes of the living body. So earth represents everything that is characterised by solidity and extension, that is all one's dense physical organs and features. Water represents whatever is fluid or liquid in one's body, from blood to saliva. Fire represents heat in the sense of temperature, which includes not just one's body heat but also both digestion and the processes of decay: one 'cooks' one's food, and one 'burns' and becomes tired, or ages. Wind represents all movements and mobility, including breathing. Sometimes a fifth great element, space (*ākāsa*), is added to the more usual four, and this abstractly represents all orifices, internal passages, and the processes of swallowing, retaining and expelling food and so on: how things are organised, exchanged and accommodated by way of space(s).

Each of these great elements, including space, is said to have both an internal and an external aspect. The abstract representations referred to in the last paragraph refer to their internal aspect, internal acknowledging the fact that though one's body is in one sense an object no different from any other object, it is also part of one's subjectivity: living bodies are the only objects that provide, or are associated with being, the locus of a consciously experiencing being. Externally, the great elements represent everything we experience (that is, including the locus of subjectivity *qua* object but also whatever is other than – 'external' to – that) that is characterised in the general and abstract sense by one or more of the great elements. Thus earth abstractly represents *all* solidity and extension; water all liquid and fluidity; fire all aspects of temperature and decay; wind all aspects of mobility and rhythm; and space all aspects of proportion and relationship.[40] One might say they represent the *principles* of solidity and extension, liquid and fluidity, temperature and decay, mobility and rhythm, proportion and relationship. And that both internal and external are similarly described serves to emphasise that the principals are generically applicable across what is often seen as the subjective/objective divide.

A central feature of the body is that it is the locus of the senses, which further emphasises that what is being referred to here is the living and functioning body and not just its substance. In Indian thought in general, six senses are usually given: to seeing, hearing, smelling, tasting, touching (the five with which we are familiar in the West) is added 'mind'. Mind is no easier to understand in the context of Indian thought than it is in the West, and many different explanations are given. But what appears to be meant by it in the early Buddhist teachings is the faculty, or sense, which filters and collates all sensory data so that it can actually 'make sense' to us. In other words, when, for example, one's eye comes in contact with a visible object (one's sense organ with its corresponding sense object), it is the 'mind' that translates that event into one of the sense of *seeing*. I have used the active terms see*ing*, hear*ing*, smell*ing*, and so on, above, but in fact without mind co-ordinating our sensory experiences all one has is a mass of sensory data arising from contacts between sense organ(s) and sense object(s). Though each of those contacts is an event that is the *sine qua non* of the sensory process as a whole, we experience them in such chaotic abundance that they need sorting out before we can understand that we *are* seeing, hearing, and so on; and also that we are seeing and not tasting, smelling and not touching, and so on. There is a strong similarity between this and Thomas Aquinas's *sensus communis*.[41] And because we *can* make sense of our sensory data there must be some inherent rationality to them: incoming data must be potentially recognisable by us. As such all sensory data, generically called *dhammā* in the texts, can be referred to as 'knowables'.[42] Or, put differently, as the objective correlate of the *sensus communis*, they might be referred to as the *mundus sensibilis*. Mind, the *sensus communis*, thus 'senses' the 'sensibility' of incoming knowables, the *mundus sensibilis*.[43]

Because sensory activity arises from an interaction between one's sense organs and corresponding sense objects, the senses are metaphorically understood as the 'doors' which link the individual with the objective world.[44] The body is thus crucial to our experience of the world as it provides us with the sense organs which act as the doors through which the objective world in its entirety is accessed by us. And it is only having come through these doors, so to speak, that sensory data can be further processed by the sophisticated mental activities which collectively correspond to the more complex and varied strata of our experiences than just discriminating seeing from hearing, tasting from touching, and so on.

It is to these sophisticated mental activities that the remaining four *khandhas* refer. Though given last in the list, consciousness is the *sine qua non* of *all* the activity of the *khandhas*. Just as it is the livingness and not the substance of the body that is relevant to understanding the first *khandha*, so it is the fact that we are aware beings and not the fact that we can be analysed into five parts that is relevant to understanding the *khandhas* as a whole. Natural periods of unconsciousness such as sleep, natural functions about which we are not consciously aware such as digestion and the circulation of blood, involuntary reactions such as a movement response to a loud noise while asleep, and those aspects of our lives which we perform subliminally such as avoiding obstructions in our path, should not be permitted to sidetrack us from the central focus of the teachings.[45] What one needs to understand consciously is how one's mind is working in fuelling one's continuity. And though that may involve a great degree of making conscious what is not already conscious, what I am referring to here as not relevant are the natural exceptions to consciousness that collectively form part of the support system, so to speak, of the more important exercise. This corresponds to the point I made above that it was only consequential actions that are relevant to understanding karma: natural unconsciousness and inconsequential actions are simply the natural functioning of the locus of what is relevant.

Consciousness, then, is the awareness that accompanies the operation of the *khandhas* as a whole. At its most basic, one does not see, hear, and so on, if one is not aware of it: what one actually sees when one looks at a scene, to use the example of the sense of sight, is only those aspects of it that become, whether immediately or with some effort of attention, part of one's awareness; anything else is *not seen*. By definition, then, seeing only *is* seeing if one knows one is seeing. And in tandem with this, awareness only is awareness because one is aware *of* something. However vague the object of awareness may be, one cannot *be* aware without one: at the very least one is aware of being aware. This point is particularly crucial in the context of the Buddhist teachings for two reasons. First, given the seemingly endless speculation, which is as prolific today as at any other time, as to what consciousness is in any context, it emphasises that what is meant by consciousness in early Buddhism is the *activity* of being conscious and not some kind of entity that one carries round with one as a sort of mind-stuff. And second, the goal of Buddhism is, as I stated in Chapter One, insight of the Truth and not some kind of trance. Trance is entirely inappropriate to Buddhism precisely because it is *absence* of awareness, *absence* of knowing anything. So even if it is the case that in Buddhism one is aiming for knowledge of a radically different kind from our normal day to day knowledge, all knowledge must be of something. This is so even if the radically different kind of knowledge involves the absence of points of reference with which we are familiar: knowledge of absence is not absence of knowledge.

I am using knowledge and awareness interchangeably here because, and I think this will become increasingly clear, the process to which the *khandhas* refer is precisely the process by which we know anything at all. Awareness, as the *sine qua non* of that entire process, is called the *khandha* of consciousness. The remaining three *khandhas* explain the way incoming sensory data, preliminarily filtered through the sixth sense, become, when coupled with awareness, different sorts of knowledge.

The first stage of what happens is that one registers one's awareness of incoming sensory data; one 'feels' it; one is conscious of having an experience of it. This is accounted for by the *khandha* of sensation.[46] It is also sometimes called the *khandha* of feeling (I have so called it myself in the past), but this is or can be misleading because it is not feeling in the affective sense of emotion that is meant here. Rather, it is feeling in the sense of the early stages of what will become a more clearly understood experience: when I know, for example, I am touching something, but I do not yet know what it is or how I might think about it or react to it. I might also know that it is pleasant, unpleasant or neutral, but I do not yet have any affective reaction to it because I do not yet know enough about it.[47] Identifying it is associated with the *khandha* of apperception: perception, that is, in the cognitive rather than in (just) the visual sense. What one is aware of as experientially embryonic is subjected to discriminatory processes in order to identify it. I know I am touching something; I begin to discern that it is something rough, something wet, something warm; ah, I realise it is a hot, wet towel. As the apperceptive process develops, what one is actually doing is imposing categories onto unclassified data: the experience becomes more and more clearly defined and identifiable. And in the process of doing this, each more clearly defined and identified aspect of what one is experiencing is separated from the others. What one is doing in this process, according to the texts, is *making manifold* and *naming* what one is experiencing.

The significance of this in the wider context of the Buddhist teachings as a whole lies in the Buddhist teaching I have previously mentioned – that all things within our cyclical experience are dependently originated. It is this that underpins their impermanence. But notwithstanding this teaching, it is nevertheless a feature of our normal experience that we identify things individually, and we assume that each individual thing is independent from other individual things, and psychologically continue to anticipate their permanence. Even if we acknowledge the ways in which one thing has certain properties relative to those of another thing, we nevertheless regard each thing as independent at least in the sense that we can relate to one without relating to another. And we think of ourselves and other living beings as existing independently too. In fact our entire conceptual framework is underpinned by the assumption that the apparent plurality of the world in which we live is transcendentally real – that is, as it is in itself, independently of our seeing it: independently, period, indeed. But according to Buddhist teachings, this is not the case: rather, such a way of viewing the world is not seeing things as they really are. Identification, then, is a process of making manifold what is in fact dependently originated, and is a feature of the pre-Enlightenment way of seeing things. Thus we read: "Men who have conceptions of manifoldness of some kind go on separating things when apperceiving; but [eventually] one drives out everything that is [thus] constructed by the mind and to do with the mundane life and proceeds to a life of freedom."[48]

Though this clearly suggests that one should understand that making manifold is part of one's own mental activity, it is important to remind ourselves that the aim of the Buddhist teachings is insight and that this involves knowing something. The apparent paradox involved in knowing something in terms other than the manifoldness with which we are familiar (how *can* something that is not separate(d) from something else be identified?) has always been accounted for by the Buddhist tradition by explaining it in terms of the nature of yogic knowledge: not only is it radically different, but we cannot know what it is without experiencing it because it involves the reorientation of all our conceptual categories. An interesting passage which contrasts a person who has died with a person who has transcended normal mental activities – that is, one who has stopped making manifold – states that the latter has 'purified his senses'.[49] Apperception with 'purified senses' is nevertheless a feature of insight, because it is cardinal to Buddhism that one knows that one knows.[50] The descriptions of the Buddha's Enlightenment indicate precisely this: the liberating experience is clearly identified as such.

A further feature of what follows from apperception is that we are able to *think about* what is or has been apperceived. And this ability contributes to our being able to conceptualise abstractly even when there is no specific experience of apperception. According to Buddhist teachings, the ability to discriminate, to name, actually to apperceive what one is experiencing by way of incoming sensory data, can function abstractly as memories, calculations, imaginings, ideas, conceptual thoughts, and any number of other similar reflections, even when there is no co-temporal incoming sensory data. Put differently, though some things are actually apperceived and some are abstractly conceived of, however complex and sophisticated they may be they are all understood by us within the same conceptual framework which involves discrimination, identification, naming, making manifold. It is an intrinsic part of the totality of our experiences that this is how we make sense of them: this is how we make them clear to ourselves.[51]

A passage I quoted in Chapter One brings together the four *khandhas* of body, sensation, apperception and consciousness in a way that clearly establishes their cognitive role: "Seeing occurs when there is contact between an eye and [visible] forms, accompanied by consciousness; this gives rise to sensations, which one then identifies; and what one thus identifies one reflects on and makes manifold."[52] And this seems to sum up the point of them. Understanding them as the individual physical and mental 'parts' of which a human being is comprised misses two crucial points. First, that it is collectively that they operate, and second, perhaps even more importantly, that what they represent is one's cognitive system: the apparatus by means of which we have all our experiences. The point is not that they offer an analysis of all that we are: in my view there is not even any suggestion that this is the case. Rather, they are what one needs to understand about oneself if one is to achieve liberation from the cycle of lives as the Buddha did. And in this sense it can be seen that they are so crucial to what one needs to understand that it is possible to understand the *khandhas* in the metaphorical sense of *representing* the entire human being. But this is not the same as stating that they are what the human being is *comprised of*.

An important feature of the description of the cognitive process quoted above is the way the structure of it indicates the way in which the processing of incoming sensory data involves their becoming clearly related as objective to the knowing subject.[53] I shall return to this point in the next two chapters.

The fifth *khandha* of volitional activities is not included in the description of the cognitive process given in the last paragraph, and the significance of this is that it is not crucial to it. The aim of the path of Buddhism is to arrive at a point when the fuel of continuity is blown out, and it is all volitions that *are* that fuel. The way they participate in the cognitive system, which indeed they do until one does achieve the goal of the path, is that they are one's affective response to whatever one is experiencing. Having identified the rough, wet and warm thing I am touching as a hot, wet towel, I respond to it negatively: because it is clammy I desire not to continue touching it. Or I respond to it positively: it is refreshing and I desire to make more of the feel of it. These negative or positive desires are volitions: I am not indifferent, or neutral, to the touch of the towel. But I *can* be neutral: I *can* simply register the touch (or whatever is the relevant sensation) and see that it is what it is simply in the factual sense. And this is the case even if the circumstance is less uninteresting than the touch of a towel: the presence of an abundance of particularly delicious food or wine, the physical pain of stubbing one's toe, seeing a supremely beautiful painting, being confined in a space in which something smells very unpleasant, hearing sublime music, travelling on the London Underground; and so on both positively and negatively. Volitional neutrality here is associated with the altruism I was referring to earlier in that acting without self-centredness is karmically insignificant.

The arising of desires/volitions need not be in response to a single experienced thing. Just as one can conceptualise as well as apperceive, so one can also have desires in general terms, again positively and negatively: to be happy, to love and be loved, to be successful, not to be disliked, not to suffer physical pain, not to be poor. Some desires are very profound and deep-seated: they are the tendencies one has to certain affective states such as sticking to tradition and custom, seeking pleasurable things, holding strongly to one's views, not wishing to acknowledge one's ignorance, desiring to continue to exist. Some of these are to do with one's karmically inherited character or personality, and one's cultural attachments, often developed and/or lying dormant over many lifetimes. Collectively these are referred to as *anusayas* – something like biases or proclivities. Even in a baby these are present.[54] And some – the last four mentioned above – are the deepest of the continuity tendencies referred to earlier in the chapter. As such they are the very last of one's affective volitional states to be uprooted, the last of the fuel to be blown out.

One's volitional activities as a whole are perhaps the most complex aspect of one's cognitive apparatus. They constitute the entirety of the psychological orientation of that cognitive apparatus. And associated as they are with one's ignorance, their continued functioning is itself conditioned by (dependently originated in) whatever is the state of one's ignorance or knowledge. As one makes progress towards seeing things as they really are, so the nature of one's ignorance changes and one's volitions, the means by which one's psychological orientation operates, are differently conditioned. But at all stages of one's cyclical experience, throughout all of which one has some degree of ignorance, they function as the causal matrix of one's continuity in every sense. It is to this that the second Noble Truth and the Buddha's definition of how karma works both refer. And the power of it is explicitly stated as follows: "What conditioned phenomena do they [volitional activities] volitionally construct? They volitionally construct the body as body, sensation as sensation, apperception as apperception, volitional activities as volitional activities, and consciousness as consciousness."[55] To draw out and grasp fully what is being said here, the *khandhas* that are described as being volitionally constructed need to be interpreted in the sense that together they represent the entire human being. So it is one's volitional activities that determine one's future coming-to-be in its entirety.

As volitional activities operate at some level until the very last stage of the path, one can see why the totality of one's cyclical experience can be understood in the psychological sense of unsatisfactoriness. But the associating of the *khandhas* as a whole with *dukkha*, as stated above, indicates the fact of experience as such, and not just that psychological aspect of it. What the *khandha* analysis shows is that experience is a combination of a straightforward cognitive process together with the psychological orientation that colours it in terms of unsatisfactoriness: entwined with the value neutral cognitive process is the affective dimension of volitional activities. In other words, experience is both cognitive and affective: both aspects are involved in one's 'cognitive lens', or perception in the broad sense of knowing discussed earlier, through which we in fact have our experience in its entirety. And though none of us can have experience as a whole in any other way, we are each ignorant (in every sense) in our own particular way and degree, and thus have volitions in our own particular way and degree. So we function as individuals each having our own particular perceptions which make up our own experience. And it is not just that we all see, understand, interpret, and respond to our experience in our own way, but that our own way of seeing, understanding, interpreting and responding *is* our experience. This point becomes clearer if one reflects on the fact that as one's perception changes, so one's experience is different: one cannot separate perception from experience. This is true at every level, including trivial examples in our daily lives. And it is why the contrast between the pre-Enlightenment state and Enlightenment can be described in terms of the contrast between ignorance and seeing things as they really are: it is the functioning of one's cognitive lens that changes. And as one's pre-Enlightenment perception is replaced by the insight of Enlightenment, so one's pre-Enlightenment experience – the cycle of lives, or experience *as we know it* – ceases. It is the meditative mental disciplinary exercises that are designed to enable one to achieve this. Meditation focuses on the operating of the mental processes so that one eventually – and it can take lifetimes – understands the way ignorance and volitions interact so that one can eventually achieve a situation whereby no further volitional activities occur.

The associating of the *khandhas* as a whole with *dukkha* also underlines the fact that we can neither separate ourselves or anything else from our experience, nor know anything of any sort other than by means of the operating of the *khandhas*. If we want to understand anything about ourselves at all, then, it is with our *khandhas* – our experiencing apparatus – that we need to start. It is significant in this context that the 'burden' that one needs to put down is not said to be thinking one is or has a self, as one might expect in the light of the traditional understanding of the doctrine of *anattā*, but is said to be the *khandhas*.[56] And precisely this, in my opinion, is what is being said in the first Noble Truth.

An interesting point, indicated by the way the operation of the experiencing apparatus is described in early Buddhism, is that what is often regarded as the duality of body and mind in fact functions as part of a single experiencing system. In the case of our bodies, none of us is a body having 'mental' experience as a contingent aspect of being alive: other than during normal periods of sleep referred to earlier, without experience a body is a dead body.[57] Nor are we able to regard our bodies as objects other than by means of our experience of them. This is as true of our own bodies, of which our experience also has a subjective dimension, as it is of the bodies of others, which we experience only objectively. In the case of our minds, we cannot separate what might seem to be our 'mental' experience from the spacial locus which the body provides: being a being of any sort *means* having a locus. This is quite apart from the fact that the raw material of experience is the sensory data which is only accessible to us by means of our sense organs which the body provides. Even our conceptualising abilities rely on our familiarity with sensory data: that is why a man who has been blind from birth has no way of conceptualising what seeing is.

Though what are commonly thought of as body and mind are thus equally integral to one's experiencing apparatus, in early Buddhism it is accepted that it is possible for one's body or physical locus to take different forms from that with which we are familiar. In particular, it is accepted that one's body might be, or become, 'subtle', what to us in the West might be termed 'ghostly' or 'ethereal': not visible in the normal way that our dense physical bodies are visible.[58] But this is still a body in the sense of the experiencing subject having a locus: it is clearly stated that consciousness only operates in association with a body, whatever level of density or subtlety that body operates at.[59] Further, though according to early Buddhism subtle beings may be spiritually advanced, the teachings are nevertheless clearly focused on the level of existence and experience with which we *are* familiar. That the attainment of Enlightenment is a *human* goal is fundamental to the fact that the Buddha himself was and is seen by Buddhists as an example others may follow. And the emphasis on understanding one's cognitive apparatus is structured in such a way that what is central to it are the processes by which we identify our experiences of the world as we know it and the way this involves our responding to them affectively. Notwithstanding the fact that other possible modes of being are described in Buddhist teachings and texts, in my opinion issues such as whether one might be able to have a non-physical body, the nature of the assumed duality between body and mind, or the nature of all the other living beings included in the Buddhist cosmos, though interesting, are tangential. They should not act as a red herrings which divert one from the point that the being that is an experiencing subject with a potential for Enlightenment is a human one.

Several points may be drawn out here by way of summary, relating both to *dukkha* and to the *khandhas*. First, *dukkha* is not descriptive of the world *in which* we have our experience: it is not descriptive of everything we *perceive out there* and then react to. Rather, it *is* our experience. Second, in stating that the continuity of that perception is fuelled by the causal matrix of our desires, or volitions, which in turn is conditioned by our ignorance, the Noble Truths are stating that one is bound to the cycle of lives *cognitively*: *dukkha* is, in short, the *khandhas*, as the textual account of the Buddha's first sermon states. Third, it is therefore precisely this cognitive process that we need to understand: in particular, we need to understand the way in which the manifoldness that so characterises our pre-Enlightenment perception is part of the cognitive process itself. Fourth, it was to the cognitive process that the Buddha was referring on the occasion of his Enlightenment when he stated that he understood experience, the cause of experience, the cessation of experience, and the way to achieve the cessation of experience: later taught as the Four Noble Truths. Fifth, though it is not incorrect to understand *dukkha* in the sense of unsatisfactoriness, it is important to recognise that it is so only from a psychological perspective: this is neither the central point nor the extent of what it means.

A further point can perhaps usefully be made here with regard to how best to approach the understanding of key terms, in this instance *dukkha* and the *khandhas*. In neither of these cases have I thought it helpful to give anything more than a passing English translation as such, because in neither case does a translation capture what the Pali terms are referring to. And this is the nub of my point: what is relevant is not the meaning of the term *qua* word but what it is referring to. As I mentioned in the Introduction, much is written on the meanings of Pali words, writing which then gives rise to more work offering different meanings. But it is by *not* attempting to define the word that one looks beyond it to what is being said in the teachings themselves. However interesting and, occasionally, helpful the exercise of establishing elaborate definitions is, it is still an exercise in trying to come up with a definition. That is to say, it gives primacy to the word itself and ignores how it came to be *used*. If one focuses on the latter point, though, one sees that the first Noble Truth in which the words *dukkha* and *khandha* are used by the Buddha was given after some insight that he had had to which he was then, subsequently, referring. The terms were what he *called* something, how he made communicable sense of his insight. More specifically – and, with regard to the way the *khandhas* have traditionally been understood, more relevantly – we can see in the light of how the cognitive apparatus works that the terms were what he *named* the process he had gained insight of. But in describing it in certain terms – the *khandhas* as five aspects, or five understandable stages, so to speak, of the process – it became reified almost as soon as the words were uttered. One might suggest that this is what making manifold has done: the operation is subordinated to terms of the apparatus. And if one does not let go of this reification, and recognise that the question What are the *khandhas*? is mis-focused, one entirely misses the point of the Buddha's referring to the *khandhas* at all.

We are now in a position to draw out an important feature of contrast between the way the Buddha's teaching is formulated, based on his Enlightenment experience, and the way both the teachings and the religious questionings of his contemporaries were formulated. With regard to the latter, I mentioned above that the search was for some permanent, immortal, thing. The *Upaniṣadic* teachers stated that it was the essence of one's self, identical with the essence of the universe. And the questions, and putative answers, of others were also formulated in terms of the self and the world. What is significant about all these is that their focus is ontological: on *what* there is, on *what* is immortal in the substantial sense. The Buddha's teaching is completely different from this in the sense that in focussing on understanding the workings of one's cognitive apparatus it is entirely epistemic. And, further, it is clear that it is here that a key aspect of impermanence, the intrinsic characteristic of experience, lies. There is nothing about the process of experiencing *qua* process that is in any sense permanent: it is, rather, at all times dynamically *in process*. Nothing that is epistemic can be anything other than impermanent. So in addition to the fact that it is intrinsic to all things, including human beings, that they age, decay, die or disintegrate, it is also intrinsic to conscious beings that their experience of that impermanence is itself impermanent. Nothing could be further from the way the ontological essentialism of the *Upaniṣads* is formulated.

Notes

1 The *Cūḷa-Māluṅkya Sutta*, M I 426ff.

2 In Pali the full expression, found in many places in the *Sutta Piṭaka, is yathā-bhūta-jñāna-dassana*: 'knowing and seeing things as they really are'. Several variations are also found: see PED, p. 549ff for references.

3 cf., for example, Bṛ. Up. 1.4.10; Ch. Up. 3.14.

4 *Sabbāsava Sutta*, MN I 8. cf. also the *Brahmajāla Sutta*, DN I, sutta 1; and the *Pāsādika Suttanta*, DN III, *sutta* 29.

5 cf., for example, SN II 223, V 418; MN I 395, 487; DN I, *sutta* 1, III 134ff. cf. also MN I 157, 426ff, 483ff; SN IV 374ff.

6 MN I 22f; AN II 211, IV 178f; and also at Vin III 4.

7 Vin III 4 gives the four *āsavas*.

8 SN II 223, V 418; MN I 395; DN I, *sutta* 1, III 134ff. cf. also MN I 157, 426ff, 483ff; SN IV 374ff.
9 Throughout the *Brahmajāla Sutta* and at MN I 487.
10 AN III 415: *Cetanā 'haṃ bhikkhave kammaṃ vadāmi. Cetayitvā kammaṃ karoti kāyena vācā manasā.*
11 See Gombrich, 1988, p. 66f, for a fuller discussion of this.
12 In particular the *satipaṭṭhāna* meditation exercises on one's state of mind (*citta*). See MN I, *sutta* 10; DN II, *sutta* 22. Other references are given, and the subject is discussed at some length, in Hamilton, 1996, pp. 110ff. See also Harvey (1995b), pp. 111ff, and Johansson (1965).
13 See in particular *Sutta Nipāta* 239ff, the chapter entitled 'Tainted Fare'.
14 The first of the three aspects of the metaphor is greed (*lobha*) in some contexts and passion (*rāga*) in others. I see no reason to think that they do not both refer to desires in general.
15 Described by Harvey (1990), p. 60ff.
16 That the 'distinction between enlightenment and final nirvana is quite clear, [but] the texts do not always make it', thus contributing to the ambiguity I refer to, is discussed and explained more fully by Steven Collins (1998, pp. 147ff.).
17 MN I 190. The same point is made for all the senses.
18 cf. Magee and Milligan, *On Blindness* (1995), in particular chapters 1–3.
19 H.G. Wells' short story *Country of the Blind* vividly illustrates this point. Interesting observations on blindness are also made in Wilkie Collins' *Poor Miss Finch*.
20 SN V 420f; Vin I 9f.
21 SN V 421; Vin I 10.
22 AN I 286; *Dhammapada* 5–7, 277–9; cf. also MN I 336; DN II 157.
23 See MN I 90: *aniccā dukkhā vipariṇāmadhammā*; and throughout the *Saḷāyatana Saṃyutta* (SN, Vol IV).
24 SN IV 175f.
25 Thag. 12: *yadatthiyaṃ bhojanaṃ bhuñjamāno.*
26 Rahula, 1985, gives the traditional Theravāda view.
27 See, for example, Damien Keown 1996 and 1998 for discussions of topical ethical issues considered in the context of Buddhist teachings.
28 See Collins (1982, Part II) for some discussion on the way *diṭṭhi*, view, is used for both 'right' and 'wrong' views.
29 See Hamilton, 1996, pp. 97ff, for a discussion on how one's state of mind might be said to evolve.
30 MN I 301.
31 SN V 421; Vin I 10. In the first sermon, the expression is *pañcupādāna-khandhā*: the five *khandhas* that are grasping. This refers to the fact that prior to Enlightement an individual is fuelled by cravings and so on. Here 'grasping' is yet another word for that causal matrix.
32 *Rūpa*, *vedanā*, *saññā*, *saṃkhārā* and *viññāṇa*: see the *Khandha Saṃyutta* (SN, Vol III).
33 *Āturacitta*. For this teaching, see the *Khandha Saṃyutta* (SN, Vol III), *passim*.
34 e.g. SN III 22: *yad aniccaṃ taṃ dukkhaṃ yaṃ dukkhaṃ tad anattā.*
35 SN I 135.
36 cf. my "*Anattā*: A Different Approach" (1995).
37 SN I 112.

38 Skilling (1995) discusses the order.

39 MN I 185ff. Though the Pali term *mahābhūtā* literally translates as great elements, and this is the English usually given, in fact one might also call them primary elements, and understand them not dissimilarly to Locke's primary qualities. In Pali, they are *paṭhavī*, *āpo*, *tejo* and *vāyu*.

40 The external aspect of space is not described in the texts: proportion and relationship are my own terms to indicate what might be abstractly represented by it.

41 cf. Copleston, 1955, p. 173f. cf. also C.A.F. Rhys Davids, 1914, p. 68ff, and Reat, 1990, p. 225f and p. 243ff.

42 This term is borrowed from Carter, 1978, and discussed in Hamilton, 1996, chapter 1.

43 cf. PED, p. 530.

44 cf., for example, DN I 63, 70, 250; SN II 218, IV 103, 117, 194. cf. also Cousins, 1981, for a discussion of the way a 'sense-door process' is developed in the *Abhidhamma*.

45 A possible exception to this point is wet dreams, which became the subject of controversy in the early Buddhist community: if they are unconscious, do they indicate a state of mind that is not free from desire?; do they constitute a volition with moral implications? (see Cousins, 1991).

46 For extensive references see the *Vedanā Saṃyutta* (SN IV 204ff).

47 cf., for example, DN III 275; SN II 53, 82, IV 204, 207, etc; AN III 400.

48 SN IV 71. The word I have rendered as freedom is the rather obscure *nekkhamma*. It seems to refer to the cessation or overcoming of passion, in the generic sense of all affective actions: the achieving of which is freedom from rebirth according to Buddhism.

49 MN I 296: *indriyāni vippasannāni*.

50 Harvey (1995b), chapters 8 and 9, discusses what he calls discernment, highlighting its importance on the Buddhist path. I do not agree, however, with the role he ascribes to *viññāṇa*, consciousness, in this process. He gives consciousness a discriminatory role that in my opinion it does not have. cf. Hamilton, 1996, chapters 4 and 5, for my own fuller discussion of both *viññāṇa* and *saññā*.

51 The two aspects of the process, sensory and abstract, are not clearly distinguished until the *Abhidhamma*. Here they are referred to as *paṭighasamphassajā* and *adhivacanasamphassajā* respectively: the former refers to what arises from sensory data and is described as 'gross' (*oḷārikā*), in contrast to the latter which refers to what arises from abstract conceptual activity, described as 'subtle' (*sukhumā*). (*Vibhaṅga* 6.)

52 MN I 111f.

53 The grammatical shift that indicates this was first pointed out by Ñāṇananda (1971, repr. 1986), and is also discussed by Kalupahana (1975, p. 122f.).

54 MN I 433.

55 SN III 87.

56 SN III 26: *bhārā pañcakkhandhā*.

57 Though there is no way for us to know the extent to which bodies in comas are part of an operating experiencing system, it is significant that even today we regard these and other similarly unconscious bodies not as functioning human beings but as being in a 'persistent vegetative state'. And from the perspective of

the Buddhist spiritual path, such a state would, I think, be regarded as one from which one needed either to recover to normal health, or be reborn into one's next life, in order to be able to be spiritually active. This is not at all to suggest that such states are to be despised or regarded as pointless; only that one would have to bide one's time in order to return to a conscious participation in one's spiritual practices.

58 See chapter 7 of Hamilton (1996) for a discussion of the 'mind-made' body.

59 SN III 53; DN I 76.

CHAPTER FOUR

The World of Experience

"Castles in the air – they are so easy to take refuge in. And easy to build, too."
Henrik Ibsen *The Master Builder* (1892) Act 3.

In this chapter I want to link certain aspects of the description of the cognitive process I have already given to some of the other teachings of the Buddha. In particular, I want to draw out the meaning and implication of the doctrine of dependent origination in more depth than hitherto. In the same way that *dukkha* is more fully understood if it is recognised as having what one might call multidimensional relevance, so too, I think we shall see, is dependent origination better understood if one draws out the complexity of its relevance. I shall illustrate and support this by discussing the way in which many Buddhist teachings have both a simple, obvious, application and meaning, and also a figurative or metaphorical application and meaning. And I shall suggest that though the former is relevant to understanding the teachings, it is only by including the latter that one can arrive at a full understanding of them. My discussion will focus on the way Buddhist cosmology is understood in terms of a metaphor of the spiritual path – the densest of 'hells' corresponding to the depths of ignorance, and the most rarefied and subtle of 'heavens' corresponding to the increasingly higher clarity of perception: cosmological 'levels', given in spacial terms, thus correspond metaphorically to 'stages' on the path to insight.

To remind ourselves of the way in which *dukkha* is multidimensional, we have seen how it refers, first, to the psychological dimension of the unsatisfactoriness of all our pre-Enlightenment experience. We accept neither the qualitative neutrality of the impermanence of all things, nor even the fact of that impermanence; and so we continue to have desires and cravings for things we want to last and experience unsatisfactoriness because they do not last. Second, though, *dukkha* refers to all experience of any sort: as *all* our pre-Enlightenment experience is characterised, to some degree, in terms of being accompanied by this psychological orientation, so what is being referred to in the first Noble Truth of the fact of *dukkha* is simply the fact that we are experiencing beings. And third, what makes us experiencing beings is our experiencing apparatus – the *khandhas*. As descriptions of the *khandhas* make clear, they operate as our cognitive lens, and it is this that *is* our experience.

What we can see from this is that the different dimensions of *dukkha* include a clear contrast between description (experience is unsatisfactory) and explanation (the cognitive system). These are not two teachings, but two dimensions of one: the Truth of experience. In what follows, I would like to suggest that all the teachings of the Buddha include this contrast between description and explanation. And, further, that the explanation is always associated with experience, or the cognitive system. In particular, I hope to show that while one can arrive at a clear and coherent descriptive picture of a human being in the world, in fact what one can also draw from the self-same picture is a clear and coherent explanation of how experience operates: of the centrality to all experience of the cognitive system. In Chapter Five I shall suggest that from this one can further extract certain significant implications about the nature of the human being and about the nature of the world.

I mentioned earlier a formula called the Three Characteristics of Existence. I stated that the first two characteristics were that everything in our cyclical experience is stated to be impermanent, and that all such things are therefore unsatisfactory (*dukkha*). The dependent origination of everything we experience in the cycle of lives is repeatedly taught by the Buddha.[1] He says he teaches the dependent originatedness of things,[2] and refers to the way things are, to the fact that there is a regularity of things, to the fact that things are dependently related.[3] In the Three Characteristics formula the dependent originatedness of all things is indicated by the Pali term *saṃkhāra*: what it states is that all *saṃkhāras* (dependently originated things) are impermanent and unsatisfactory. More usually translated 'conditioned thing', it is in this case worth noting that the term *saṃkhāra* itself gives us a clear indication of the point being made here. It comes from the verbal root which means to make or do (*kṛ* – mentioned earlier in connection with the words karma and Sanskrit), and to this is added the prefix *saṃs*, which gives 'make' the more specific meaning of 'put together', 'compose', 'construct', 'form', or 'condition': such things – constructions – are not, therefore, independent. It is *because* all things are conditioned that they are impermanent: permanence requires independence, autonomy. And, as I stated earlier, it is because all conditioned things are impermanent that they are unsatisfactory.

Here we can see that this is clearly descriptive of how things are. All of the things within our cyclical experience are conditioned by other things. Whether they are chairs and tables, trees and shrubs, musical notes or scientific formulae, toenails or fingers, ideas or abstract analyses, laughter or tears, cats and dogs or human beings: nothing exists independently of the context that conditions it; whatever their nature, all things are dependent on conditioning factors of some kind. If we look around us and consider the way things are, we can without too much difficulty in fact see that nothing occurs out of context. To give but obvious examples, we can readily see that chairs and tables are constructed; trees and shrubs grow from seeds and are dependent on sun, water, and so on; musical notes and scientific formulae are played on instruments, worked out; toenails and fingers are connected to other parts of bodies; ideas – however spontaneously they seem to come to us – and abstract analyses are dependent on a human being's mental processes; laughter and tears arise because of things that are funny or sad; cats and dogs and human beings have, at any point in time, a history that can be understood in any one of a number of ways, biological and geographical to name but two. And in each case other conditioning factors are also readily apparent. For example, a further aspect of the conditionedness of all things is that the occurrence of anything involves factors such as their colour, pitch, temperature, weight, density, location, and time relative to the colour, pitch, temperature, and so on, of other things. All of these factors indicate that as well as more overtly conditioning factors, things are also what they are by virtue of what they are not. Though we can identify and interact with things individually, neither they nor we are in fact independent of this aspect of context at any stage of that identification and interaction.

Because the Buddhist teachings as a whole are focused on the fact that human beings experience cyclical existence, a fundamental aspect of the dependent originatedness of human beings themselves is explained in a formula of the various conditioning factors which give rise to the birth, ageing and death of an individual in any given life. It describes not just the generally applicable factors contributing to how all human are conditioned, but also why human being A is different from human being B: why our 'cognitive lenses' vary in the way I have described earlier. The number of conditioning factors varies (in some places eight, in others twelve[4]). But the point made by the formula is that the fundamental conditioning factor for any given life of each individual is that individual's ignorance. Prior to Enlightenment, every individual is *ipso facto* ignorant to some degree, and in some specific-to-him way(s). And it is this ignorance that has and will continue to condition his affective causal nexus, collectively his past and present volitional activities. This in turn conditions his awareness, the operating of his psycho-cognitive faculties in general, and his birth, ageing and death.[5] Being cyclical, the process continues in subsequent lives, at the start of each life the conditioning factors operating in whatever state they have become at the end of the previous life. And the point is explicitly made in the texts that as ignorance is the *sine qua non* of the birth, ageing and death of an individual, when one has achieved a state of insight (Enlightenment), which is the cessation of ignorance, so there will be no further births, ageings and deaths: the conditioning factors for them will have ceased.[6]

At this level of understanding the doctrine of dependent origination, we have a description of a similar kind to the descriptive level of *dukkha*, which was that what is impermanent is unsatisfactory to us. Here we know that all things are conditioned by other things: though our conceptual framework operates as if all things are individually separate, in fact they are not. Dependent origination is thus simply and obviously understood.

But if one links this description of the dependent originatedness of all the things in our cyclical experience with the way the functioning of our cognitive apparatus *is* in fact that experience, one arrives at a significantly different, or extended, understanding of dependent origination. We saw that the cognitive process is one of making sense of incoming sensory data, and of discriminating in more detail the content of any given experience. This involves what is called 'making manifold', and is a process that continues unless and until one achieves Enlightenment, as is clear from a passage I have quoted before: "Men who have conceptions of manifoldness of some kind go on separating things when apperceiving; but [eventually] one drives out everything that is [thus] constructed by the mind and to do with the mundane life and proceeds to a life of freedom."[7] From this, it follows that though at a descriptive level dependent origination can be understood in the sense that all the factors of our experience are conditioned in ways such as those mentioned above – as it were by each other, in fact at a more explanatory level one can see that what all things are *actually* dependently originated in is our cognitive apparatus. It is in the processing of all our incoming experiential data that the identity of any of the factors of our experience is acquired: in making sense of those data, it is we who give them names. Put differently, what the existence of any of the factors of our experience *in the form in which we know them* is dependent on is our cognitive apparatus.

The centrality of this link between the operating of the *khandhas* as our cognitive process and understanding dependent origination is made in a passage in the texts where repeated examples of *khandha* activity, giving rise to various cognitive events – occurrences of visual, auditory, olfactory (and so on) consciousness, is how it is put – are regularly interspersed with: "Whoever sees dependent origination sees the *Dhamma*; whoever sees the *Dhamma* sees dependent origination. Such things [the cognitive events] are dependently originated: that is to say, the [operating of the] five *khandhas*."[8]

And as the operating of the subjective cognitive apparatus itself functions as a dependently originated process, so it also constructs the phenomenon that the objective factors of our experience can be seen to be what one might call laterally conditioned by each other. Thus it is the case that though the subjective and objective aspects of our experience – that is, our cognitive process and what it constructs for us – appear to parallel each other in terms of being two dependently originated processes as it were alongside, or 'opposite', one another – one might say discretely linear – they are in fact the linked 'poles', again as it were, of a single process.

That this is the case has some very significant implications, and it is with drawing out certain aspects of these that most of the rest of this book is concerned.

In order to draw out further the way our cognitive apparatus is what one might call the origin on which our objective experience is dependent, I would like here to suggest and discuss the way this is implicit in many aspects of Buddhist teachings and writings if one interprets them metaphorically. And for this I think the most obvious place to start is to look at the way the term for the 'world' (*loka*) is used in the texts. In common with many of the key terms of early Buddhism, it is used in a wide variety of contexts.[9] But what I would like to draw out is the way it is specifically used as a metaphor for the life of an individual human being. What I mean by this is that in many contexts the term 'world' is used not to refer to the external world, either in the sense of what we see, or of the planet earth in space, or of the universe as a whole, but, rather, to stand for or signify the 'world' of an individual: *one's* world. This is a not uncommon metaphor in modern terms: we talk of one whose worldview is utterly alien to our own as living in a different world; advertising agencies create imaginary worlds in order to persuade us to purchase certain goods in order to enhance our world; we can say of friends or acquaintances whose occupations are completely different from our own that we know nothing of their worlds; if one has travelled extensively one might think of someone who has spent his entire life in a tiny remote village that his world has limited horizons; and the same might be said of those with minimal imagination or who lack a capacity for abstract conceptualising. In all such cases what is meant by 'world' is the world of one particular person's experience. And as such the term signifies that experience in its totality: each person's world is nothing other than everything within his experience throughout his or her life. And in early Buddhism we find a similar metaphorical use of the term as one of the correlates of the centrality of human experience to the Buddha's teachings.

In fact the metaphorical usage of 'world' pre-dates the Buddha's teaching and is to be found in the *Vedic* sacrificial religion. There, in spite of its having the conventional spacial meanings with which we are familiar, it always had what has been described as an 'inherent vagueness'.[10] One of its applications was that it indicated a state of happiness or stability (perhaps in the sense of orderliness). Its earliest meaning was a "free, open space" or a "safe, sacred space",[11] which was of particular significance in the context of the very early stages of the Brahmanical religion because of the importance when they were but newly settled in India of clearings, forest glades, and so on. This importance went on to be indicated in the sacrificial ritual, when a sacred space is constructed to represent the 'world' that is desired. In this way the term became associated with cosmological planes (desired worlds), which tended to be interpreted spacially. But the association of security and happiness with the sacred space also came to be extended metaphorically so that the desire for a certain world (which might be attained by means of the sacrifice) was seen in terms not of the spacial location but the security and happiness of the individual's state of mind. The term for 'world' thus came to have two principal meanings: the one spacial and the other psychological.

In Theravāda Buddhism as a whole, 'world' is also used in several senses. The most well-known usages are, first, that it has the conventional spacial sense, in particular used to indicate cosmological levels: each level is itself a 'world'. These cosmological worlds are populated variously: earth by human and other animal beings, and other levels by various of the not-normally-visible beings referred to earlier. Some of these are languishing miserably as demons in hells, and some are subtle beings who have achieved advanced stages of the spiritual path and are enjoying the advantages of one or other of the heavens.[12]

And, second, there has long been accepted that there is a metaphorical correspondence between the different cosmological 'worlds' and the different levels of meditation, which are themselves also called 'worlds'. Meditative levels are described as it were vertically – states of mind that are characterised in certain ways are said to be attained by 'ascending' from one to the next, each attainment requiring extensive meditative disciplinary practice. And just as one's normal everyday conceptual framework corresponds to the normal everyday world we see around us, so the characteristics of the state of mind acquired at each meditative stage are said to be similar to the characteristics of a corresponding cosmological world. This correspondence has produced what the Theravāda tradition sees as a psychological cosmology.[13] That is to say, they see the various different levels of the external world, the cosmos, as paralleling the different subjective levels attained in meditation: a lofty heaven corresponding to an appropriately advanced meditative level.

This psychological cosmology in turn lends itself to the suggestion, which I first made in *Identity and Experience*,[14] that the whole notion of Buddhist cosmology is underpinned by the metaphor of the spiritual path of the individual. This is particularly appropriate in that the characteristics of both the various cosmological levels and the corresponding meditative levels are given in terms that relate to the gradual dissipation of our normative conceptual categories and the resulting clarity of one's state of mind. As, incrementally, with meditative practice one's perception becomes freed from the restraints of all the 'conceptions of manifoldness' that condition what one 'constructs by the mind' at the everyday level, so one's world becomes, in similar incremental stages, characterised in terms that correspond to the absence of those manifoldnesses and constructions. And the characteristics of those incrementally notable changes in one's state of mind correspond to the way cosmological levels become more subtle and rarified: as it were empty of manifoldnesses, which characterise the more dense level with which we are familiar. What I think we are seeing here is a reference to the correspondence of denseness to ignorance and clarity to increasing insight.[15] Not only is this a metaphor which is not unfamiliar to us in our own culture, but one can also readily extend it to include the correspondences between light and happiness, darkness and despair, illustrating the way the metaphor covers not only the cognitive but also the affective aspects of the state of mind concerned.

It is significant to the appropriateness of the metaphor of the spiritual path that in Buddhism the universe is unbounded, and that there is no cosmological level associated with nirvana, the goal of the spiritual path. A famous textual passage states of the sphere where there is neither earth, nor water, nor heat, nor wind (that is to say, the sphere where there is no trace of the four great elements which characterise the world around us, discussed in the last chapter), that "it is *this* that is the end of *dukkha*".[16] And the end, or cessation, of *dukkha* is nirvana, as stated in the third Noble Truth. Another term for nirvana is *sukha*, the converse of *dukkha*. As *dukkha*, in psychological terms, means unsatisfactoriness, so *sukha* correspondingly means happiness. By extension, too, as *dukkha* refers to the level of experience in which one's world is characterised by the restrictions or dis-ease of ignorance, so *sukha* refers to the level of experience in which one's world is characterised by freedom from ignorance, or the ease of insight. Conceptually, these applications of restriction/dis-ease and freedom/ease are also appropriate to the contrast between manifoldness, which involves the restrictions of identificatory boundaries, and absence of manifoldness, which is free of them.

In spite of the development within the Theravāda Buddhist tradition of the psychological cosmology as described above, this metaphorical link between meditative attainment and cosmological level is not found in any formally established form until the *Abhidhamma*. And though since then the Buddhist tradition has accepted the cosmological aspect of the correspondence as reflecting the 'external' world in all its complexity, if one looks at the earliest material, as I am doing here, the correspondence between subjective state and cosmological level is at best unsystematically implicit. For example, the attainment of certain meditative states is sometimes said to be a prerequisite either of being reborn into or of contacting other beings in corresponding 'worlds'.[17] And it is made clear that no matter how good such a world might be, it is to be eschewed in favour of attaining nirvana.[18] It is now commonly assumed that such unsystematic references are the embryonic form of the later more detailed metaphorical structure.[19]

In fact in the earlier texts, and it is this I want to draw out here, it is as a metaphor for the entire life of the individual human being that 'world' is more specifically used. This is most clearly indicated in the section of the texts which is primarily concerned with the analysis of the individual in terms of the five *khandhas*.[20] As we have seen, the *khandhas*, as the experiencing apparatus of the individual, constitute the focus of the Buddhist teachings: it is this that one needs to know and understand about oneself. And as such, the *khandhas* can collectively be understood metaphorically to represent the individual as a whole. We saw them used this way in the passage quoted in Chapter Three which stated that the coming-to-be of the entire human being was constructed by one's volitional activities. And by extension from this metaphor we sometimes find the *khandhas* collectively referred to in terms of an individual 'world'. So, for example, we read that the five *khandhas* together comprise a "phenomenon which is a world in the world".[21] The context is one in which the Buddha states that he has no quarrel with the world or with some of the teachings of other teachers in the world. But he wants to establish a teaching which is not given by those other teachers, that of the *khandhas*, which he has thoroughly penetrated and realised. Here the point is made that the world with which he is concerned is the subjective world of experience.

Similarly, 'world' is sometimes used interchangeably with *dukkha*, the same passage repeated first with world (*loka*) and then with *dukkha*. We are already familiar with the way *dukkha* is itself identified by the Buddha as subjective experience when he defined it in terms of the five *khandhas*. So the interchangeability of 'world' and *dukkha* implies the metaphorical usage of 'world' I am suggesting. The Buddha's teachings, as we know, are aimed at no longer being subject to rebirth, and frequently this is expressed as the "ceasing of all the *khandhas* which are *dukkha*".[22] This means to the point where the individual, whose on-going rebirth is signified by the continued functioning of the five *khandhas*, achieves liberation from bondage to that rebirth process. Passages such as this should not be taken in the literal sense that at Enlightenment, or nirvana, the five *khandhas* suddenly cease working altogether. Rather, the individual, on achieving liberating insight, is no longer contributing to his continued pre-Enlightenment experience (*dukkha*) by means of his cognitive lens operating in the same old way. He is able to function volitionlessly (in the affective and consequential sense) in order to meet the needs of his normal and *in*consequential functioning. By contrast to the way the *khandhas* signify individual continuity, therefore, he will have reached a state which might be indicated metaphorically by the expression 'the ceasing of all the *khandhas*'. And this is the same as the ceasing of *dukkha*. As *dukkha* is explained in terms of the *khandhas* in the first Noble Truth, the cessation of the *khandhas* is the same as the cessation of *dukkha* – and the latter is, indeed, how the third Noble Truth expresses the goal of the path.

It is in this sense that the word *dukkha*, the entire experiential life of an individual prior to Enlightenment, is interchanged with the word 'world' (*loka*): as nirvana is the cessation of *dukkha*, so it can be stated to be the cessation of one's world. Illustrating the metaphor, we read, for example, that the Buddha states: "I will teach you how *dukkha* arises and how it ceases ... Visual consciousness arises because of sight and (visible) objects (and so on through all the senses); contact is the combination of the three; feeling is conditioned by contact; craving is conditioned by feeling. This is the arising of *dukkha*".[23] The cessation of *dukkha* comes about when the craving which is normally conditioned by feeling no longer occurs: when craving utterly fades away and ceases, then grasping, becoming, birth, and cyclic existence cease. And immediately after this we read exactly the same about the world:

that the Buddha is teaching how the world arises and ceases.[24] Elsewhere, this point is made in a description of what an Enlightened person has achieved: the arising of the world is understood and abandoned, and the cessation of the world is understood and realised.[25] The individual's experience, then, can be metaphorically expressed as the world: his experience *is* for him the world.

This same point is made elsewhere where it is stated that "It is these five types of sensual desire that are called the world in the discipline of the noble one [that is, one on the path]".[26] The Buddhist is to become detached from sensual desire and practise appropriate meditation. And when he eventually sees that his continuity tendencies are completely destroyed, he "is said to have come to the end of the world, he lives at the end of the world, he has overcome attachment in the world".[27] And elsewhere we read: "I declare that the end of the world is not to be learned, seen, or attained by going to the end of the world. Nor do I declare that the end of *dukkha* can be made without attaining the end of the world".[28] It seems clear that 'world' is being used in two senses here, and that what is being stated is that the world one needs to understand, and bring about the cessation of, is the world of experience. And in that sense, the attaining of the end of experience – *dukkha* – is the attaining of the end of that world: but this attainment has nothing to do with world in the spacial sense, of travelling to a *place* that is the end of the world.[29] Later in this chapter, the individual's 'world' is again defined in terms of the senses, as in the passage above. The relevance of the senses in both these contexts is that all our incoming experiential data come through our senses in the way we have seen. It is because we cognitively process that incoming data as we do that we continue to have cravings; and it is because of such cravings that our 'world' has continued existence: this is how the individual continues. And it is this – this particular 'world' of experience – that the Buddhist disciple seeks to understand.

A very similar passage to that just discussed is more explicit in making the point I have suggested when it states: "Where there is no more being born, growing old, dying, passing from birth to birth – the end of *that* world is not known, seen or reached by going to it".[30] The interlocutor of the Buddha to whom this is taught is a hermit called Rohitassa who had acquired all sorts of supernormal psychic powers including the ability to travel at great speed. He had thought that that ability would give him the means to travel to the end of the world, where there would be no more rebirth. But he realises from what the Buddha tells him that what he is seeking would not be found by spacial travel even if he were to continue for a hundred years.

Two other passages state that the world is defined by virtue of the fact that it 'breaks up' or is 'subject to dissolution'. In one the breaking up is brought about either by knowing that the senses, and the way they operate as part of our cognitive system, are *dukkha*.[31] In other words, one's world of experience continues as it is for so long as one is ignorant of its nature. In the other passage, it is stated that it is the cognitive process, associated as it is with sensory data, that is called the world because it is that process that is subject to dissolution.[32]

Though these two passages explicitly link sensory data with the world through the characteristic of breaking up and dissolution, in fact the sensory basis of the cognitive process is repeatedly stated to be the foundation of *dukkha* because it is this sensory-cognitive process that is impermanent (it is to impermanence that both breaking up and dissolution refer).[33] In Chapter Three, I discussed the psychological association of unsatisfactoriness (*dukkha*) with whatever is impermanent, but here it is suggested that the impermanence of the cognitive process is in fact what underpins *dukkha* in the sense of experience. This passage gives textual backing to the point I made in the last paragraph of Chapter Three: that nothing that is epistemic can be anything other than impermanent. So while it is impermanence that gives rise to the psychological response that things are unsatisfactory, we here have a clear explanation of *why* it is that experience itself is intrinsically impermanent. And also of why the experiential world of an individual (*dukkha*) is defined in terms of the impermanence of that epistemic process.

It is because of the fact that it is the world of experience that needs to be understood that the Enlightened person is called one who has reached the end of the world, or, as one translator suggestively puts it, a 'world-ender'.[34] Anyone who has not understood the 'five types of sensory desire that is called the world in the discipline of the noble one', referred to above, is called one who is 'belonging to the world'.[35] And each time one is reborn one comes to 'another world',[36] and it is this process of being world-bound that one is seeking to bring an end to. For, as quoted above, the Buddha said that what he taught was how the world arises and how it ceases.

This point ties in with the common use of the contrasting terms 'worldly' (*lokiya*) and 'trans-worldly' (*lokuttara*) to refer, respectively, to one who is still struggling at early stages on the path and to one who has achieved either Enlightenment itself or at least a very advanced stage along the path to liberating insight. I have suggested elsewhere[37] that these terms should be understood in terms of the metaphor I am discussing here. That is to say, a worldly person is one who has yet to understand the way his world is in fact created, and indeed limited, by his own cognitive apparatus: he is bound to the way it 'normally' operates, and, in being bound, is reborn again and again to 'another [such] world'. In contrast, a trans-worldly person is one who has grasped the nature of his experiential world and is (or is almost) no longer bound by or limited to it.

In my view, the use of world in this metaphorical sense serves to emphasise the extent to which the Buddha consistently draws attention away from the 'external' world, and the issues associated with it which were the focus of the religious concerns of so many others at the time, to the need to understand the subjective role in the world of experience. And this is because his concern is consistently focused only on what needs to be addressed in order to solve the problem of bondage to the cycle of rebirth.

Other key aspects of the Buddha's teachings appear to be expressed metaphorically, or involve the metaphorical or figurative use of certain words or phrases. There are a great many instances of this, and an overview of some of them will provide more of a context in which to assess the significance of the way 'world' is used metaphorically.

We have in fact already come across one of the most important metaphors found in early Buddhist teachings: that of fire.[38] Picking up on the centrality of fire to the Brahmanical sacrificial religion, the Buddha transposes the symbolism of the fire from something that the householder should keep alight to something that the seeker of the Truth should strive to burn out. As I have already explained, so crucial is it that the brahmin householder maintain his three sacrificial fires that they came to symbolise his very identity and continuity throughout his entire life, eventually being used for the last time to ignite his funeral pyre – the man's death thus coinciding and being associated with the dying out of the fire.

And this symbolism of the householder's identity and continuity is linked to his performing his sacrificial duties, which use the fire as the locus of the rituals, and thus to the maintenance of social and cosmic order: to the performing of his own-*dharma* in order to maintain *Dharma*. The Buddha also symbolically associates fire with continuity, but rather than being something that should be tended and kept alight in order to fulfil one's religious duties, it is understood in terms of the fuel of the continuity of *dukkha*: that which one is aiming to overcome by means of bringing about its cessation. Greed, hatred and ignorance represent the three sacrificial fires, and it is this cognitive and affective causal matrix, which we have discussed before, that one needs to 'blow out'. Following this, fire is a central practical metaphor in some forms of Buddhist meditation, any negative states of mind being understood in terms of the binding fuel/fire analogy.

Richard Gombrich has recently pointed out[39] that the fire-as-fuel metaphor is also implicit in the word *upādāna*, roughly translated as 'graspings'. I briefly referred to this term, which is often found associated with *khandha* in the texts, in Chapter Two. The expression *upādāna-khandhā*, which is used in the context of an individual who, prior to attaining Enlightenment, is 'fuelled' by desires (graspings), is commonly translated as 'the *khandhas* of grasping'. But in fact 'the *khandhas* which are fuelled', or 'the *khandhas* which are on fire', would better draw out the metaphor. Interestingly, it may also be that the term *khandha* itself is part of the fire metaphor in a passage to which I have previously referred in which the Buddha speaks of the five *khandhas* which are on fire as being the 'burden' one needs to understand the taking up and putting down of.[40] The *khandhas* here metaphorically represent the 'bundles of fuel' one needs to put out: this is the burden to be laid down. In contrast, the brahmin householder would need bundles of firewood as the fuel to keep his sacrificial fires alight: this is the fuel he needs to collect. Elsewhere, the *khandhas* are more explicitly stated as being on fire,[41] and all sensual pleasures, the nature and arising of which are identified and understood as one understands the operation of the *khandhas*, are likened to a pit of charcoal that would cause pain and death (and, by implication, rebirth: not, therefore, nirvana) if one were to fall into it.[42] In metaphorical terms, such references are in perfect harmony with the teaching of the first two Noble Truths about the fuelling of *dukkha*. And they are in perfect harmony with the common expression that one who has attained nirvana is 'completely cool'.[43]

Another common metaphor in early Buddhism is that of the house, or home, or village, and sometimes the fire metaphor is associated with it too.[44] The image of house (or home or village) is used to symbolise individuality in place of the *khandhas*, in the sense that the *khandhas* are said to be a house or home or village. One finds, for example, the *khandhas*, representing the individual who is vulnerable to being enslaved to sensual desires of all sorts, likened to the way an old house, whose thatch is highly flammable, is vulnerable to fire taking hold and sweeping through it.[45] Similarly, a foolish man who experiences states of mind such as fearfulness is likened to a house which is built in such a way as to burn up easily.[46] Such states of mind reflect self-concern and are therefore associated with the way one's cognitive apparatus works prior to Enlightenment: fear is an affective reaction which is no less part of the causal nexus than overt desire. The point is to see that it is important to save what one can from the burning house: that is to say, to leave behind fear and other negativities; it is this that matters and counts, not what is consumed. This can be done by the overcoming of self-centredness, and the practice of qualities such as generosity.[47]

We saw in Chapter Three that it is the *khandha* of volitional activities that volitionally constructs the coming-to-be of the entire individual in his next life. This point is made metaphorically when desire is said to be the house-builder who builds another cyclical life that is *dukkha*.[48] Each life is, metaphorically speaking, a house.[49] Linking more directly with the *khandhas*, another reference states that the home that consciousness dwells in is provided by the other four *khandhas* of body, sensations, apperception and volitional activities. What ties these together is desire. And by understanding how the *khandhas* operate, and the states of mind associated with desire, such a home is abandoned.[50] This renders one 'homeless': one is free from the home in which one is tied to and by one's desires. The aim to relinquish one's association with the home in which one is so tied is indicated when the expression 'homeless' is used in early Buddhism to signify that an individual has embarked on the spiritual quest for Truth. Following the example of the Buddha when he himself began his search, on becoming a monastic Buddhist one is said to 'go forth from home to homelessness'.[51] This use of the metaphor also alludes to the contrast between Buddhism and the Householder religion of the brahmins. In the latter, both the fulfilling of one's religious duties and one's identity (symbolised by the household fires) require one to be tied to one's status and role as a householder. In the former, the understanding of the nature of one's experience as an individual has nothing to do with such ties. Rather, the aim is to see the way in which one has and continues to create one's home-as-metaphor-for-this-life, and to achieve the cessation of that process.

Part of the complexity of the house metaphor relates to the fact that the householder life is particularly associated with indulgence in and attachment to sensual pleasures, which is one of the extremes that the Buddhist Middle Way, here metaphorically described as one of homelessness, avoids.[52] It is having abandoned the sensual pleasures that one goes forth from the house, one text states.[53] Another explicitly links abandoning home with abandoning all that the heart holds dear, all desires, and ignorance.[54] And the senses themselves are metaphorically represented as the doors (of the house that is one's body, the locus of one's individuality) by means of which the individual subjectively relates to the objective world, as I have previously stated. As a village needs to defend itself, so the individual needs to guard his sense doors. This guarding is not so much to keep all sense data out, but to control how one deals with and reacts to it. Given that it is subjectively that one interprets and responds to incoming sense data, the point is that one should not have an affective (and therefore consequential) response to what one is experiencing: one should not be entranced with views about its various characteristics, is how one passage puts it.[55] Referring in this instance to the sense of sight, it goes on to state that one should be intent on restraining those things which give rise to unwholesomeness, evil, covetousness or dejection which flow over one for as long as one lives with one's sense of sight unrestrained; one should guard the visual sense and attain restraint over it. The attainment of such restraint over one's reaction to incoming sense data is what distinguishes the advanced Buddhist from a person who is allowing his cognitive apparatus to function 'normally': while ignorant, we *do* react affectively to our sense data; when liberating insight is attained, we 'see things as they are' *without* reacting to them. This point is made, also using the metaphor of guarding the village, in a passage where the incoming sense data are referred to as 'village plunderers': in finding the data entrancing, our cognitive apparatus is 'plundered' by them and led astray.[56] And elsewhere village becomes town, the gates of which have to be guarded by wise door-keepers.[57]

The metaphor of the house (or home, or village, or town), then, is used to signify individuality. It serves several purposes simultaneously. First, it indicates the locus provided by the body: each individual is spacially identifiable. Second, it suggests the way one is attached to that individuality by relating the nature of the attachment to the way one might also be attached to family and/or community. This is, in particular, an attachment which functions by means of the way one reacts to one's incoming sensory data. In associating the metaphor with the life of the householder, what is being emphasised here is sensual desire (associated above all with the reproductive duty of the brahmin householder, who has to produce sons). And by extension from this specific desire, *all* affective responses are included. Third, it implies the way in which our sense of identity is associated with our sense of place, both spacially and in terms of our relationship with our family and/or community. We do not exist out of spacial context, and our sense of and attachment to our 'self-hood' is very much associated with our place in family and community. These are the strongest psychological ties we have, corresponding to the fact that the strongest of our physical desires is sexual, triggering the biological process of reproducing ourselves in order to provide continuity of lineage in terms of family and community. All of this has to be left behind one, and the process by which it is perpetuated 'guarded against', if one is to attain the liberating insight described by the Buddha.

This symbolism has been interpreted literally by the Theravāda Buddhist tradition in that it is thought that in order to practise the mental discipline necessary for liberating insight one needs to become a member of a monastic order. It is thought that one cannot achieve mental detachment from home, family and community unless one is physically separated from those things. Such physical separation is enabling of the psychological separation, it is thought. Whether or not the physical separation is actually necessary, as the tradition has it, it is the achieving of the psychological detachment that is the aim, and that is the prerequisite to seeing things as they really are.

Perhaps in part suggesting the strength of the attachment and psychological orientation associated with our normal identification with our place in home, village and community, which have to be uprooted, another powerful metaphor used in early Buddhism associates the normal functioning of one's cognitive apparatus with a stream, and its re-orientation as going 'against the stream'. That the cyclical series of rebirths are collectively called *saṃsāra* in Indian religions as a whole in fact suggests a 'flow' or 'stream'. Precisely this was the original meaning of the verbal root, *sar*, from which *saṃsāra*, more usually interpreted as 'going round', derives. A well-known and repeated story describes the stream of the cycle of lives as vast and frightening, but states that there is a further shore (nirvana) that is secure and not frightening: fear here again indicating the self-concern that is associated with rebirth. What one needs to do is to use a raft, powered by one's hands and feet, so that one might cross over to that further shore. The raft is the Buddhist teachings, and using one's hands and feet here indicates the energy and effort one needs to apply to following the teachings successfully.[58] Elsewhere, the cycle of lives is referred to as the 'stream of Māra' (Māra representing death, and here more specifically the repeated deaths at the end of each life), and when one has uprooted the continuity tendencies one has 'cut across the stream'.[59] In slight contrast, but using the same metaphor, the tackling of the task of going against the stream by following the Noble Eightfold Path is referred to as 'entering the stream',[60] and there are numerous references to one who has done so as a 'stream enterer'.[61] This perhaps refers to the disciple's conscious engagement with understanding the stream in order to cross it; and having entered the stream for this purpose, the benefit of this, referred to as the 'fruit' of stream entry, is reaped.[62]

The mechanics of the stream are identified in a passage where the causal nexus of volitional activities, whose foundation is ignorance, is likened to a hilltop upon which rain is falling in thick drops. The water flows down the slope, filling cracks and gullies, streams, lakes, rivers, sea and ocean.[63] Similarly, the causal connection flows between faith, joy, equilibrium, happiness, concentration, seeing things as they really are, detachment from volitional activities, and liberation. Elsewhere the same point is made when it is stated that just as the ocean, as it flows, makes rivers and tributaries and lakes and streams also flow, so ignorance causes the flowing of the continuity of rebirth. And again the ebbing of ignorance causes the ebbing of continuity just as the ebbing of the ocean reduces the flow in other waterways.[64]

Life as an individual is described as a 'flooding tide', a 'whirlpool', adrift on the 'current of rebirth'.[65] In the cycle of lives, one 'floats down the stream of becoming (i.e rebirth)'.[66] Though ignorance is the foundation of the causal nexus, the consequential aspect of rebirth in the cycle of lives is perhaps more graphically stated in terms of sensual desires, as indicated by the sense doors needing to be guarded in the metaphor of the village. So it is not surprising that these passages also refer to the whirlpool or current in terms of insatiable sense desires, and of the passion for existence. Giving free rein to one's passions and sense desires is 'going down with the current'.[67]

A slight variation on the metaphor makes the same point when an individual life is likened to a log floating down the Ganges at risk of becoming grounded on one or other of the river banks, of sinking mid-stream, of getting stuck on a sandbank, or caught in a whirlpool.[68] The banks are interpreted as the operation of one's senses, sinking mid-stream as the desire for pleasure, getting stuck on a sandbank as self-centredness, and being caught in a whirlpool (somewhat repetitively) as sense pleasure. If one can avoid such things, one will, like the log floating down the Ganges to the ocean, 'float' to nirvana. In not being caught by these things, one will have the cognitive clarity ('right view' – *sammādiṭṭhi*) which is the means by which one floats towards nirvana.

Though no mention is made of reversing the current in the example given in the last paragraph, usually the stream or current of continuity needs to be reversed if one is to attain liberation from that continuity: if one is to 'go against the stream'. This is clearly stated to be very difficult; indeed, it is deep, subtle and difficult to see.[69] But its possibility is beautifully illustrated by the symbolism of the lotus flower. Though its roots are in water and the plant grows in water, yet its stem rises and stands above the water to flower, and the flower is untouched by the water.[70] Needless to say, this involves abandoning passions and desires: this, together with the cultivating of insight, enables one to go against the current.[71] But going against the stream will not be achieved by those who remain enslaved to passions and desires.[72] One who manages to achieve a significant degree of detachment from consequential volitional activities is referred to as 'one who goes upstream'.[73]

A Theravāda Buddhist legendary tale about the Buddha's life indicates the significance of 'going upstream' when it relates that on the night of his Enlightenment, as he prepared himself for deep meditation, he floated a rice-bowl on a nearby river and stated that if he was about to achieve liberating insight it would float upstream, and if not it would float down 'with the current'. The bowl floated upstream, 'against the current'.[74]

The common application of needing to go 'upstream' or 'against the current' in order to make progress on the path to liberating insight relates to the fact that that insight involves undoing and reorientating (reprogramming, as it were) the way one's entire cognitive process works. 'Seeing things as they really are' is radically different from anything with which we are cognitively familiar: and in being so fundamentally different, it can be likened to the huge effort that would be involved in ceasing to be carried along by a current flowing downstream and bringing oneself to the point of moving against the current. The fact that for so long as one has any degree of ignorance one's volitional activities also continue to function means that the stream or current is referred to as one of desires in general. But the real reorientation that is aimed for is cognitive. The point is that what we think of as our normal cognition is in fact flowing uncontrolled like a stream. And what one has to do, therefore, and this is implicit in the term 'mindfulness' which refers to the form of Buddhist meditation that leads to seeing things as they really are, is to understand or control the workings of one's mind, so that one can gain insight into the way in which normal cognition operates and change it. This ties in with the fact that the doors or gates to the house or village need to be guarded, or the fire of continuity quenched. The metaphors are linked in their relating to the workings of one's cognitive apparatus.

There are many other metaphors to be found in the early Buddhist texts, some with a wider application than others. But those discussed here will, I think, suffice to illustrate both the importance of the use of metaphor – importance in terms of being commonly recognised *and* of the centrality of the issue to which they relate – and the way they are used to relate to the cognitive process which is the means by which one experiences cyclical life.

In my view the metaphor of the world ties in with these other metaphors. What really matters is understanding one's experience: it is this, no more and no less, that brings liberating insight. And in focussing his teachings solely on the means to achieving that insight, the Buddha metaphorically relates the different aspects of what we think of as the world around us to one's subjective experience. In explaining how the *khandhas* work, he focuses in particular on the fact that we cannot have access to anything else:

all our experience is mediated to us by means of them. And our 'world' is simply that. We cannot have access to an 'external' world because we cannot get outside of our experience. Our experience, then, *is* our world. And as such it is peculiarly appropriate that Buddhist cosmology be understood as a metaphor for the spiritual path: our world 'expands', so to speak, with the diminishing of the restrictions of ignorance. In Buddhism the expansion of the world is associated not just with more and more lateral experiences, so to speak, with more factual knowledge acquired, but with the different perceptions associated with deeper insight and clarity of understanding of how things really are: with the developing of a different way of knowing. But in principle this metaphor is not difficult to empathise with in our own culture: we all experience, however minimally, the liberating effect of knowledge, particularly in the sense of understanding different forms of knowledge and different ways of thinking, and the fact that one might understand these as the broadening of the limits of one's 'world', sometimes to the point that we are able, with the new knowledge, to view the world very differently – even if not radically so in the Buddhist sense. And we commonly use corresponding metaphors such as something having 'widened one's horizons' or brought about a more 'far-seeing approach to life', of a new experience 'opening up a whole new world', that one 'will never see things that way again', and so on.

Conversely, and applying different appropriate metaphors, we can and do as it were 'shut down' or 'draw in' our worlds for a variety of reasons, which may be either positive or negative. For example, one might for a time withdraw to a special shared and imaginarily created 'world' with a loved one in order to 'shut out the ['external'] world'. One might do something similar to amuse a child (such are the 'worlds' created by the storytellers), for a period of work, or for a retreat or in preparation for an undertaking of some kind. Or one might temporarily 'withdraw from the world', creating for oneself a 'gentle, protective world' or an imagined 'safe place', in order to heal after some hurt, to recover from bereavement, and so on. All of these withdrawals are as it were smaller 'worlds within the world' which we create temporarily for ourselves. Less constructively (though only in the beneficial sense of constructive), perhaps, and often also less wittingly, one might in varying degrees make use of fantasy worlds – the pipe dreams of Eugene O'Neill's *The Iceman Cometh*: the castles in the air of

Ibsen's *The Master Builder* – in order to cope with aspects of oneself or one's life one cannot face or come to terms with. In this way one can 'take refuge from reality', deluding oneself sometimes extremely successfully, creating a 'cloud cuckoo land' in which to live.

For each and every one of us, then, our world is the world of our own experience, dependent on the workings of our cognitive apparatus. Though as common human beings we seem to share a structural framework within which the apparatus works – we each bring the same mechanics to bear on the data – we are each different in detail according to our individual degree of ignorance and the way our volitional activities are conditioned by that. So our capacity for certain refinements varies, and our tastes, inclinations, preparedness to face the deconstructing of pipe dreams, and so on, are, in the broader framework, determined by our individual karmic history: the way our ignorance and volitional activities have cyclically produced a complex causal nexus over many lifetimes.[75]

And what follows from this, as I said earlier in this chapter but as we can perhaps see more clearly now, is that what is clearly indicated in the way the Buddhist teachings are given is that all of the factors of our experience, whatever they may be, are dependent for their existence *as that* on our cognitive apparatus. This explains the famous early Buddhist expression "In this fathom-long living body, along with its apperceptions and thoughts, lies the world, the arising of the world, and the cessation of the world".[76] And this is why the factors of experience are referred to as 'conditioned things' – *saṃkhārā*. They are conditioned *by us*. And the fact that the Pali term (as a past participle, *saṃkhata*) also means 'constructed' or 'made' refers to the fact that all of the factors of experience are constructed or made *like that* by our cognitive process. It is we ourselves who construct the world as we know it from the mass of incoming sensory data we continually receive. One can see more clearly from this the significance of the fact that the term *saṃkhāra* is from the same verbal root as the word karma, as mentioned earlier. Karma, according to the Buddha, operates by means of our intentions. And our intentions, in their broadest sense – including all volitional activities – are effected by the *khandha* of volitional activities, which is called by the same word: the *saṃkhāra-kkhandha*.

In fact two aspects to the construction of the world by our cognitive apparatus are indicated by the way the word *saṃkhāra* relates to all conditioned things, as well as to volitional activities in particular. All conditioned things are conditioned whether they are volitions or not: there is no difference between a road and greed, in this respect. So one might say that there are both cognitive and affective constructions, so to speak. What appear to us as objects are of the same constructed nature as affective volitions: both are both constructed in the same way and also have consequences in terms of continuity – the former in the sense that they occur because of one's ignorance, itself underlying continuity, and the latter in the sense that they have direct or specific consequences. So in fact the distinction is hypothetical because one's entire world, which includes roads and greed, continues for so long as one's cognitive apparatus is operating from a basis of any degree of ignorance. And that goes hand in hand with the operation of the affective dimension of that apparatus: the two are not distinguished until Enlightenment occurs, when the cessation of ignorance brings about the cessation of all self-centred desires. This is made clear in the description of the rooting out of the continuity tendencies.

It is clear, I think, by now how it is we ourselves who construct the world which is our experience: what one might call the objective world. But if we recall the structure of the textual description of the cognitive process to which I have referred before, we can also see the way in which the notion of subjectivity is also part of the cognitive construction. The passage is as follows: 'Seeing occurs when there is contact between an eye and [visible] forms, accompanied by consciousness; this gives rise to feelings, which one then identifies; and what one thus identifies one reflects on and makes manifold.' As noted earlier, what is suggested is the way the developing of the polarity between subject and object is a part of the way the process operates. As objectivity becomes increasingly and more clearly manifold, so subjectivity is also more clearly polarised from that objectivity. This corresponds to the point I made earlier that though the dependently originated processes of the objective world and the cognitive subjectivity appear as two processes, actually they are parallel aspects of one process. I suggested earlier that what the objective world is dependently originated in is the subjective cognitive process, but in fact the point is that each of the two aspects of the one process is *mutually* dependently originated: neither could function without the other.

The implications of this for the nature of subjectivity are highly relevant in the context of the Buddhist teaching of *anattā*. And it is with this that the next chapter is concerned. Before proceeding to that, however, I will conclude this chapter by suggesting that the final dimension of *dukkha* is metaphysical.

Standing as it does as the first Noble Truth, it relates to our experience in every respect. As unsatisfactoriness, it indicates its psychological aspect. This is itself related, by means of the functioning of the *khandhas*, to the mechanics of continuity. What continues is experience: this is the explanation of the first Noble Truth, which states the fact of experience (*dukkha*), that is to say what is mediated by the operating of the *khandhas*. And as such *dukkha* indicates that the nature of the Truth which the Buddhist seeks to understand is epistemic: no other aspect of the Truth is in fact accessible to human beings. So dukkha in the Four Noble Truths is to be understood both in terms of the way desires fuel the continuity of the psychological experience of unsatisfactoriness, and also, more profoundly, the way our cognitive process fuels and reveals to us a world that is *ontologically not other than* our experience.

Notes

1 Recorded in particular in the *Nidāna Vagga* of the *Saṃyutta Nikāya* (Vol. II), and the *Mahānidāna Suttanta* in *Dīgha Nikāya* (Vol. II).

2 *Paṭiccasamuppādañca vo bhikkhave desissāmi paṭiccasamuppanne ca dhamme.*

3 SN II 25: *dhammaṭṭhitatā dhammaniyāmatā idappaccayatā. Idappaccayatā* is usually rendered 'causally related'.

4 cf. SN II 25 for the twelvefold version, and throughout the *Nidāna Saṃyutta* for this and other variations.

5 This interpretation of the formula of dependent origination is suggested and discussed, and other interpretations are referred to, in Hamilton, 1996, chapter 6.

6 Throughout the *Nidāna Saṃyutta*. That the dependently originated continuity of the individual can cease in this way is also implicit in the frequently given general formula: 'this being so, that occurs; this ceasing, that ceases'. This formula is discussed further in Chapter Eight.

7 SN IV 71.

8 MN I 190f.

9 Many are discussed in Harvey (1995b), chapter 5.

10 Gonda, 1966, p. 110 and *passim*.

11 Ibid, pp. 1–41.

12 See Steven Collins (1998), chapter 4, part I: "Life in the Heavens".

13 The cosmology itself is described in Gombrich (1975) as well as Collins (1998). The correspondence is discussed in Collins, 1982, p. 217, and Masefield, 1983, p. 78. Masefield favours, as I do not, a literal interpretation of cosmological references in purely spacial terms.

14 See Hamilton, 1996, p. 99 and chapter 7 where I was building on an earlier suggestion by Richard Gombrich (1975, p. 134) that one of the higher, formless, cosmological levels, the *arūpadhātu*, is "an elaborate spacial metaphor for spiritual progress".

15 This contrast echoes the contrast between the 'grossness' of sensory impression and the 'subtlety' of conceptual activity mentioned in Chapter Three, n.51: in effect the contrast between abstract and concrete aspects of experience.

16 *Udāna* 80: *Es' ev' anto dukkhassa 'ti.*

17 cf., for example, AN.II.126–130; MN.II.37, 194f.

18 MN.II.37.

19 cf. the entry for *loka* in Nyanatiloka's *Buddhist Dictionary* (1980, p. 108f), which reflects the commonly accepted view: "Though the term *loka* is not applied in the Suttas to those ... worlds ... there is no doubt that the teaching about the ... worlds belongs to the earliest, i.e. Sutta period of the Buddhist scriptures...."

20 The *Khandha Saṃyutta*, SN, Vol III.

21 SN.III.139: *loke lokadhammo.*

22 *Evam etassa kevalassa dukkhakkhandhassa nirodho hoti*, found frequently throughout the *Nidāna Saṃyutta.*

23 SN II 71ff.

24 The Pali is identical save for *lokassa* in place of *dukkhassa.*

25 AN II 23.

26 AN IV 430.

27 AN IV 431f.

28 SN IV 93.

29 In this I disagree with Peter Masefield (1983), who sees "no reason why we should not take such [spacial] expressions quite literally" (p. 81; and cf. also p. 83).

30 AN II 48.

31 SN IV 52.

32 SN IV 53.

33 Throughout the *Saḷāyatana Saṃyutta* (SN, volume IV).

34 AN II 6, with this translation of *lokantagū* by Woodward in the Pali Text Society translation. At AN IV 432 the Pali is *lokassa antam*, and at AN II 48ff we find *lokantagū*, *lokantaṃ* and *lokassa antaṃ*.

35 AN IV 431: *lokapariyāpanna.*

36 MN II 73: *upeti gabbhañ ca parañ ca lokaṃ*, literally: 'he comes to a womb and to another world'.

37 Hamilton, 1999.

38 Fire as a metaphor in early Buddhism is discussed in further detail in Gombrich, 1990 and 1996.

39 Gombrich, 1996, p. 67.

40 SN III 25f.

41 SN III 71.

42 SN IV 188f. All of the points in this paragraph were first suggested and further discussed by Gombrich (1996, p. 67ff.), who also points out that the fire metaphor is used in the famous Parable of the Burning House in the *Lotus Sūtra*, one of the most important texts of Mahāyāna Buddhism.

43 For example, AN IV 84.

44 House imagery is discussed in Collins, 1983, pp. 165ff.
45 SN IV 185.
46 AN I 101.
47 AN I 156.
48 *Dhammapada* 153–4.
49 DN III 145.
50 SN III 9f.
51 *Agārasmā anagāriyaṃ pabbajati*: for example at DN II 16, 241ff.
52 cf., for example, MN I 504.
53 *Sutta Nipāta* 337.
54 SN I 15.
55 DN I 70.
56 SN IV 175.
57 SN IV 194f.
58 SN IV 174f; MN I 135, 260.
59 MN I 225f. cf. also *Sutta Nipāta* 715, 948.
60 SN V 347.
61 For example, DN I 156, III 107f, 132, 227; AN II 89; SN II 68, III 203f, 225f, V 193f.
62 For example, MN I 325; AN I 44, III 441, V 292f, 372f; DN I 229, III 227; SN III 168, 225, V 410f.
63 SN II 30ff. The metaphor of rain is used for a slightly different purpose in the Mahāyāna Buddhist Parable of the Raincloud.
64 SN II 118f.
65 SN I 15. cf. also *Sutta Nipāta* 319.
66 SN IV 128.
67 AN II 5.
68 SN IV 179f.
69 MN I 168.
70 MN I 169; SN I 138. The lotus flower, symbolising the possibility that a human being might attain the flowering of insight even though this grows from the mire of ignorance, is perhaps the most well-known and widely used metaphor in the Buddhist tradition as a whole.
71 AN II 5.
72 SN I 136.
73 AN I 233; DN III 237.
74 J I 70.
75 The development of the complex causal nexus is discussed at length in Hamilton, 1996, chapter 4.
76 AN II 48ff.

CHAPTER FIVE

The Experience of Subjectivity and Objectivity

"For my part, when I enter most intimately into what I call *myself*, I always stumble on some particular perception or other, of heat or cold, light or shade, love or hatred, pain or pleasure. I never catch *myself* at any time without a perception, and never can observe anything but the perception."
Hume, *Treatise of Human Nature*, Book I, part iv, section vi.

"It does not follow that there is no simple Self; it only follows that we cannot know whether there is or not, and that the Self, except as a 'bundle of perceptions', cannot enter into any part of our knowledge."
Bertrand Russell, *A History of Western Philosophy*, p. 637.

I said in Chapter One that one of the main reasons why the term *anattā* is ambiguous, which in turn has allowed different interpretations of it to arise, is because the Buddha never clearly explained how it was meant to be understood. In particular, he never actually stated 'What I teach is that there is no self at all', and he never answered the question Does one exist after achieving liberation from rebirth? by saying No. I explained that in my opinion to interpret *anattā* in the sense of a doctrinal statement that there is no self was a misinterpretation which had arisen because the context in which the Buddha was teaching was one in which virtually all the seekers of the Truth were obsessed by the notion that in one way or the other that Truth was to be found by understanding whether or not one was or had a permanent and abiding self or soul. The *Upaniṣadic* teaching of the brahmins, for example, stated that liberation from the cycle of lives was to be attained by realising that the essence of one's self, *ātman*, was identical with the essence of the universe, Brahman. And others were asking a plethora of questions all of which were formulated in terms of the existence or non-existence of such a self, and, indeed, of a similarly permanent external world. I explained that I thought that the Buddhist teachings were different from all other religious teachings of the time in the very respect that they were *not* about whether or not one is or has a self or soul – what one is – but that they were about understanding how one works. Any concern with the notion of self-hood, whether it be negative or positive, was, I felt, to focus on the wrong thing and to miss the point of the teachings – that attention should, rather, be directed elsewhere – and, moreover, I suggested that selfhood was neither *the* question nor *in* question.

I have also now shown in more detail where, in my opinion, the Buddha's teachings were seeking to direct attention: to understanding the nature and mechanics of experience, by means of one's cognitive process. An important passage where the Buddha deals with all sorts of possible permutations of what might be considered to be the self actually makes this point. After several pages of establishing that this, that or the other aspect of oneself is not in any way one's essential self (which is why this passage tends to be interpreted simply as stating 'there is no self'[1]), the Buddha goes on to state that *all* ideas framed according to the concept of (permanent) existence, *and this explicitly includes non-existence*, are misconceived (*akallaṃ* – which one might also render as inappropriate, or even as absurd). This is because, the text states, what needs to be understood are verbal expressions, and the way in which (or the 'system' according to which) things are so expressed, the explanation of things, and the way in which they are explained, the identification of things, and the way in which they are identified, the occurring of things, and the way in which they occur: it is by means of insight into all *this* that one achieves liberation.[2]

I also stated earlier, though, that given the Buddha's teaching that *everything* within the world of experience as a whole is dependently originated, it follows that the manner in which experiencing human beings occur is not as independent selves. Any self-hood one may have, then, cannot be permanent and unchanging because independence would be a pre-requisite of such qualities.

Bearing all this in mind, and in the light of the discussion in the last chapter on the way dependent origination operates, what I would like to do now is to draw out from that some of the implications relating to the nature of self-hood, and to show why it is that I think that in the Buddha's teachings it is neither *the* question nor *in* question. This will involve discussing the relation between the nature of selfhood and the nature of the world, building on what we have already discussed in previous chapters. In focussing on these two subjects we shall, of course, be dealing with the central two topics of all those other seekers of the Truth to which I have just referred. What I hope we shall see, though, is why they were not the explicit topics of the Buddha's teachings, as well as the crucial way in which they relate to what he did teach. We shall see that in focussing on experience as he did, the Buddha was indicating that the only access one has to understanding anything about the nature of selfhood and of the world was by means of understanding (at least relevant aspects of) the nature of knowing. Moreover, by this means one arrives not only at an understanding of what one can know, but also of what cannot be known.

Before beginning a more specific discussion on the nature of selfhood, I would like first to consider some textual passages where the expression *anattā* is used in a key context. And what I would like to suggest is that if one reads the passages somewhat differently from how they are commonly understood, they can be seen to suggest the association between *anattā* and experience, in the sense of one's cognitive process. I have referred several times to passages in the doctrinal treatises which state that whatever is impermanent is *dukkha*, and I have related this to the impermanence of the experiencing process: and as experience is all we have, so *dukkha* relates to the entirety of the experience of the cycle of lives. Most of such passages go on to include the further point that whatever is *dukkha* is *anattā* – selfless, or not self.[3] And usually, this last point is explained not in the light of understanding *dukkha* as experience as I have done, but in the light only of the more common psychological understanding of *dukkha*. That is to say, given that the notion of self-hood at the time of the Buddha was intrinsically associated with permanence and unchangingness, and hence the bliss – perfection – of immortality, it followed that whatever was impermanent, and therefore unsatisfactory (*dukkha*), could not be a self of that sort (so what is *dukkha* is *anattā*).

But this explanation has two serious limitations. First, in being wholly associated with understanding *dukkha* in the sense of its psychological dimension alone, it is problematic because the aim in Buddhism is to achieve the converse of *dukkha*. Nirvana is, as

I have previously mentioned, often referred to as *sukha*, the 'bliss' or 'ease' that is the converse of the dis-ease that is *dukkha* in the sense of representing unsatisfactoriness that needs to be 'cured'. And given this context, one might well be tempted to infer that the bliss of nirvana could be associated with self-hood in some sense. In order to avoid making this inference, which would be erroneous, one has to draw on other teachings to establish that this is not the case. There is nothing stated in the descriptions of Enlightenment, for example, which would corroborate the inference. More decisively, it would clearly be in conflict with the third of the three Characteristics of Existence to which I have previously referred. The first two Characteristics are that all conditioned things – that is, everything within our cyclical experience – are impermanent and *dukkha*, exactly as is said in the passages I am discussing here. But the third Characteristic states that *all* things – that is, not [just] conditioned things – are *anattā*. Buddhist tradition has understood this 'all things' to include the insight of nirvana, which, in contrast with cyclical existence is said to be 'unconditioned', in addition to the conditioned things referred to in the previous two lines. And they have taken it to support their view that not only is no conditioned thing one's self, but the achievement of the bliss of nirvana – the converse of *dukkha* – is existentially realising that there is *no* self. But one can alternatively, and in my view more helpfully, interpret the third Characteristic in the sense that nirvana has nothing to do with achieving knowledge of a permanent self: it is neither *about* (one's) selfhood nor is the insight structured *in terms of* (conceptual categories which predicate) selfhood. Rather, the bliss is entirely associated with the coolness of the cessation of the burning of the fuel of continuity. Cognitively one is no longer restricted by ignorance, and affectively one is no longer burning with desires. Of neither or both of these would it be correct to state that they are, in contrast to whatever is *dukkha*, the experience of a self. On the contrary, the notion of self-hood is both irrelevant and inappropriate to the situation. Whether one interprets the third Characteristic of Existence traditionally or not, though, in the context of the limitation to which I am referring one has to draw on it to avoid making the erroneous inference about what is realised at nirvana.

The second limitation of understanding the expression that whatever is *dukkha* is *anattā* in the light of the psychological dimension of *dukkha* alone is that it takes no account of the extent to which *dukkha* relates to the cognitive process as a whole. And this limitation is perhaps particularly unfortunate because it has arisen in spite of the fact that the passages in question are concerned with the operation of the senses. In each of them, the senses are in turn stated to be impermanent, and therefore *dukkha*, and therefore *anattā*. They go on to state that whatever is *anattā* is "not mine, I am not it, it is not my self".[4] Because of the way the senses are separately itemised over and over again in each of these very similar passages, it can, and indeed has, been taken that what is meant by such passages is that one should not regard any one of these individual senses to be one's abiding self: that though we have these 'things', none of them is to be thought of in the mistaken sense of individually being associated with self-hood. This is very much in line with the traditional understanding of the *khandhas*: that though we have five *khandhas*, none of them is one's self. And just as I think this way of understanding the *khandhas* is, while not literally wrong, an extremely limited and potentially misleading interpretation of them in the context of how they are more properly to be understood, so I think this way of understanding these passages about the senses is also extremely limited and potentially misleading.

In my view, these references to the senses should, like references to the *khandhas*, be understood to be referring to their role in the cognitive process. Indeed, each of the senses has no purpose whatsoever *except* insofar as it is the means by which we experience the appropriate sensory data which are then made sense of by the rest of our cognitive apparatus. In the midst of the plethora of somewhat repetitive short passages on the senses, there are some variations that, if one takes an overall perspective, give a much clearer indication that what is being referred to is the cognitive process as a whole. We find, for example, that what is being included is divided into 'internal' and 'external'.[5] What this means is that though the senses are perhaps given stronger emphasis and are referred to most frequently, in fact they are clearly seen as only one aspect of a process that involves the interaction between the senses, what is 'internal' or 'subjective' – the knower – and the corresponding objects of sense, what is 'external' or 'objective' – the known. The sense objects, each corresponding to the senses, are separately itemised in exactly the same way as the senses.

These references to sense objects would be odd if what is being stated in all these passages referring to the senses is that none of them is one's self. The inclusion of the added point that 'what is not self is not mine' in many of these passages means that it is one's personal self that is being referred to here, and not the independent status of other things as 'selves' in the generic sense. But it would hardly occur to one that the *objects* of sense – visible things, sounds, smells, and so on – would be one's self, so why is the point being made so explicitly? I think this anomaly is easily overcome if these passages are understood to be referring to the cognitive process as a whole. The oddity then disappears and the inclusion of the sense objects becomes perfectly understandable. Even if one leaves aside the fact that according to the Buddha all things are dependently originated, experience is not something in which subjectivity is self-sufficient: it is the process of subjective-objective interaction that is involved. One section of the text suggests the inclusive nature of experience when it explains that the senses and their corresponding objects are 'the all'.[6] It is suggested that the all can be abandoned if one fully knows and understands it. And what is involved in fully knowing and understanding it are the senses and their corresponding objects. Furthermore, without fully knowing and understanding and abandoning the all in this way, one cannot bring about the cessation of *dukkha*. Using one of the metaphors discussed in the last chapter, this all is said to be on fire,[7] a fire associated with all the various desires that bring about rebirth. This process has to be overcome by detaching oneself from sensory desire, and then one is free from rebirth.

In my view, this is clearly relating the sensory process to one's entire experience – expressed here as the all in much the same way as the world is used metaphorically to refer to one's experience in its entirety. And it is for this reason that none of it, none of the senses or their corresponding objects which underlie the metaphor as a whole, is in any sense a self. Rather, it is the process as a whole that is impermanent because what is being referred to is of epistemological status; and, further, it is referred to as *dukkha* not just because what is impermanent is psychologically unsatisfactory but because the term *dukkha* is used to indicate that it is one's experience. It follows from this that whatever is *dukkha* is *anattā*.

It is worth making a slight digression and reminding ourselves of a feature of a later period of the Buddhist tradition which is relevant in the context of what is being suggested here. In the early centuries of the common era, there arose a trend or movement within the Buddhist community as a whole which gave rise to what was and still is called Mahāyāna Buddhism. 'Mahāyāna' means 'great way' and the name was used to indicate that the people who espoused this sort of Buddhism regarded themselves as having a better understanding or interpretation of the Buddhist teachings than did earlier Buddhists, who they collectively referred to by the derogatory (and no longer used) label Hīnayāna, indicating that theirs was a 'lesser way'. One of the points on which Mahāyāna Buddhists claimed superiority was their understanding of what was meant by *anattā*. The way they referred to this was not as *anattā* – not-self – but as 'emptiness' or 'voidness', meaning that all things were empty or void (*śūnya*) of independent existence, expressed as 'own-being' (*sva-bhāva*). *Anattā* was therefore referred to by Mahāyāna Buddhists as *śūnyatā* – emptiness. The impersonality of the term emptiness made, and still makes, it easier to understand that what is being indicated is the absence of independent existence of all things. As I have previous commented, one of the problems of understanding *anattā* is that the word 'self' is usually used so personally that it is perpetually difficult to understand that its reference is generic.

This difficulty seems to have been a problem for the early Buddhists themselves, as well as for later Buddhists and scholars alike. In the passages we have just been discussing, for example, the early Buddhists seem to have missed the generic application of *anattā* to all of the factors of the cognitive process. They indicate their misunderstanding by stating of the objects of sense just as much as of the senses that they are 'not mine'. They are, it seems, only concerned with reiterating that the Buddha's teaching, unlike others, was not about finding a permanent self that is 'me' or 'mine'. And this, I suggest, has led to a compilation of a mass of short and repetitive passages in a way that indicates that the full implication of what they were saying was not clearly understood. And it also paved the way for early Buddhism making itself vulnerable to the charge by Mahāyāna Buddhists that it did not properly understand the emptiness of all things.

Mahāyāna Buddhists conceded that early Buddhists had understood the subjective aspect of *anattā*: that personal identity is dependently originated rather than an independent, permanent and unchanging essence. The early teaching of the formula of dependent origination which shows the way in which individuals are conditioned, in each life, by their ignorance and volitional causal nexus from previous lives clearly indicates an acceptance of the conditioned nature of subjectivity. And there was in any case the widespread focus on the repeated reference to the fact that this, that or the other part of the person is not the self, as I am discussing here. But it was claimed by Mahāyāna Buddhists that early Buddhists had not grasped the objective aspect of *anattā*: that *all* of the factors of cyclical experience, in being dependently originated, are also empty of own-being. This claim was made by stating that while early Buddhists understood what they called *pudgala-nairātmya*, the not-permanent-selfness of persons, they did not understand *dharma-nairātmya*, the not-permanent-selfness of *all* things. We have seen that in fact this teaching is very much a part of early Buddhist teachings, both implicitly in the focus on experience and explicitly in the formula of the Three Characteristics of Existence (all things are *anattā*). And so in fact the Mahāyāna claim is, at least in principle, not a valid one. But from what we have seen it also seems not unlikely that over the course of even a relatively short period of time the early Buddhist teaching *was* misunderstood, even within its own tradition, and that the stress was placed only on the subjective aspect of not-permanent-selfness. And that in turn became interpreted simply as meaning that there is no self.

The overwhelming degree to which seekers of the Truth during the early period of Buddhism associated their search with finding the essence of themselves is very much evident in the passages we have been discussing about the senses. The emphasis on none of the senses or sense objects being one's self is coupled with repeated references to the need to become detached or neutral about each of them. The point of such references is clearly that the disciple of the teachings was likely to have a tendency to crave an experience of permanent self-hood above all other cravings: an experience, disciples thought, of immortality. And it was to overcome this that the impermanence of each of such things was so explicitly and repeatedly stated. This, in my view – and unsurprisingly, contributed to the missing of the point of the generic nature of the dependently originated subjective/objective process, and that the impermanence that was not-self was not of each 'separate' thing but of the cognitive process as a whole.

What I am suggesting here, then, is that the statement that what is *dukkha* is *anattā*, repeatedly found in the texts, is best understood if one recalls that in the first Noble Truth *dukkha* is summed up as the *khandhas*. This indicates that *dukkha* refers to experience, mediated by means of ones cognitive apparatus. This is confirmed in the passages to which I have referred where the senses and sense objects are said to be *dukkha*, and therefore also *anattā*. Nothing about this is saying anything specifically about *one's* self. What it is saying is that, as experience, none of it is or has any independent selfhood. There is thus a clear association between *anattā* and experience.

There are several other implications about the Buddhist teaching of *anattā* that arise from understanding the central focus of the teachings in terms of understanding experience and the factors of the cognitive process by which that occurs – which, indeed, *are* the process of experience. I would like now to draw out some of these implications.

A key point derives not just from the cognitive process as described but from the place given to knowledge and to the nature of knowing – or, more accurately perhaps, how knowledge is understood in the Buddhist texts. I have said on at least two occasions above that it is cardinal to Buddhist teachings that the goal of the path is known to the individual. That this is the case, and why it is the case, is clearest from the textual descriptions of the Buddha's Enlightenment. On that occasion, he achieved insight – described as seeing things as they really are, which is also the cessation of the ignorance that is the causal foundation for cyclical continuity. What this means is that at the very end of the path the individual functions as a *knower* of the Truth. Though meditative disciplinary practices are designed to remove mental clutter, and to transcend the restrictive norms by which the cognitive process is usually limited, it is cardinal to Buddhism that the aim is not to achieve a total obliteration or cessation of knowing. To think that one who has achieved insight does not know and see is said to be absurd (*akallaṃ*).[8] And it is expressly stated that far from suppressing one's ability to see, which is no better than being blind (or to hear, which is no better than being deaf – and so on through the senses), one needs to cultivate one's perceptive faculties so that one arrives at understanding of the nature of what one experiences.[9] The point is that it is only by knowing how things really are – how experience operates, in this case – that one can set about reversing the process by which one continues to be bound to the cycle of rebirth. That bondage, as we have seen, is cognitive, in the broadest sense: that is, the way our perceptions are intimately associated with our affective reactions to them. And knowing and seeing this process as it really is enables one to 'uproot' the binding continuity tendencies of desires coupled with ignorance – both aspects of the bondage.

That this is the case was one of the reasons why, as I said in Chapter One, I had found perplexing the view that the goal of the path of Buddhism was the realisation that one is or has no self. Quite apart from the incoherence of such a goal, it is not something that is compatible with the way the teachings are structured and the way the Buddha's experience of Enlightenment is described.

But what is entailed in the centrality of insight – knowledge *of* the Truth – is that whatever is known by the individual who follows the teachings to their goal *cannot be* his self. This is because the way the arising of knowledge is described in the texts clearly indicates that in order to be known, the known thing must be in a relationship of objectivity to the knower: the polarity between the knowing subject and the known thing is intrinsic to the process of knowing. There is thus no way a knowing subject can know itself because it is not, and nor can it become, objective to itself. So *nothing* that an individual knows can be his self. For this reason, it is possible to state of whatever one *does* know, of *all* of it, that it is not-one's-self. If one accepts the early Buddhist account of the nature of knowledge, or something equivalent to it, then this is as true today as it was at the time of the Buddha. So at a time when most thought that what they were seeking to know *was* their true self, the Buddha made the point that "Whatever has form, is past, future or present, internal or external, gross or subtle, inferior or superior, far or near, *all* form: all this is not mine, not me, not my self".[10] More simply, and even more inclusively, he could state categorically of anything knowable, as he did in the third line of the Three Characteristics of Existence formula, that it is 'not-self'. Similarly, it is stated that one with insight (in this instance literally 'who has view') sees that knowables are not-self.[11] And one might also helpfully phrase the expression discussed above that 'whatever is *dukkha* is *anattā*' in the by now familiar to us idiom: whatever is experienced (*dukkha*) is not-self (*anattā*). This is the case not just because what is experienced has epistemological status, and is therefore not a permanent self, but also because whatever is known (experienced) by a knowing subject cannot be his self – even though he can gain knowledge of how experience itself works.

What is involved in the process of knowing can be drawn more fully from the description of the cognitive process given in the context of the operating of the *khandhas* so that one can see more clearly the relationship between objectivity and what is known. In the discussion of the *khandhas* in Chapter Two we saw that experiential data are accessed by us by means of the senses, and are then processed by the cognitive apparatus in increasingly refined and sophisticated stages so that they make sense to us in the light of our cognitive norms. At the very early 'stages' – in practice of course the process functions imperceptibly fast – the data are minimally made sense of in that they constitute the bare awareness of an as yet unidentified sensory event. One may initially be aware of it as visual, tactile, auditory, etc., possibly at a vague level pleasant or unpleasant, but no more: and all of the multiple aspects of the experience that contribute to one knowing what is going on have then to be identified. This identifying is the most significant stage of what subsequently happens for the point I want to make here. Described in the texts in the context of the *khandha* of apperception and conception (the *saññā-khandha*), this is the stage at which one knows what one knows.

As I pointed out in my discussion of this *khandha*, the identification process is one which involves naming: this is intrinsic to knowing what experiential data are – to identifying them. Naming is indicated implicitly by the fact that one of the meanings of the classical Sanskrit equivalent of the Pali name for this *khandha*, *saṃjñā*, is 'name'. But it is also made explicit in the early Buddhist textual descriptions of the way identification is part of sorting out incoming experiential data in that naming is but another way of putting what is called the 'making manifold' of those data. One might say that the process of making manifold in order to identify is the process of making nameable the aspects of one's experience. For this reason the Pali term for making manifold, *papañceti*, is sometimes alternatively translated 'verbal differentiation'. One does not verbally differentiate what is not made manifold: one does not refer to a bucket full of water in terms of drops, for example, a log of wood in terms of carved bowls, or an indeterminately foggy photograph in terms of individual items in it. If one does not see or introduce credible and meaningful manifoldness, one does not verbally differentiate. But if one sees the bucket of water sprayed as drops, bowls carved from the wood, the focus of the photograph improved, the ensuing perception in terms of manifoldness would simultaneously prompt verbal differentiation: many drops, bowls plus offcuts of wood, the image of a person in a street.

It is, in fact, the most fundamental aspect of the way we understand our experience that we identify and verbally differentiate – give names to – things: this underpins the entire conceptual framework by which we function in our day to day lives. Even if we are unfamiliar with something we verbally differentiate it as 'it', 'that', 'x', and so on, and in so doing one gives it a meaningful place in one's experience. Even if something remains vague or muddled, one nevertheless similarly refers to 'it', 'the jumble', 'the gist', and so on. However concrete or abstract something may be, identifying it involves verbally differentiating it: this is the case just as much with a feeling or a concept or a sound as a stone or flower.

In the broadest sense, all this verbal differentiation is what we call language, without which we could not think or communicate or understand the world of our experience in its entirety: the process of 'making sense' is one which involves the introduction of identifiable categories and references which can be indicated by means of language. Of course there are other, non-linguistic, ways in which non-human animals and sub-normal human beings can communicate. But they do not share the same cognitive norms, and the ability to communicate by means of language is one of the primary indications of normality or natural healthiness among humans. Though it is possible for people who are not naturally healthy to learn other ways of communicating, those ways have to be based on the common conceptual framework if they are to be understood by others: one needs somehow to be able to ascertain what someone is 'trying to say'. Those other ways of communicating are interpreted by others *into* language. Language is thus the basic tool we need to enable us to function normally. This is not at all to say that language is the *only* means we have of communicating or of understanding our own inner experiences. Most of us, consciously and unconsciously, use non-verbal ways of communicating and of understanding. Indeed much can be communicated and understood (if not always accurately) through facial expressions, what we call 'body language', what clothes one is wearing, through actions or inaction, through remaining silent (and so on). And I imagine most of us have experiences that we understand very clearly but that we feel at the same time entirely incapable of articulating verbally to anyone else. There is, too, the profound communicative power of music, sometimes even referred to as 'the language of music'; and likewise of colour. But language in the sense of verbal differentiation nevertheless does underpin the entire edifice of the conceptual world in which we live as healthy human beings. And this is one in which we are able not just to understand the immediacy of what we experience through sensory impression – to fit our immediate perceptions into that entire conceptual edifice – but also to 'think about' things as abstractions, ideas, possibilities, hypotheses, rational arguments, and so on. Full understanding of our experience involves making sense both immediately and abstractly,[12] but *all* making sense requires verbal differentiation. Furthermore, not only is this perhaps the key feature of what distinguishes us from lower animals, and an indication of natural healthiness, but the more complex, abstract, subtle and sophisticated it is the more we tend to associate it with superior intelligence. At least in Western culture the more complex, abstract, subtle and sophisticated the degree of ability to differentiate verbally the more highly it is prized: sometimes to the point where it is prized not for the wisdom, insight, brilliance, illumination, clarity of what is being said but simply for the skill of saying it.

Though verbal differentiation, the use of language, is a constant feature of our experience because it provides and works according to the conceptual criteria and framework by which we make sense of anything at all, what we are generally not conscious of during the process is the significance of just what it is that is happening. Provided we are making sense both for ourselves and for the purpose of communicating to others, indeed we have no need to be conscious of it. But what is happening is that the process of verbally differentiating data is the way in which those data are objectified in relation to a knowing subject. *All* the data, concrete and abstract, of our cognitive experience are organised according to a system of objectification in this way. Unless and until this happens, experiential data are *unknown*: and *in becoming knowable* they are objectified. Perhaps more correctly, all data that *are* experienced – in fact one's experience itself in its entirety – are objective. Experience is experienc*ed by* the subject. This is why consciousness, in the textual descriptions, refers to the process of *being* conscious, to consciousness *of* something. Experience and consciousness are experience and consciousness only in this sense. Furthermore, this entire process is one that we do for ourselves: in order to make sense of *our* experience, *we* objectify all our experiential data. In order for something to be known *at all*, it is necessary for there to be a subject who is objectifying it. And conversely, objectivity, which one may also understand in terms of all of what is known, is itself entirely dependent on the functioning of a subject. According to the Buddha's teachings this is the process that needs to be understood. But while the subject may be able to understand the *process*, he cannot as it were change places with his known object and become objectively known to himself. *Whatever* is known is thus objective in relation to the knowing subject *because this is what knowing is.*

Objectivity understood by means of the way the texts describe how the cognitive process operates, then, shows that whatever is known is not-one's-self because the manner in which one knows anything precludes that possibility.

There is a further aspect to the point being made here, which relates more specifically to self-hood. And this is also indicated by the way the cognitive process is described in the texts, and how we have been discussing it above. We have seen in some detail the way in which the processing of experiential data, in the broadest sense of the way we continuously make sense of everything within and according to our conceptual framework, is a process of objectification. And because nothing *is* experience except by this route, so to speak, one might go so far as to refer to experience itself as objectivity. But it is not *only* objectivity. If experience is so to speak acquired by the processing of data, this entire process is incoherent without the simultaneous presence of a subject. As I said above, experience is experienc*ed*. Put differently, objectivity is dependent on subjectivity *per se*. In a sense, this again is to do with the nature of knowledge. But one needs to remind oneself that the knowledge that is referred to here is not just knowing one discrete item x, or experiencing another discrete event y, but the knowing that represents our cognitive experience in its totality. From the day we are born to the day we die we are experiencing human beings. This is what makes us human beings – certainly in the sense of those for whom the Buddha's teachings were intended. And it is the totality of *that* that is referred to here. So though one might say that the dependence on subjectivity of objectivity is to do with the nature of knowledge, in that there is no such thing as knowledge without both a knowing subject *and* a known object, in fact what is being indicated here is that the entire world of experience is one which is *comprised of* the polarity between subjectivity and objectivity. A more Buddhist way of putting it would be to say that subjectivity and objectivity are mutually dependently originated.

If we tie this in with where we got to at the end of the last chapter, one might say that it is not just that for each and every one of us our world is the world of our own experience, but that it is intrinsic to there being such as thing *as* human beings in the world that it is polarised in this mutually dependent way. This intrinsic interdependence of both objectivity *and* subjectivity is indicated in the grammar of the description of the cognitive process mentioned at the end of the last chapter. But we can now more comprehensively see the full significance of both knower and known being indicated in that description.

Furthermore, what we can also now draw out is that in addition to the knowing subject not being able to know himself, whatever else one *can* know is also limited by that subjective-objective polarity. That is to say, one cannot get outside of it, as it were, either to check it or to look at what else there is or may be 'out there'. *Whatever* one can know is part of the mutual polarity, and one *can* know *only* that. This is not at all to say that what one can know is limited in any narrow empirical sense. Far from it. Indeed, just as we do not know *a priori* the limits of what we call the empirical world, so we do not know *a priori* the extent to and ways in which the subjective-objective polarity might stretch (for want of a better way of putting it). I shall discuss some of the ways the Buddhist worldview specifically relates to this point below. But it is nevertheless the case that knowing and seeing only *are* knowing and seeing in the context of such a polarity.

The mutual dependence between subjectivity and objectivity adds a further specific indication to the way in which *anattā* might be understood. We have already seen that if all of the factors of our experience are objectified *by us*, then the status of each of 'them' is not that of an independent 'self'. We have also seen that whatever one can know as a knowing subject is not-one's-self. And we can add to these the fact that in being mutually dependently originated with objectivity, the whole notion of subjectivity is of the same impermanent status as objectivity. Though this might seem obvious to us from where we have got to now, it is in fact worth stating specifically because what we have seen highlights the dependent originatedness of subjectivity in a way that is not *existentially* obvious. Experience does not *seem* to us to be structured in the way the textual sources describe and imply. Not only is one not aware of the operating of the cognitive process as a whole, but one is also not aware of the mutual interdependence of subjectivity and objectivity. Though the Buddha did state that his teaching was 'intelligible to those who study it', it was not for nothing that he also stated in the same context that it was deep, difficult to see and difficult to understand.[13]

There are three points that it might now be helpful to discuss in the light of the foregoing so that the point we have arrived at can be seen in an appropriate perspective. The first point is to remind ourselves of the fact that according to the Buddha's teachings, liberating insight is not merely an intellectual understanding of what the nature of Reality might be. The second, which is related to the first, is a consideration of the way in which such a trans-intellectual liberating insight can be understood in terms of knowing and seeing the Truth. And the third is the relationship between the understanding of subjectivity and objectivity as described above and the notion that thinking implies, indeed involves, a thinker. What I would like to suggest – and this is contrary to what is normally said about Buddhism – is that the place of selfhood in Buddhism is not incompatible with this dictum: this is, in my view, why selfhood is neither *the* question nor *in* question. As I said at the beginning of this chapter, though neither self nor world are the specific focuses of the Buddha's teachings in the way they were the specific focuses of the teachings of others, what we are seeing here is the way they in fact crucially relate to what he did teach.

First, then, the nature of liberating insight. I can perhaps draw out the point I wish to make in the context of the way it is sometimes rhetorically asked if the Buddha was a philosopher. His teachings encompass many philosophical issues, are in many respects of interest to philosophers, and can be summed up in terms that represent them as 'a philosophy': they can be coherently explained – or, at least, they can be explained no less coherently than many other philosophies can. Attempting to explain them coherently is, indeed, much of what this book is about. But whether or not one wishes to call the Buddha a philosopher, there are two aspects to his teachings which crucially differentiate him from the way this might normally be understood – certainly in the West. First, the Buddha himself stated repeatedly that the insight he gained at the experience of his Enlightenment gave him the certainty that he would no longer be subject to cyclical rebirth. In other words, the insight that he gained affected his own future far more radically than gaining knowledge normally does. And it is cardinal to Buddhism that by following the Buddha's teachings and fully putting them into practice others will be able to have the same insight and thus to achieve the same liberation from cyclical rebirth. Second, and I referred to this as a characteristic of the pan-Indian worldview in the Chapter Two, it is a fundamental feature of the Buddha's teachings that the insight he gained had been realised in the sense of his having experiential knowledge of it. Though the insight was of metaphysical Truth, it was not something he had inferred or arrived at by reasoning or logical deduction. Rather, he experienced its truth directly. Indeed, these two points are intimately related because the first and second insights were of the fact and mechanics of rebirth: the Buddha was able to see his previous lives and other beings being born and reborn according to their past actions.

It is clear from the nature of what is described as being seen that Enlightenment requires that one's cognitive apparatus be functioning radically differently from the way it normally does. In this book I have somewhat arbitrarily indicated the difference by referring to the knowledge gained at Enlightenment as insight rather than knowledge. But one might, as previously suggested, understand the order of the cognitive shift that is aimed for as corresponding to that between a blind person and a sighted person. And it is to achieve this ability that meditative disciplinary exercises are practised for a very long period of time. The Buddha taught that these mental disciplinary exercises bring about such a reorientation in the way one's cognitive apparatus 'sees things' that one is enabled clearly to see metaphysical Truth for oneself. I feel that as one becomes clearer about the implications of the Buddha's teachings, and as one thereby understands some of the more significant aspects of the nature of the world, of identity, and of what is involved in liberation according to his teachings, it is important to remember this point. However much greater clarity about the meaning of the teachings is achieved intellectually, this should not detract from the fact that for Buddhists the Truth has to be experienced. Put differently, there is nothing to suggest that an intellectual grasp of the teachings of the Buddha will radically affect one's future in the way that experiential realisation of the Truth to which they point is said to. Indeed, the teachings are primarily intended to be applied in a practical way: they are not a theoretical description. To overlook this is to overlook not only the most significant aspect of the experience that the Buddha himself had, but also to overlook his entire purpose in giving his teachings at all. He did not teach because what he had to say was interesting in the context of the history of ideas – however interesting we might find it to look at the teachings in that context. He taught because he believed that if others were able to achieve the same insight as he did then they too would have the benefit of freedom from bondage to the cycle of lives. This is *why* the teachings are a method and not a theoretical description.

Leading on from this, the second point I wish to discuss here is the way liberating insight relates to knowing and seeing in the sense that this involves knower and known – the subjective/objective polarity I have been discussing above. I have already stated more than once that it is cardinal to Buddhism that liberating insight is insight *of* the Truth of how one is bound to the cycle of lives and, therefore, how to free oneself from that. But if this is trans-intellectual, to what extent can it be understood as knowledge as we normally think of knowledge? To achieve the cessation of ignorance it is explained that one needs to empty one's mind of the clutter of its normal conceptual framework and of all the discursive activities, in their broadest sense, that are associated with that. And I have only just stated above that what is aimed for involves a radical reorientation and re-application of one's cognitive apparatus. In particular, to paraphrase a textual passage to which I have referred before, it is ceasing to 'have conceptions of manifoldness which give rise to separating things when apperceiving'. But I also stated in the context of discussing the *khandha* of apperception and conception that liberating insight is identified no less than anything else. The textual passages which describe the Buddha's insight clearly state that he knows that he knows the Truth he has been seeking. And this appears to be a singular, verbally differentiated, known experience. How can these aspects of the situation be reconciled?

The question is a significant one because it is so clearly indicated that what has to be experienced is the cessation of verbal differentiations of any sort: ceasing to make manifold. But we make things manifold in order to identify and know them. So if one has an experience which is not part of verbally differentiated manifoldness, in what sense can it be known? Put differently, if metaphysical Truth is transcendent of the criteria by which we know anything, how can one actually know it?

I think the key to understanding this point is once again to do with the nature of knowledge rather than of what is known: it is to do with the way we know that we know something rather than the nature of the known thing. If we recall the description of the cognitive process, and the way subjectivity and objectivity become polarised, we are given two powerful clues to how one might understand the situation. First, it indicates that whatever is immediately experienced has to be *translated* into knowledge. And second, it follows from this that whatever *is* immediate is not *itself* organised according to conceptual criteria: it is in knowing it that it becomes so. Indeed, the entire cognitive process by which one knows anything at all involves 'making manifold what is *not* really manifold'.[14] So it is always the case that it is only in the process of translating immediate experience into knowledge that the conceptual framework comes into play. And this applies to understanding an insight into things as they are no less than to understanding things more mundanely as we usually do. There is an indication of this in a textual passage which describes the way insights gained in deep meditation, when one's mind is empty of differentiating criteria, leave an 'abstract impression'.[15] One becomes conscious of those insights at the level of understanding only when one emerges from that deep meditative state. This is contrasted with, but operates in an essentially similar way to, the process of 'sensory impression'[16] which is the operating of the normal cognitive state of mind with which we are more familiar.

There is another factor which is relevant here, and which should be clear in the light of where we have got to in our attempt to understand the teachings of early Buddhism in the way I am suggesting. In the textual passages which record the Buddha's Enlightenment, he is said to have gone into deep meditation before experiencing the Enlightenment insights. And there seem to be two aspects to what he actually experienced. One is that he gained insight into metaphysical truth in the sense of what is involved in the operating of an individual history. The other is that he gained insight into the nature of the ignorance that characterises – or, better, underpins – 'normal' perception. What both of these involve, above all, is insight into the fact that the matrix of continuity is subjective, and that the error upon which continuity depends – that is, verbal differentiation – is part of the way we process our experiences. One might sum it up by saying that what the Buddha gained insight into is *what is happening*: he saw *that it is we who make manifold* rather than manifoldlessness as an objective something in itself (as it were). Put differently, it may be that having been in deep meditation what the Buddha came to realise was that what the entire structure of our experiential world is correlated and mutually dependent with is subjectivity, and that the operating factor of this correlation for any given individual is his cognitive apparatus. This would have involved his gaining a clear insight into the status of both the subjective and objective aspects of the correlation – of the fact that all things are dependently originated. But it need not have involved his gaining access to anything other than an understanding of his own mental processes.[17]

This understanding, moreover, is such that it is not difficult to see that it might be gained from having an experience of one's subjective cognitive apparatus *not* functioning manifoldly, as in deep meditation which involves the stilling of the activities of the mind. Coming out of such a state might well leave one with an impression that translates into knowledge of what *usually* happens. In other words, knowledge of the absence of activity gives one knowledge of what the nature of the activity usually is. And it is this knowledge which arises as it were subsequent to the clearing of the normal clutter of activities that constitutes insight: the experience needs understanding and interpreting. This is what distinguishes Buddhist meditative practice from other Indian meditations that concentrate solely on achieving the stilling of normal cognitive activities. A Buddhist, rather, interprets or *gains insight* into the truth of what is going on, thus giving rise to the name 'insight meditation' to refer to the mental discipline involved.

The situation is in practice considerably more complex than this makes it sound. In the first instance, it is clear that Enlightenment insight is not something that is gained quickly. It takes long periods, Buddhists would say lifetimes, of mental discipline, before the impressions of deep meditative states of mind actually do translate into meaningful insight. And during this process, it is clear from the descriptions of the Buddha's Enlightenment that one also acquires the ability to use one's cognitive apparatus differently from the way one normally does: in seeing what usually happens one can reprocess it, as it were. The textual descriptions of the Buddhist insight meditation known as 'mindfulness' show how this ability is built up. This kind of meditation is practised alongside others that are intended to achieve stillness and clarity. Mindfulness meditation focuses on a variety of meditative objects: parts of the body in various states of health or decay, the different feelings one is experiencing, one's different states of mind, and various doctrinal teachings or abstract conceptual thoughts. In any given session of meditation one selects any one of these,[18] and the point is to become proficient in concentrating on each one very precisely, excluding every thought other than that it is what it is. The aim is not just to see *it*. Rather, the point is to understand, by means of as it were studying the process of attempting to 'isolate' each meditative object, the impersonal nature of *all* things, of whatever nature: however different and individually characterised they may appear to be, all things are similarly dependently originated. The texts describe this as follows: "... mindfulness is present precisely to the extent necessary for knowledge, sufficient for mindfulness, and one proceeds unattached, not grasping [i.e. seeing as independent] anything in the world."[19]

By practising this sort of meditation as well as others which concentrate on stilling the activity of the mind, the meditator builds up the ability to understand the way in which one's entire cognitive system operates. By concentrating on gaining understanding of the nature of all things at the same time as working on stilling one's normal mental activity, one can see the way one's affective reaction to one's perceptions is something that arises because of *not* understanding that all things are similarly dependently originated and therefore impermanent and impersonal. It is because things are seen as independent and therefore permanent that one craves – affectively reacts to – them in one way or another. In this way one achieves insight into the way we ourselves fuel the causal matrix of continuity because we react affectively to perceptions. And this in turn gives insight into how things operate, or things as they really are.

This process is generic to all human beings, and *qua* process has to be understood alike by everyone. But one also has to understand the state of one's own particular causal matrix: one's own particular degree of ignorance. Each person's state of mind conditions the way that person makes sense of his experiential data – that is, verbally differentiates, or conceptualises in terms of language – in his own way. As an old text puts it: "As one knows, so he speaks."[20] Both the generic and the specific aspects of the process become clear by means of meditation because the meditative disciplinary exercises are centred in one's own mind.

In spite of the complexity and duration of the practice of reorienting one's mind to prepare it for Enlightenment insight, the point I want to make here is that the centrality of knowledge *of* the Truth in Buddhism can be reconciled with the fact that it is at the same time trans-intellectual. In being described as being 'beyond reasoning'[21] (as well as deep and difficult to see), the point of the exercise is to see that reasoning – that is, the naming process which involves language – is a subjectively introduced aspect of the way we see things, and that the conceptual framework which underpins this is part of the cognitive process as a whole rather than a feature of things as they really are. The Pali translated here as 'beyond reasoning' might also be translated 'transcending logic',[22] in which case the logic of the relationship between the subjective and objective aspects of the cognitive process is more clearly indicated, as well as the language used to express it. Insight into (knowledge of) both the logic and the reasoning involved in expressing it involves understanding the process as a whole from the inside, as it were: 'beyond reasoning' and 'transcending logic' mean penetrating the nature of the reasoning and of the logic, rather than getting outside of the system as a whole. Though one may be able to reorient the way one uses the apparatus by which one has one's experience – so that one can gain from it an understanding that as it were 'transcends' one's normal understanding of experience – one cannot get outside of the world of experience completely because it is so structured that one is a *sine qua non* of it. What is happening, then, must be of the order of extending the frame of reference beyond its normal boundaries. It is in this respect that the analogy of a blind person becoming sighted is relevant, in that one can analogously see from this the way in which the world of experience is transformed and extended: it is not that in becoming sighted the formerly blind person has somehow gained access to something 'other' or 'outside'; rather, his experiential apparatus has provided him with a radically different way of understanding his experience that is as it were transcendent of its previous limitations.

This leads me to my third point here, the relationship between the understanding of subjectivity and objectivity as described above and the notion that thinking implies and involves a thinker. Buddhism is sometimes used as an example of a system of thought that is diametrically opposed to this suggestion, usually drawing on Descartes' *cogito ergo sum*.[23] The Buddha's use of the term *anattā* is interpreted as his stating that there is no self, in the way I described in Chapter One, and, given this, it is then taken that thinking is not a reliable indicator of whether or not there is a self. Unlike Descartes, the suggestion is, the Buddha did not fall into the trap of erroneously inferring the existence of a self from the activity of thinking. All one can know from the fact of thinking is that there is thinking: it is not that 'one thinks', but that 'thinking is occurring'. There is no doubt that Descartes' separation of mind and body, and the radically separate ontological status he attributes to each, are incompatible with how Buddhism understands the functioning of the cognitive apparatus. But I nevertheless do not think the associating of a thinker with thinking is at all incompatible with what is suggested by Buddhist teachings. As we have seen, there is a clear indication that it is not just that the notion of objectivity emerges with the cognitive process as a whole – with the emerging of verbal differentiation – but that the notion of subjectivity is integral to the meaningfulness of this process. If this process is not one that involves thinking then I do not know what else thinking might be. And if subjectivity is not the self-conscious experience that we understand in terms of 'I' and 'me' then I do not know what else subjectivity might be either. It is thinking – in the broadest and most generic sense of the cognitive process as a whole – that effects and is the linchpin of the entire experiential edifice of subjectivity and objectivity. So it seems to be entirely compatible with what is found in the early Buddhist texts to suggest that thinking is indeed an indicator of the subjective experience of 'I am'. Put differently, according to what one finds in the Buddhist texts, if there were no such thing as the cognitive process, there would be no notion of a self in the world. And all aspects of this correlation – thinking, self, world – are integral to it. This is why understanding the role of the cognitive process makes one a 'world-ender'. And it is also why understanding the truth of how things really are can be understood as the realisation that the Buddha's teaching on *anattā* refers to dependent origination. Both the world, as the objective aspect of the process as a whole, and the correlated and co-dependent notion of subjective individuality, are linked and understood by means of the cognitive process.

Just as knowledge is a meaningless term unless it refers to knowledge *of* something, so the structure and chief characteristic of thinking is such that it involves the very notion of the thinker. In my opinion, it is drastically to distort the meaning of what thinking is to suggest that it can be understood in terms of 'there is thinking'. One does not for long have to talk along the lines of 'it is thought that a dinner party will be had this evening', 'there is the thought that the smell of sulphur is disliked', 'thinking occurs that one should have nothing but porridge for breakfast', and so on, before having to indicate *by whom* such things are thought. Furthermore, if one cannot so indicate, one at best renders oneself open to the charge of waffling – and at worst of talking nonsense. Intrinsic to thinking is the notion that it is an 'I' that thinks.

But – and it is an important but – the metaphysics of this has to be understood clearly. What it is *not* legitimate to infer from thinking is that the 'I' that thinks is a permanent or independently existent Self. There are many accounts in the texts of instances when the Buddha refers to thinking that 'this is mine, I am this, this is my self' in terms of being part of 'wrong view'.[24] In the *Alagaddūpama Sutta* it is stated that thinking in such a way leads one on to all sorts of other 'wrong views' about that mis-conceived self, a self which is simply not like that.[25] All views formulated in terms of a permanent self – including, according to this text, the non-existence of such a self – are part of the ignorance that binds one to continued rebirth. In fact it is in being associated with thinking that the very notion of 'I am', though it is intrinsic to the process, is most clearly exposed as being dependent. This 'I' represents the subjective aspect of the experiential phenomenon of there being 'me' in 'the world'. And it is this interrelationship, this process by which the entirety of that experiential phenomenon occurs, that has to be understood. Persisting in thinking in terms of permanent existence precludes the possibility of realising this, which is why one reads in a highly metaphorical textual passage: "This shore and the far shore are left behind, like a snake sheds its old worn-out skin, by one who has completely eliminated any notion of conceit."[26] And this is why that understanding can be described metaphorically as having arrived at the point when one is a 'world-ender'. One attains liberation from cyclical existence, experience as we know it, when one understands its nature: that the metaphysics of the situation is the same for both the world and the notion of 'I' – the thinker – in it.

Though one can say that thinking involves a notion of 'I am', then, the ontological status of that 'I' is that it is dependent. All questions to do with permanent existence, including non-existence, are misconceived in this context. Rather, what is being said is that in the context of something being 'known and seen' (to use the Buddhist rather than the Cartesian way of putting it), there is the 'one who knows and sees' it.[27] The Buddha's teaching was concerned with giving to others the ability to understand the nature of their cognitive process, because it is that that creates and perpetuates cyclical experience. Though one can state that nothing that is known is one's self, we can see perhaps more clearly now that the issue of whether or not there *actually* is a self is, in one sense, not in question – the operating of the cognitive process involves such a notion. And, in another sense, whether or not there actually is a permanent self is not *the* question, because it is not relevant to understanding the process involved. And so this was a subject on which the Buddha remained silent. Questions about whether or not one has a self that is eternal, and so on, are, as we have already seen, part of what are called the 'classical unanswered questions'. According to the textual passages in which they are recorded, what he did say when faced with these questions was that what he teaches, and what the questioner should concern himself with instead of such questions, is the reality of human experience, *dukkha*, its cause, the possibility of its cessation, and the path leading to its cessation.[28] This is, of course, a reference to the Four Noble Truths and their emphasis on subjective experience as I have discussed.

Elsewhere, an important related point is made when the Buddha states that when one understands dependent origination one *will no longer ask* (my italics) questions about the self, in the past, future, or present, such as "Am I, or am I not? What am I? How [or Why?] am I? This 'being' that is 'I', where has it come from, where will it go?".[29] I have referred to this passage (which in many ways is similar to the *Alagaddūpama Sutta*) before, and in my view its significance in the context of understanding the Buddha's teachings has hitherto been very much overlooked by Buddhists and scholars alike. In fact its real significance is only evident when one has understood that dependent origination fundamentally indicates the activity of the cognitive process: that by this means objectivity and subjectivity are mutually dependently originated. And it follows from this relationship that when one does understand that, one will see the futility of asking questions about self-hood: one will see that they cannot be answered because the answers cannot be known. This is because what is known by the knower cannot be his self;

thus the dependently originated self of the experiential world cannot be known. And the knower cannot get outside that cognitive framework of experience to see whether or not there is a transcendentally existent self; thus whether or not there is such a self cannot be known either.

This unknowability has been overlooked both within the Buddhist tradition and outside it, perhaps partly because of some well-known words of a famous and highly influential Theravāda Buddhist of the fifth century CE, Buddhaghosa, a figure of a St. Augustine or St. Thomas Aquinas-like stature and role within the tradition. Buddhaghosa stated: "Mere suffering exists, but no sufferer is found; the deeds are, but no doer is found."[30] The standard interpretation of these words, here given by an eminent contemporary Theravāda Buddhist, is: "If you remove the thought, there is no thinker to be found."[31] And though this is *literally* not incompatible with the point I have been making – that is, that where there is thinking there *is* a thinker – the statement was intended by the author to mean, and is taken by others as meaning, that there is therefore no *permanent* self. Whether or not there is a permanent self is not only unknowable, but is also both not necessarily associated with thinking as well as being completely irrelevant to the Buddha's teachings.

To link my understanding of how thinking involving a thinker is compatible with Buddhist teachings, I would refer back and link it to my discussion above on the nature of knowledge and that the goal of the path in Buddhism is known. The Buddha lived for 45 years after his Enlightenment insight, continuing to function and teach as an individual like any other. He did not fizzle out of existence. Thus though the ontological status of the 'I' that thinks is one of mutual dependence with the experiential world that involves thinking (taking thinking here as a term to refer to the entire cognitive process of 'making manifold'), there is no sense in which insight into that triggers the instantaneous cessation of its continuity. It is essential to one's understanding of what is involved that the metaphor of the 'world-ender' be seriously taken as a *metaphor.* The whole process is one which involves a deeply serious spiritual path of the transformation of human understanding. And that understanding itself occurs within the world of experience as a whole: the knower of the Truth is the thinker of thoughts. Though in theory his ontological status might sound precarious, it is in reality deep and difficult to understand, given its deep involvement in Reality.

Put differently, the problem that needs solving, according to the Buddha, is an epistemological one, and following the Buddha's teachings leads to insight into the arising and nature of knowledge, and into the status of what one knows. But the process that leads to that insight, and the solving of the epistemological problem, does not itself affect Reality. A popular analogy for this is given within the Buddhist tradition. If one is attempting a climb to see a mountain peak but the mountain is enfolded in clouds, one can but struggle blindly in what one hopes is the right direction. It is only if and when the clouds are blown away that one can see the mountain and the peak clearly. While this has radically changed the experience for the climber, the mountain peak itself remains unchanged. Similarly, bondage to continuity in the cycle of lives is underpinned by 'false' knowledge (ignorance), and liberation from that bondage is achieved by 'correct' knowledge (insight).

To conclude this chapter, then, we have been focussing on the two central topics of all the other seekers of the Truth at the time of the Buddha – self and world. And we have seen that in coming to an understanding of their nature one can better see both why they were not themselves the focus of the Buddha's teaching, and also the crucial way in which they relate to what he did teach. In focussing on experience as he did, the Buddha was indicating that the only access one has to understanding the nature of self-hood and of the world is not by focussing on either or both of them separately, because this is not how they are; rather, it is by means of understanding the nature of knowledge.

I think many misinterpretations of Buddhist teachings, and the attribution to them of invalid implications (that there is no thinker of thoughts, to remind ourselves of just one), arise from a fundamental failure to understand that their focus is limited to the world of experience. When this is properly grasped, other aspects of the teachings fall into place and are less vulnerable to misunderstanding. I have already discussed several of the most important of these aspects, and have in this chapter been looking at some of the factors surrounding the issue of self-hood. The next two chapters will draw out how the experienced world is structured: that is, the way the texts suggest that experience conforms to certain criteria, as well as some of the ontological issues that arise from the dependent status of the world of experience as we have now come to understand it.

Notes

1 cf, for example, Collins (1982) pp. 98f and Gethin (1998) pp. 137f.
2 DN II 68.
3 See in particular the *Saḷāyatana Saṃyutta*, SN Vol IV: *yaṃ dukkham tad anattā.*
4 *Yad anattā taṃ netam mama neso ham asmi na meso attāti.*
5 *Ajjhattam* and *bāhiram.*
6 SN IV 14ff: *sabba.*
7 SN IV 19.
8 DN II 68: *tad abhiññā vimutto bhikkhu na jānāti na passati iti 'ssa diṭṭhīti tad akallaṃ.*
9 MN III 298ff.
10 For example, at MN I 139f: *tasmātiha bhikkhave yaṃ kiñci rūpaṃ atītānāgata paccuppannaṃ, ajjhattaṃ vā bahiddhā vā, oḷārikaṃ vā sukhumaṃ vā, hīnaṃ vā paṇitaṃ vā, yaṃ dūre santike vā, sabbaṃ rūpaṃ: n' etaṃ mama, n'eso 'ham asmi, na meso attā ti.*
11 MN III 64; cf. also MN I 300; SN IV 31; AN III 444. My interpretation of this passage, and others relating to *anattā*, differs from that of Steven Collins (1982, pp. 95f.).
12 These two aspects of the cognitive process are referred to by the terms *paṭighasamphassa* and *achivacanasamphassa* respectively, as previously mentioned.
13 For example, at MN I 167; Vin I 4.
14 AN II 161: *appapañcaṃ papañceti.*
15 *Mahāniddesa*, Vol I, p. 222. cf. also pp. 53–3. The Pali I have translated as 'abstract impression' is *adhivacanasamphassa*, which in other contexts refers to the way one abstractly conceptualises – thinks about – the factors of sensory experience also; Chapter Three, n.51, and n.12 above. cf. also DN II 62.
16 *Paṭighasamphassa.*
17 In some later forms of Buddhism (and with a slightly differently context in certain other Indian traditions) the process of verbally differentiating is referred to in terms of grasper and grasped, indicating more overtly than in early Buddhism the way objectivity is linked with subjectivity.
18 In the Buddhist tradition, one would have a meditation teacher or spiritual guide who would assist in this.
19 MN I 56; DN II 292.
20 *Sutta Nipāta* 781: *yathā jāneyya, tathā vadeyya*
21 MN I 167: *atakkāvacara.*
22 This is Kalupahana's translation (1975, p. 183).
23 See, for example, Rahula (1985) p. 26, and Gombrich (1996b) p. 40.
24 The Pali is *etaṃ mama, eso 'ham asmi, eso me attā.*
25 This is how I understand the use of the expression *asati*, as explained in Chapter One, n.14. Even if one takes it more literally as 'does not exist', the context requires that one understands this as 'does not exist *like that*' – i.e. permanently. Richard Gombrich (1996b, p. 38ff) also discusses this *Sutta*, saying of the Buddha: "... from the fact that there is a process of thinking he would refuse to draw the conclusion that 'I exist'. But remember that for the Buddha existence implies stasis: it is the opposite of becoming."

26 *Sutta Nipāta* 4. 'Conceit' is a common expression for thinking one is or has a permanent self: it alludes to self-centredness in the separative sense in every respect.

27 DN II 68.

28 cf., for example, DN III 136; MN I 431; SN II 223, V 418.

29 SN II 27.

30 *Visuddhimagga* p. 513.

31 Rahula, 1985, p. 26.

CHAPTER SIX

The Structure of Experience

"Man is the measure of all things."
Protagoras in Plato's *Theaetetus*, 160d.

It is cardinal to early Buddhism that the Buddha was a man like any other man. The crucial point of this is that his teaching is not seen in terms of revelation from some higher, superhuman source, but as a guideline so that others may achieve the same liberation that he, as an example to them, had achieved before them. His Enlightenment insight was one which he clearly stated was attainable (in principle – each person would have their own karmic limitations governing each particular life) by all other people. And the exemplary nature of the Buddha is emphasised by the fact that the focus of his teachings is experience. As human beings, not only is experience the most fundamental thing that we have in common with each other, but it is also the case that we do not have access to anything *other than* our own experience: we are *characterised* by being subjectively experiencing beings.

In the last chapters I have been suggesting and discussing the way in which early Buddhist teachings should be understood to be drawing attention to the point that in order to understand our experience we need to understand the way our cognitive apparatus works. My suggestion was primarily based on the fact that this seems to me to be the way the teachings themselves indicate they should be interpreted. Not only is the Buddha's insight a cognitive one, but what has to be understood in order to have the same insight is the working of the *khandhas* – which the texts in my opinion clearly indicate to be the cognitive apparatus itself. Further, in seeing the *khandhas* in this way the point to note is that understanding of them is required not in terms of what part of the apparatus each of them is but in terms of how they operate together as a process. Apart from this, my suggestion was based on the compelling factor that it is by means of our cognitive apparatus, and by this means alone, that we have the totality of our experiences.

I have also discussed the way in which the cognitive process is one which involves the inter-dependence of subjectivity and objectivity, how experiential data are objectified in order to be knowable by an experiencing subject. And I have discussed various factors regarding the issue and nature of selfhood that seem to be implicit in this structure.

What I would like to do in this chapter is to look further at what is involved in the objectifying process. In particular, I will discuss further the ways in which the characteristics of what we take to be external to us are subjectively conditioned. In the light of this, and of my discussion in Chapter Four on the way the 'world' is referred to metaphorically in the texts, what I want to discuss further here are the implications one can draw from the early Buddhist material regarding the structure of the world in which the Buddha, as a human being like the rest of us, experienced his earthly existence.

I have discussed in previous chapters the way the texts describe the cognitive process as one in which objectifying experiential data in order to make sense of them involves 'making manifold', and the way that this can be understood in terms of 'the giving of names', or verbal differentiation. This correlates, I suggested, with the fact that central to the criteria according to which we both construct and understand our conceptual framework is language. What I want to do here is to add to this a further discussion the way this use of language involves the delineation of things, and what this implies. In the narrow sense, such delineation involves, in the giving of boundaries, the means whereby one can identify the factors of what it is one is experiencing – in its complex entirety, 'making manifold' is the process by which one 'makes sense' of all experiential data. But at the same time, and in a more profound sense, it also involves the rendering of experiential data into what represents to us the 'real' world. Put differently, it is not *just* that the experiential data of events x, y and z need to be made sense of, and that these events are as it were individually the referents of the descriptions of the *khandhas*-in-action process. Rather, what the *khandhas*-in-action process is referring to is the organisation by us of *all* experiential data in terms of every aspect of our whole world, including all of the characteristics and criteria according to which it is taken by us as being 'real'. What I want to discuss more fully here, then, are both these aspects of what is involved in the process of verbal differentiation: that is, that delineating refers both to the giving of individuality and also, more profoundly, to the way the world of our experience is reified.

Before drawing out in more detail the implications of various textual references to this process, in particular references to name-and-form (*nāma-rūpa*) and the senses, I think that reflecting on a few mundane and familiar instances of the way we associate language and making manifold will help by way of analogy to illustrate what it is that our cognitive process is doing all the time, though in fact it operates almost entirely without our being aware of it. From this I think we shall see more clearly the point I want to draw out here with regard to the significance of the reification involved in the process.

Let us imagine, first, that a person enters a darkened room. So dark is it that his first feeling is one of disorientation – even imbalance: he may even instinctively put out his hands in order to steady himself. In order to feel even minimally oriented, he needs to derive from the darkness some degree of 'sorting it out'. Perhaps most basically, in order for him to feel that he is standing on a stable foundation he needs to ascertain that it is 'a room', with walls, floor, ceiling, and so on: otherwise it is simply amorphous disorienting dark space. And in order for it more specifically to be *that* room, he has to ascertain the shape, corners and limits of it. Having done this, if he is dimly aware that there are various dark shapes in the room, it is not until he identifies them specifically – table, chair, sofa, standard lamp – that he knows any more about the room than its shape and that it is not empty: it is a sitting room. Gradually, he fills in more detail – pictures, books, photographs, empty wine glasses, a cushion on the floor, and so on. Each stage contributes to the way that the room as a whole becomes identified to him so that having initially encountered simply dark space he comes to 'know' the room and its contents as a complex whole. From the amorphous darkness a 'real' room is discerned.

Taking a slightly different example, countless times a writer reaches for his pen without thinking about it or what he is doing. But if it is not where he reaches for it, it temporarily becomes an object that is very clearly identified in his mind that he needs to find. He finds himself with a clear and precise picture in his head of the pen that he is looking for and might actually say to himself 'Now where did I put my pen?' or even 'Pen, where are you?'.

Again differently, the writing of an article or book transposes from one's mind literally countless facts, references, thoughts, feelings, ideas, understandings, insights, suggestions, and so on, all of which co-exist in some degree of muddle, into (one hopes) a clear, coherent, communicable form so that other people have access to it. To do this one has to sort out what it is necessary to say and how one needs to put it in order to make it clear. This is the case whether the topic is the worldview of ancient India or how to cook an elaborate meal. Conversely, when one reads an article or a book written by someone else – about, say, the political situation in Italy, or what black holes are – however clear and interesting one may have found it at the time, one sometimes ends up feeling left with what one might call the impression of an interesting topic. Occasionally one is even left with no detail about the subject at all, such that one would be unable to tell another person what one has read. In such circumstances one needs to formulate a way of registering key points so that we actually 'know what we know' about the topic. Depending on how complicated it is, we might consciously mark off the points as we go along, talk it though in our minds at the end of each chapter, make a written note of key headings, or even try explaining it to someone else.

Similarly, if we are puzzling over something we cannot quite understand, we often find that similar kinds of techniques will clarify it for us. Talking over a problem or worry often enables us better to sort out and see more clearly what exactly the problem is or the worry about. And having to describe to someone else a trivial day-to-day action – the setting of one's central heating timer, say – actually explicates to us what it is we are doing in a way we are not normally aware of even though we do it frequently.

In each of these cases, the process of putting into words the relevant point(s) is one in which things become delineated: the room and its contents, the pen, the conceptual factors of the Indian worldview or the items needed for the meal, the logistics between the different political parties, people and influences in postwar Italy or the criteria that explain the occurrence of black holes, the factors of the problem or the worry, exactly where all the knobs and switches are and what one is doing to them in setting the clock timer. Until we do this, at least for the first time in any given situation, we only know it at best as a vague and not necessarily accurate impression, expectation, idea. In verbally differentiating things, whether items, concepts, relationships, actions or feelings, what language is doing is sharpening the delineations in order to clarify things. Put differently, one might say that in order to identify something, and so bring it within our linguistic and conceptual framework, we give it boundaries: we delineate it from what it is not.

This delineating or giving of boundaries is what the expression 'making manifold' (*papañceti*) refers to. And what is happening as the relevant data become more clearly delineated in this way, and the boundaries of each object, thought, idea, and so on, are more clearly identified, is that each of the factors of the experience concerned become in a more meaningful (to us) sense an identifiable part of what is to us our real world. In this way, all the factors of our experience become *reified*. Furthermore, in becoming conscious objects of our experience in this way, each becomes real to us not only in the temporary sense of understanding *that* experience, of putting the building blocks of each specific scenario in place, so to speak. Rather, it is by this process that *anything* one experiences acquires reality for us. Put differently, one might say of the entire mass of incoming experiential data that in order for them to become in any meaningful sense one's *experience*, the process by which they are objectified corresponds to what we understand to be the real world.

If we go through one or two aspects of our examples, we can see the extent to which this 'making real' is actually happening in a very real way. It is our identifying of the sofa that gives it reality to us as anything more than a dark mass. And the identifying of it involves not just the giving of a name tag in an abstract sense, but the recognition that it is *that* sofa. It has a specific location, dimensions, density, colour, texture, and so on. It has a history, what one might call character (it is scruffy or smart, for example, old or modern, squishy or hard, clean or stained), and so on. As the pen looms large in the forefront of our minds it temporarily takes on what one might call a 'more real' status. At the same time its existence and place in our world is confirmed. It is our ability clearly to identify and assimilate the conceptual factors of a different worldview that give it a present and meaningful reality rather than a vaguely acknowledged otherness. As we identify the root of a problem as some emotional trauma we were previously unaware of it becomes a real part of our psychological make-up. And so on.

Delineating and identifying things, verbally differentiating them – making them manifold – is, then, the way we reify our experiences: by naming them as we do we as it were pin them down so they can become a real part of our total reality. This is what seeing them – in the sense either of apperceiving or conceiving of them – and knowing them *is*. If something is to have a place in our world, it has to go through this process: what is not subject to this process, as far as we are concerned is not part of our world. If a sofa cannot be delineated from the darkness then that part of our world does not include a sofa as part of its reality. In becoming known, though, things are reified: they take a place in and become an accepted part of our world.

The role that language plays in reifying things is also exemplified in other ways. The way it is ritually used demonstrates its power in the reifying of symbolic movements, for example. In the Christian eucharist the priest does not just break the bread and pour the wine but he says he is doing it. The physical movements of the Brahmin priest at a sacrificial ritual are accompanied by words that are quite literally believed to have creative – reifying – power to bring about the desired result of the sacrifice. At the ceremonial conferring of a Knighthood, the British sovereign does not just touch the recipient's shoulder with the point of a sword but also says 'I dub thee Sir Knight'. And we do a similar thing at a more commonplace level all the time. When we raise a glass to someone we nearly always say 'cheers', '*salut*', 'it's good to see you', to acknowledge that the salutation is being made. When we shake hands, we say 'how do you do', 'good morning', 'hello'.

A verbal explanation of a non-verbal symbol acts in a similar way. If we do not understand a mathematical symbol we see on a page a verbal explanation of it 'makes real' to us what it represents – and this example indicates that reifying in this sense of making something a real part of one's experience applies to what is abstract just as much as to what is concrete. A verbal explanation of the symbolic shape of a religious building can 'make real' to us an enormous amount not just about the building but about the religion as a whole. We may be able to guess that the spire symbolises the devotee's aspiration towards God, and the series of carved rings around the spire the stages on the path over a series of many lives. Or in a different context we may more appropriately guess that the spire represents the hierarchy of priestly authority in an ecclesiastically mediated religion, and the rings the various levels in the hierarchy. But in either case, this degree of clarity requires us to verbalise the symbol, inwardly to ourselves if not out loud. And if we do not already know enough to make the appropriate guess then an explanation will tell us much about the structure of the religion concerned.

I think what matters in understanding what making manifold, verbal differentiation or naming, and the use of language, mean in the context of the cognitive process in Buddhism is to see what it is that is happening: what it is that the process is actually doing to the 'raw data' involved. The point is not that every single moment of our experience is laboriously delineated in verbal detail. Rather, what is occurring when we do this is not just that we delineate experiential data in a way that they are not delineated otherwise ('one continues to make manifold what is *not* really manifold', is how the text puts it), but that in making sense of them the data to which we do this (so to speak) are transformed by us so that they correspond to what we think of as being 'real'. Furthermore, *in order* to make sense of the data we have to do this. Undifferentiatable experiences such as *dark space* – rather than 'a' dark space – or undifferentiatable white space, are so sense*less* that they can be used as torture to drive one mad: in being *un*reifiable they can be subversive of our normal sense of reality. Similarly, it is not possible within our conceptual framework for me in this book to refer to the raw – not-yet-reified – experiential data which are transformed by the process to which I am referring in terms which are not at the same time reifying. That is to say, the word 'data' in itself predicates a degree of plurality to what according to the texts is 'not manifold'.

To put all this somewhat differently, one might note that the use of our verbal differentiating apparatus is something that has to be learned, is something that only operates normally if one is healthy, and varies from person to person. Babies are not born with their cognitive apparatus fully functioning, and even parts of their own bodies are not clearly delineated and identifiable by them. People with neurological disorders do not delineate experiential data in the same way as others do, a point famously illustrated in Oliver Sacks' book *The Man who Mistook his Wife for a Hat*. And the reality of people's worlds of experience varies very considerably because of constraints of intelligence, circumstance, cultural worldview, interests, and so on. In each such case, the degree, extent, nature of reality of one's world is subjectively determined. Each such person, including the baby, *has* a world of experience that is real to them. Indeed, unless one is born profoundly unconscious, then from birth all human beings are characterised by being experiencing subjects, with an experienced objective world, as I have previously stated. But unless and until experiential data are subjectively processed *as* a real part of one's world, one's reality does not include them. And unless and until experiential data are subjectively processed in a manner that is shared by healthy cognitive apparatuses, one's world will not be real in the same way as it is to others. This is partly a matter of physical maturity: the cognitive apparatus of baby, toddler, child, adolescent, functions in increasingly more efficient and sophisticated ways until access to what is commonly referred to nowadays as the adult world is experienced. But though the fundamentals of that adult world are shared as common experience, the extent of the reality of that world varies, and continues to vary, from person to person depending on all sorts of conditioning factors. Each person has to reify for himself the factors of his own world.

For each healthy individual, in order for the factors of experience to be meaningfully interpreted and communicable, all those factors – in their multitudes of varieties, tangible and intangible, concrete and abstract – are verbally differentiated by means of language.

The structure of this cognitive system, and the association of naming with recognisability, and therefore with having a place in the order of reality of the experiential world, is indicated in the early Pali texts by the terms *nāma*, name, and *rūpa*, form, often found together in the compound *nāma-rūpa*, 'name-and-form'. The association of name and form with the structure of the cognitive system is indicated in an old text where the understanding of the manifoldness that is the 'root of both subjective and objective disease' is equated with the understanding of 'name-and-form'.[1] The Pali term for 'disease' in this passage, *roga*, is clearly a synonym for *dukkha*, in the sense of experience. So name-and-form is the structure that underpins the manifold world of experience.

The compound *nāma-rūpa*, and the separate terms *nāma* and *rūpa*, are also found in very early non-Buddhist texts, including the *Ṛg Veda*, the *Upaniṣads*, and the *Śatapatha Brāhmaṇa*.[2] In these contexts *nāma* is associated with the 'conferring of a name' and with the fact that something or someone 'is called so-and-so', and *rūpa* is associated with the differentiation of something or someone in terms of its/his form or appearance. These two means of representation or manifestation – what something is called and its appearance – are described as the two great forces (literally, 'monsters') of Brahman, and it is by means of these two that what is undifferentiated becomes differentiated. Whatever constitutes reality (*satya*) is characterised in this way, the 'name' of something being conferred by speech and its 'form' arising from the eye. It is possible for things to have either name or form alone, suggesting, though no explanation of this is actually given, that included are both conceptual (things with names but no form) and as-yet-unnamed (except perhaps as 'thing', 'it', and so on) visible aspects of our experience. The point with both name and form in these contexts is that they indicate delineation, differentiation, identity. And, as these ancient texts state, it is by this means that the entirety of the reality of what is called the 'manifest' world is apprehended.[3] Subsequent exegetes of these ancient texts have interpreted the manifestation process and ontological status of the manifest world differently, but none questions name and form as referring to the structure of its manifestation.

In Buddhism, in fact, the expression 'name-and-form' has usually been interpreted differently from this, as referring to 'mind and body'.[4] In my book *Identity and Experience*, I suggested that this was inappropriate, and that in the Pali texts the expression should be interpreted similarly to the way it had been used in the pre-Buddhist sources.[5] Specifically, I suggested that name should be taken to refer to abstract identity and form to physically (though not necessarily visibly) recognisable identity, the former applicable to what is conceived of and the latter to what is apperceived, the two, separately and/or together, covering the range of whatever is either conceived or apperceived – that is, the entirety of what is cognisable.[6] Referring in this particular context to human beings I stated that *nāma* should be understood as: "… not *mere* name, but, rather, 'name' as the entire conceptual identity of the individual. *Rūpa* provides 'form' or recognisability to the individual in the sense of giving shape to that abstract identity which, eventually, is apperceivable by means of sensory impression."[7]

That this suggestion was focused specifically on human beings was because one of the key contexts in which the term name-and-form is found in the texts is a formula, called the formula of dependent origination, which is associated with how human beings come to be. The formula was given, perhaps, in response to questioning along the lines of: 'If all things are dependently originated, how does this apply to human beings?'. This context is why 'name and form' came to be interpreted as 'body and mind', in that these might not unreasonably be thought to be part of the make-up of each person. There are various versions of the formula, but the most common is as follows:

> Ignorance is the condition for [the occurring of] the formative causal matrix[8]
> This causal matrix is the condition for [the occurring of] consciousness
> Consciousness is the condition for [the occurring of] name-and-form
> Name-and-form [together] are the condition for [the occurring of] the senses
> The (six) senses are the condition for [the occurring of] contact
> Contact is the condition for [the occurring of] feeling
> Feeling is the condition for [the occurring of] craving
> Craving is the condition for [the occurring of] attachment
> Attachment is the condition for [the occurring of] becoming
> Becoming is the condition for [the occurring of] (re)birth
> (Re)birth is the condition for [the occurring of] old age and death.[9]

This formula has been interpreted in different ways within the Buddhist tradition, but in my opinion it makes most sense if it is taken as explaining why people are born not randomly but as individuals A, B and C: how it is, in other words, human beings are in fact recognisable from each other and are not merely numerically differentiated clones; and, further, how it is that individuals A, B and C are not X, Y and Z: how it is, in other words, that human beings are *specific* individuals, each associated with a conditioning causal lineage that affects that particular series of lives. So, to put it in general terms, my view is that the formula is explaining the way that in any given life the identity of a conscious individual human being is conditioned by (dependently originated in) his previous karmic make-up, which in turn is dependent on his particular state and degree of ignorance. For each such individual, all of these are in turn the conditioning factors of his collection of affective and cognitive faculties, with which he becomes an actual person, is born, ages and dies. And one can see from the formula – which in fact is given in reverse order in the texts to emphasise this point – that when, at Enlightenment, ignorance ceases, the *sine qua non* of this whole cyclical process is no longer operative and one has achieved liberation from rebirth.[10]

Name and form in this context, then, refer to the fact that an individual will have an appearance – what he will look like physically, the 'form' he will take, when born; and to the way that individuality is abstractly indicated: 'name' is the verbal differentiation, so to speak, of the form as 'person'; name identifies the form. And in this context of referring to the recognisability of a person, name and form are said to be mutually dependent. Referring to this formula, the Buddha states that in the absence of those characteristics by which 'name' is conceived of, it would not be possible to verbally differentiate a 'form'; and in the absence of those characteristics by which 'form' manifests itself, it would not be possible to conceive of a 'name'.[11] What I think this is saying is that a person cannot be either just name or just form: neither a name without form, nor a form without a name, can be a *person*. In the latter of these two, the name is not the given personal name – Jane, John, and so on – but the name 'a person'. To *be* a person, there must be form that is nameable 'person'. This is particularly emphasised in one version of the formula where it is stated not just that name-and-form is dependent on consciousness, in common with other versions of the formula, but also that consciousness is dependent on name-and-form.[12] So not only is name-and-form dependently associated with consciousness, indicating specifically that all human beings are aware beings, but for each such aware being name and form together constitute the identity blueprint, as it were, of him as an individual.[13]

The terms name and form, and the compound form name-and-form, are also found in other contexts in the Pali *Nikāyas*, which suggest that they indicate how *all* things are delineated and identified, verbally differentiated. As cited above, understanding manifoldness, the 'disease of subjectivity and objectivity', is equated with understanding name-and-form. This suggests that in early Buddhism, as in the pre-Buddhist understanding of name-and-form, the entirety of cyclical experience – the world of subjectivity and objectivity – is organised according to, and understood by means of, a name-and-form structure, illustrated in the mundane examples discussed above. To put this differently, one might say that what the world of subjectivity and objectivity is characterised by is named form(s).

This point is also made elsewhere, in that the answer to the question 'Where are name and form completely destroyed?' is that it is by the cessation of consciousness.[14] The Pali form of this question and answer (I have cited only part of it, and will return to it in full below) is a somewhat stylised verse form of a riddle. Though I have followed its grammar in my English phrasing of the question above, slightly adjusted but more illuminating ways of putting it would be: 'at what point does [the] name and form [structure] cease?', or, better, 'what is the limit of [the] name and form [structure]?'. In answer to either of which the response given in the text, that it is by the cessation of consciousness that name and form are completely destroyed, would indicate that name and form characterise the cognitive world of experience, and that it is not until, on attaining Enlightenment, one achieves the cessation of that – ignorant – perspective that one is no longer subject – in the sense of being bound – to such a world. 'Cessation of consciousness' refers, then, to the cessation of ignorant cognition, and this corresponds to the limit of the name and form structure. Other passages variously confirm this when they refer to the cessation of consciousness as the cessation of *dukkha*, experience,[15] describe liberation from rebirth as the cessation of name and form,[16] and state that the continuity tendencies which bind one to rebirth cease to function in one who is no longer in thrall to name and form.[17] If one bears in mind that the Buddha lived for forty-five years after his Enlightenment insight, one can better understand that in all such references the point is not that on Enlightenment one becomes *un*conscious but that in attaining insight bondage to continuity has been overcome.

Though name and form are mutually and necessarily dependent in the context of a human being, as discussed above, and together characterise the structure of the experiential world, we also find name referred to on its own in the texts. Where there is no actual 'sensing' of a visible form, a sound, or an odour (and so on through all the senses), one can still abstractly refer to what is *called* (that is, what has the name) 'vision', 'hearing' and 'smelling' (and so on).[18] In this passage what is being referred to is a stage of meditation in which form as a characteristic of one's cognitive experience has been 'transcended' and where the activity of sensory apperception has 'ceased'. As well as acknowledging the existence of non-visible beings that have 'subtle' form, the texts refer to a form-less level of experience. That this is associated with the most advanced pre-Enlightenment levels of meditation suggests that the meditative discipline, which is progressively effective, brings one to the point where one's cognitive apparatus can function increasingly abstractly. One might suggest that one gains control over the way it operates by means of understanding what is going on. In the process of achieving what is referred to in this context as the complete 'cessation of making manifold' – that is, its 'normal' uncontrolled way of operating – 'form' characteristics are as it were transcended, or 'seen through', first. In descriptions of the meditative exercises, this level of experience is referred to as 'the plane of no-thing'.[19] And one can perhaps see from our discussion the sense in which this term is used in this context: the meditator is learning to suspend, so to speak, the operating of his cognitive apparatus in the usual making manifold (thing-like) way.

But I suggest that one can also perhaps generalise from what is said here about 'name' a point that is not explicitly made in the texts: that name on its own refers to conceptual or abstract aspects of experience. Descriptions of the cognitive process to which I have referred in earlier chapters clearly indicate the way in which thinking abstractly, in every sense, is encompassed within the process of making manifold or verbal differentiation. In other words, while thoughts, feelings, ideas, hypotheses, and so on, have no form, they *are* part of the verbally differentiated manifold world: they are delineated and identified in the same manner that forms are, save for the fact that the former are only abstract whereas the latter, in addition to their having an abstract identity or name, are also concrete and, as such, have density and other characteristics associated with form. So for the sake of plausible clarity one might say that though in general terms, as I said above, the world of subjectivity and objectivity is characterised by things that have names (name and form), this generality has to be understood to encompass both concrete and abstract aspects of that world, the latter of which, more precisely, are formless.

Though one has to extrapolate the generalisation I have made with respect to 'name', the texts have more to say about 'form'. And these passages give us more information about the extent of what is involved in the cognitive process of making manifold. It is consistently stated in the texts that whatever has form is characterised by one or more of the four great elements of earth, water, fire and wind mentioned in Chapter Two in connection with the *khandha* of the body, which in Pali is also known by the same term as form in the more generic sense, *rūpa*. In the *Sutta Piṭaka* the four great elements are said to be the 'primary' characteristics of form. So fundamental to the world of experience are the elements as primary characteristics, in all their multiplicity of combinations, that the verse riddle I referred to above which asks the question 'where are name and form destroyed?' begins by asking: "Where do solidity, fluidity, temperature and mobility [the four elements abstractly understood] not have a hold?".[20] The same point is made when the insight gained at Enlightenment, nirvana, is elsewhere referred to as "that condition wherein solidity, fluidity, temperature and mobility are not".[21]

The Pali term for primary, *no-upādā*, more literally means either 'underived' or 'not clinging or grasping'. Nothing is said in the early texts about why this term is used, but armed with an increasing understanding of the cognitive and ontological context one can perhaps make a reasonably informed suggestion. I suggest there are in fact two ways in which the four elements are what one might call 'primary' which are respectively compatible with both 'underived' and 'not clinging or grasping'. Corresponding to 'underived', it seems likely that the four elements are primary in the sense that each of them abstractly represents a *characteristic* of form rather than something that is itself an *example* of form. Thus whereas the elements earth, water, fire and wind abstractly represent the characteristics solidity or extension, fluidity, temperature and mobility respectively, a pot of coffee, a burning candle, a vase of flowers, a human body, are actual examples of things that have form that can be analysed in terms of a combination of those abstract characteristics.

With regard to 'not clinging or grasping', in fact this term is most commonly found in the early texts in association with the five *khandhas*, in the non-negative sense of 'clinging or grasping' (*upādā*). Here it refers to the causal momentum of volitions (clingings or graspings) which fuel the pre-Enlightenment continuity of each individual, who is represented metaphorically simply by the (his) *khandhas*. In the light of this, one can perhaps suggest that in the context of the four elements, *not* clinging or grasping corresponds to the way the elements are primary in the sense that they represent not the actual forms – the examples that have been, as it were, 'grasped' – but the *potential* characteristics of *all* examples. Thus while *whatever* has form has the characteristics of one or more element, the elements themselves are 'primary' in the sense that they are abstractly representative of all potential form(s). Occasionally in the early Pali texts space is mentioned as a fifth element, and in fact whatever has form is spacial, both in the sense of being spacially locatable and in the sense that, in not being abstract, form has some sort of spacial extension. One needs to bear in mind here that according to the early Buddhist texts, form is understood to range through a wide range of degrees of density and subtlety; it need not be visible.

The primary status of the elements is further suggested in both these cases in that experience is characterised *according to* (name and) form. For so long as one remains unenlightened, all one's experience is characterised in this way. That there is a place for abstract aspects of experience, what one might called name-*without*-form, in no way compromises this. Such abstractions would have no meaningfulness outside of, or except in contrast to, the context of a world of name-*and*-form.

The way abstract potential becomes – and it is important to grasp that this is very much 'as it were': abstract potential is not some*thing* that is literally transformed – the multiplicity of examples of form that are separately and collectively understood by us in terms of the world of experience is indicated by two different aspects of the teachings given in the texts. First is the general process we have already discussed which explains experience in terms of subjectivity and objectivity. As we have seen, that process can also be referred to in terms of name and form. Prior to Enlightenment, each individual 'makes manifold', that is he verbally differentiates or 'gives names' to whatever is part of his experience, be it concrete or abstract: this is how raw experiential data is transposed into meaningful cognition. And the ability of each individual to process that data meaningfully – to verbally differentiate in terms of name and form – is correlated, perhaps, with the way form is understood according to certain potential characteristics – experiential data being the *mundus sensibilis* referred to in Chapter Three.

Second, though, is the more suggestive point that *rūpa*, form, as well as being characterised by the four 'primary' elements, is said to have a 'secondary' or 'derived' aspect. A standard description of form is that it is "the four great elements and whatever is secondary to, or derived from, those four elements".[22] I say that this point is suggestive rather than informative because nothing is said in the early texts (or even in the commentary on this description of form[23]) as to what is meant or referred to by 'secondary': it is only in our present context of an increasing understanding of the relationship between cognition and the experiential world that one can draw out a plausible explanation. Given the general understanding that we already have one might immediately suggest that secondary or derived form refers to the *additional* characteristics of form beyond solidity and extension, fluidity, temperature and mobility: the characteristics of, say, colour, texture, smell, taste, shape, and so on. It is by means of these that we know that a form is in fact a jug of coffee and not a lighted candle. Both are primarily characterised by solidity, liquid (in the case of the lighted candle the liquid wax below the flame), temperature and a degree of mobility (apart from the obvious mobility of the liquid and the flame, they can fall, spill, roll off a table, and so on). But, secondarily, they look, feel, smell, taste, and so on, quite different. Indeed, while primary characteristics may be primary in the process of making manifold, they are not sufficient for anything more than the most rudimentary of identification to take place – of the nature of 'lump of warm stuff' – and many familiar items of our everyday experience would not be meaningfully discernable by means of these characteristics at all. And the identifying of primary qualities does not render things interchangeable. No cognitively healthy person could as it were stop at the level of lump of warm stuff and randomly treat it either as a jug of coffee or as a lighted candle as it suited him.

Later Pali texts in fact support this suggestion with regard to how secondary form should be understood, though it is only in the context of our greater understanding of the cognitive process, and the ontological implications of that, that the support becomes clear. In later texts secondary form is stated to be the senses and corresponding sense objects.[24] Following these texts, the Theravāda tradition has continued to state that secondary form is the senses.[25] But both the Pali and other Theravāda sources give definitions rather than explanations and the relevance of the senses to secondary form is, to say the least of it, far from clear within the tradition. The reason the definitions alone are unhelpful is because the context in which secondary form is referred to is in descriptions of the *khandha* of the body – the 'form' (*rūpa*) *khandha*. As explained in earlier chapters, this *khandha* has been understood by the Theravāda tradition to refer to one's body in the sense of 'matter': 'form' is understood in this material sense. So one might find form – including secondary form – defined, to quote from an exemplary Theravāda source, as follows: "In [the *khandha*] of Matter are included the traditional Four Great Elements …, namely, solidity, fluidity, heat and motion, and also the Derivatives … of the Four Great Elements. In the term 'Derivatives of Four Great Elements' are included our five material sense-organs, i.e., the faculties of eye, ear, nose, tongue, and body, and their corresponding objects of the external world, i.e., visible form, sound, odour, taste, and tangible things, and also some thoughts or ideas or conceptions which are in the sphere of mind-objects. … Thus the whole realm of matter, both internal and external, is included in the [*khandha*] of Matter."[26]

In the context of attempting to understand one of the *khandhas*, in a tradition which has persisted in seeing them as an analysis of the individual into five aggregate parts, there being in their view no 'self' as such, this definition, faithful though it is to the later Pali texts, is hard to follow. Though one might without difficulty accept that a *khandha* of matter would include one's physical sense organs, beyond this the definition seems wholly incompatible with such a *khandha*. And notwithstanding my previous suggestion, on the basis of factors such as breathing, temperature, decay, mobility, and so on, indicated by the abstract meanings of the four great elements, that one should see the form-*khandha* as the living and functioning body rather than mere matter, it is still difficult to accept the inclusion *here of* 'some thoughts or ideas or conceptions'. It is difficult not only because thoughts, ideas and conceptions are so clearly described in the context of the way the other, non-form *khandhas* contribute to the cognitive process, but also because the ways in which the livingness of the body is indicated (breathing, temperature, decay, mobility and so on) are not suggestive of thoughts, ideas and conceptions, or, indeed, of whatever is meant by a 'sphere of mind objects'. The author is attempting to explain the inclusion in the Buddhist texts of 'mind' as one of the senses, an inclusion which is rendered even more conceptually troublesome than usual if one understands the form-*khandha* in the traditional material sense.[27] More relevantly to us here, though, it is simply not compatible with the traditional Theravāda understanding of the *khandhas* as the five parts of which human beings are comprised that the form-*khandha* should include, as part of secondary form, sense *objects*. Either this is not the way one should understand what the *khandhas* are, or this is not what secondary form is. Even if one adapts the context to embrace one's understanding of the form-*khandha* as the living, functioning body, the inclusion of sense objects as part of the definition of the *khandha* is puzzling, to say the least of it. I think, though, that the wider frame of reference we have been building up will help to sort out the puzzle.

Given that one of the *khandhas* is referred to by the term form, *rūpa*, and it is in the context of referring to this *khandha* that the texts state that form has both primary and secondary aspects, it is unfortunate that nothing is stated about how secondary form should be understood. In fact, this absence of explanation of secondary form in the early texts, and the bald definitions of it as the senses in later texts, may well have been contributory factors to the long-standing misunderstanding of what the *khandha* teaching is about and, in turn, of the more specific way in which it is crucially important to the teachings as a whole. The lack of clarity has been exacerbated by the fact that though in later texts, followed by the Theravāda tradition, the senses have been identified in the defining of secondary form – that is, as part of the form-*khandha* – in the early texts the only *khandhas* the senses are explicitly associated with are the non-form *khandhas*. In the *Sutta Piṭaka*, descriptions of each of the four non-form khandhas begin with the statement that they are six-fold according to the six senses. The description of the sensation-*khandha*, for example, states that sensations are classifiable according to whether they arise from visual, auditory, gustatory, olfactory, tactile or 'mental' contact.[28] The 'contact' here refers to the fact that in order for there to be sensation at all, there has to be what is called a 'coming together' of sense organ, sense object (that is, the relevant experiential data) and consciousness.[29] This threefold 'sensory event' gives rise, in the case of consciousness together with eye and visible object, say, to the experience of a visual sensation.[30] Similarly, the descriptions of the *khandhas* of apperception and conception, volitional activities, and consciousness state that these too are sixfold in the same way.[31] And with regard to sixfold consciousness, it is further explained that it is not that there are different *kinds* of consciousness, but that "Consciousness is known by this or that name [i.e. visual, auditory, olfactory, (and so on)] because an appropriate condition arises. If consciousness arises because of eye and visible form, it is known as visual consciousness (and so on)."[32] The text continues by way of analogy to explain that this should be understood similarly to the way fire is defined according to what is burning: if it is burning sticks, twigs, and so on, it is known as a stick or twig fire.

In the early texts, then, the senses are never stated to be part of the form-*khandha*, as the later texts and the Theravāda tradition would have it. And other than the references to the senses in the context of the non-form *khandhas*, governing according to sense the nature of the *khandha* activity in question, they are referred to in a plethora of unrelated ways in the early texts. In the early material there is, in other words, a distinct absense of clarity not just with regard to the form-*khandha* but about how the senses themselves should be understood.

I said above that I think the wider frame of reference we have been building up will help to sort out the puzzle. More specifically, I think that the most meaningful route to understanding both secondary form and the senses, and, as it were, the relationship between the two, lies initially in understanding the *khandhas* teaching to be referring to the cognitive apparatus as a whole. It has been via this route that we have now reached the further stage of understanding the way the cognitive process is instrumental in the experience of subjectivity and objectivity, which in turn is referred to in the texts as 'name and form', the basis of our present discussion.

I have elsewhere discussed in considerable detail the plethora of references to the senses to be found in the early texts, as well as other related issues and terms.[33] Arising from that discussion, I suggested that though the sense organs are, as physical body parts, literally parts of the form-*khandha* along with all other bodily organs, the senses as such are best understood neither in terms of sense organs having corresponding sense objects, nor as things that can be identified as part of any particular *khandha*. Rather, they should be understood figuratively as the faculties of vision, hearing, smelling, and so on. These are figurative in that the manner in which they are present, so to speak, is quite different from the presence of the sense organs. "An eye" (for example), as a later text puts it, "does not see because it is not conscious; nor does consciousness see, because it is not an eye."[34] The point of the sense referred to as eye is *seeing* – both the ability to see, and the activity of seeing. This is the case with all the senses: the point of an ear is hear*ing*, of a nose smell*ing*, and so on. In knowing that a human being has senses, what one knows is not just that he physically has eyes, ears, nose, but that he can see, hear, smell.

So crucial is all this to the entirety of our experiential world that the texts state that in order for something to *be* an experience it must first be a 'conscious sensory event': the description of the cognitive process begins with 'visual consciousness arises ...'.[35] And the same is the case whatever sense is involved or appropriate to the event. As such, one can, in the context of what I am now suggesting with regard to experience as a whole, see that the senses are not just niceties, or refinements, but are the ways in which the factors of our experience acquire their defining characteristics. In fact one might suggest that just as the primary aspects of form, the four great elements, abstractly represent the primary characteristics of all examples of form, so the secondary aspects of form abstractly represent the secondary characteristics by which all form is more fully identified, by which, indeed, one is subsequently able more precisely to 'name' form. Thus the raw experience that is initially processed at a rudimentary primary level as 'lump of warm stuff', say, which is the most one might understand of form at its most basic, is further processed and named the jug of coffee or the lighted candle because the more specific and infinitely variable secondary characteristics of colours, smells, textures, tastes and sounds are 'sensed'.

Further, one might understand the 'secondariness' of the sense-determined characteristics in two ways. It lies first in the fact that all lumps of warm stuff share underlying primary characteristics, whether they are jugs of coffee, lighted candles, etcetera, but differ in their secondary characteristics. And it also lies in the fact that though there is no sense in which one could conceive of a jug of coffee without any of the relevant primary characteristics, identifying it as coffee might not involve all of the relevant secondary characteristics. In other words, if the lump of stuff is not characterised partly by liquidity it cannot be coffee; but if it is so characterised, one might not need to see it as brown to interpret it as coffee: smelling it might be sufficient for this. And the secondary characteristics necessary for identification would also vary from item to item and time to time: having a stuffy cold which impaired one's ability to smell would mean one would need to see the coffee, for example; and tasting fine white sugar would help in distinguishing it from salt in a similar container.

What becomes clear in understanding secondary form in the light of the broader frame of reference we have been establishing, rather than in the narrow and unclear context of the traditional interpretation of the *khandhas*, is the way in which it is appropriate rather than inappropriate to refer both to senses organs and sense *objects* in this context. If one understands the senses in terms of the sense organs alone one is limited to seeing them simply as various lumps of flesh. But in understanding them, like the living functioning body and all the other *khandhas*, as part of the cognitive process by which all experience is mediated, one can see that in operating as see*ing*, hear*ing*, tast*ing*, and so on, the objectified aspect of the experience – what is experienced as seen, heard, tasted, and so on – is as much a part of it as is the presence of the sense organ. Though as I mentioned above one can refer abstractly to seeing, hearing, tasting, and so on, by name alone, the activities of seeing, hearing, tasting, and so on, are necessarily experienced as part of the world of subjectivity and objectivity. One sees, hears, tastes, *something*. As such, though one refers separately to sense organs, sense objects and what is sensed – nose, cheese and smell, for example – this separation is in fact an abstraction from the experience 'smelling cheese-smell'.

And once again the point here is not that individual experiential events operate in this way but that the entire world of our experience is characterised in this way for so long as it persists. As such, both primary and secondary aspects of form fundamentally characterise the manner in which experience is understood. The point made above that the secondary aspects need not all be operating in order for identification to take place does not compromise this. It remains the case that it is by means of the operating of the senses that experience is meaningfully mediated: one literally 'makes sense' of one's experience. The fact that the characteristics of experience occur in an infinite variety of combinations is referred to in the 'Section on Variety' of a chapter entitled 'Kindred Sayings on Characteristics'.[36] All variety arises, this chapter states, because of the variety of sensory events.

Moreover, it is because such sensory events mediate, so to speak, the structure of our experience as a whole, that the characteristics of that structure, referred to either in terms of the senses or more specifically as the four great elements of form, are associated with affective states of mind. All feelings, apperceptions, intentions, desires, passions and quests are, the 'Section on Variety' goes on to state, dependent on the variety of sensory events.[37] And if there were not the four great elements (each is referred to in turn in various ways), there would be no experience, negative or positive.[38] The point is to understand the nature of the elements and the senses, their arising, and their cessation.[39]

The generality of this is why the senses are referred to metaphorically as 'doors' (*dvāra*), as mentioned in previous chapters. And these 'doors', by which all experience is mediated, need to be 'guarded'.[40] As I have previously explained, 'guarding' refers to the way one interprets and responds to one's experience. The aim is to understand the process as it is and not to become involved in affective, and therefore binding, responses to anything that is a part of one's experience: to as it were disengage the affective response from the cognitive operation. In one textual passage it is stated that though the Buddha sees, and so on – in other words, his senses continue to function in the operating of his cognitive process as other people's do – in his liberated state of Enlightenment he does not respond with desire and lust to what he sees.[41] In having seen, at Enlightenment, the way the process works, he is aware that affective responses are based on ignorance as to the nature of one's experience and has uprooted this binding continuity tendency. Similarly, the Buddha explains that when an advanced Buddhist sees a visible object with his visual faculty, for example, he "is not entranced with views about its various characteristics". Rather, the passage goes on, he is intent on restraining those things which give rise to unwholesomeness, evil, covetousness or dejection which flow over him for as long as he lives within his sense of sight unrestrained. And he guards his visual sense, attaining restraint over it.[42]

The reference here to negative affective states 'flowing over' the disciple alludes conceptually to the stream metaphor discussed earlier, and through the Pali (*anuvāssaveyyuṃ*) it also relates what is being said to the deepest binding tendencies (the *āsavas*) which need to be rooted out on achieving Enlightenment. Again this indicates the fundamental role of the senses in the cognitive system as a whole: they are part of the cognitive process per se, and though the Buddhist may be aiming for detached understanding of the process, for insight into the way it works so that he is able to cease fuelling its continuity, this does not mean their operating literally ceases. What ceases with insight, itself the cessation of ignorance, is the affective response, as described in the last paragraph. References to the 'cessation of consciousness', the 'cessation of the *khandhas*', the 'cessation of sensory contact',[43] the 'end of name and form', the 'cessation of experience (*dukkha*)', all need to be understood in this context. Rather than taking them in literal terms, one should grasp the way they are all metaphorically referring to the cessation of the ignorance which is the fundamental condition for one's cognitive apparatus with attendant affective responses continuing to function in the 'normal' pre-enlightenment way.

If we return to the mundane examples discussed above of the way we delineate and reify our experiences by means of verbal differentiation, we can perhaps now see more clearly the extent to which the early Buddhist material suggests that we do this. Though one can extrapolate examples, as I have done, in order to be able to imagine more easily what the cognitive process is doing, it is clearly implicit in the Buddhist texts that the entire world of experience is as it is because it is dependent on our cognitive processing apparatus. It is by means of this process that the world of experience is made real for us. In being a world of subjectivity and objectivity, the *structure* of the objective world is not independent of the subjective process. Whatever conforms to this structure, what we experience as its contents, so to speak, are not in themselves, independently or inherently, x, y and z. Rather, in the process of making manifold they are apperceived, conceived of, verbally differented and named x, y and z *by us*.

This is why textual passages which refer to the *khandhas* include references to sense objects. These passages are not referring to the *khandhas* as the five constituent parts of which human beings are comprised, as the Theravāda Buddhist tradition has interpreted them, but to the way the world of experience as a whole is subjectively dependent. More clearly than heretofore, we can see why it was to this process that the Buddha directed attention.

Notes

1 *Sutta Nipāta* 530: *anuvicca papañca nāmarūpaṃ ajjhattaṃ bahiddhā ca rogamūlaṃ sabbarogamūlabandhanā pamutto.*

2 ṚV X 71.1; Bṛ. Up. 3.2.12; Śat. Br. XI 2.3.3ff. cf. also Bṛ.Up. 1.4.7 and Ch. Up. 6.3, 8.14.

3 These references are all discussed in chapter 6, entitled *Nāmarūpa*, in Hamilton, 1996.

4 See, for example, Radhakrishnan, 1988, p. 172; C.A.F. Rhys Davids, 1914, p. 23f; Johansson, 1969, p. 78; E.J. Thomas, 1951, pp. 63ff; Harvey, 1995b, p. 116f and *passim*.

5 See chapter 6, *Nāmarūpa*.

6 In Buddhism, as in other Indian religions, it is accepted that there are a multitude of entities that exist in a form that is not visible to the naked eye. Though the range and types of entities as it were allowed for in those traditions differ from anything usually conceived of in the West, we do nevertheless also acknowledge the existence of non-visible entities. Indeed, many are attested to by scientists.

7 p. 127.

8 More colloquially, one might express the Pali term *saṃkhārā* in this line of the formula as 'package of previous karmic influences'.

9 SN II 25 and throughout the *Nidāna Saṃyutta*.

10 Other interpretations, and detailed comments and suggestions are given in Hamilton, 1996, chapter 4, The *Saṃkhārakkhandha*. See also Collins, 1982, pp. 203ff.

11 DN II 62.

12 DN II 56; see also SN II 104, 113.

13 It could be argued that this formula also refers to the way the cognitive apparatus of those human beings works in the sense of 'where there is consciousness there is the perception of name and form, the senses as its secondary characteristics, and so on'. (See, for example, Reat, 1987, p. 18, and Reat, 1990.) While there do appear to be superficial parallels with my discussion in this chapter, in my opinion the fact that so much of the formula leads up to birth clearly indicates that in this context the purpose is to explain the way human beings are conditioned as individuals, as I have described.

14 DN I 223: *kattha nāmañ ca rūpañ ca asesaṃ uparujjhati? ... viññāṇassa nirodhena etth' etaṃ uparujjhati*. SN I 15 gives a slight variation on the riddle, and see also *Sutta Nipāta* 1036–7.

15 *Sutta Nipāta* 734: *viññāṇassa nirodhena n'atthi dukkhassa sambhavo*.

16 SN I 13, 35.

17 *Sutta Nipāta* 1100. In *Identity and Experience* (pp. 124f.) I suggested that in the contexts discussed in this paragraph name and form should be interpreted in the traditional way as mind and body. I am no longer of this opinion, except possibly in the sense that mind and body might be understood as a metaphor for one's pre-Enlightenment experience.

18 AN IV 426f.

19 For example at MN I 41: *ākiñcaññāyatanaṃ*.

20 D I 223; S I 15 gives a variation of the riddle.

21 *Udāna* VIII.i: *tad āyatanaṃ yattha n'eva paṭhavī na āpo na tejo na vāyo*.

22 For example, SN III 59: *cattāro ca mahābhūtā catunnaṃ ca mahābhūtānam upādāya rūpaṃ idaṃ vuccati bhikkhave rūpaṃ*.

23 SA III 276 makes no comment on *upādā*.

24 The earliest reference to the senses and sense objects being referred to as 'secondary' is in the canonical but late Pali text the *Paṭisambhidāmagga* of the *Khuddaka Nikāya*, I 76–8. In this context no reference is made to *rūpa*, form, however. Specific statements that the senses and their objects, collectively called *āyatanas*, are secondary form are found at *Dhammasaṅgaṇī* 594–6; *Vibhaṅga* p. 70ff; and *Aṭṭhasālinī*, p. 305ff.

25 See Buddhaghosa's *Visuddhimagga* p. 444; and for two modern examples Walpola Rahula, 1985, p. 20f., and Ñāṇavīra Thera, 1987, p. 98ff.

26 Rahula, 1985, p. 20f.

27 Nowhere in the early texts is 'mind' in this context equated with the brain, and, in spite of its materialistic understanding of the form-*khandha*, the Theravāda tradition as a whole has not interpreted mind to mean brain. As explained in Chapter Two, in the early texts 'mind' seems to refer to the most preliminary stage of filtering and organising of experiential data according to whether it is seen, heard, smelt, tasted, touched or non-sensory (that is, abstract).

28 SN III 59f.

29 MN I 111: *cakkhuñ c'āvuso paṭicca rūpe ca uppajjati cakkhuviññāṇaṃ tiṇṇaṃ saṅgati phasso*. The form of the Pali is the same through all the senses.

30 *Phassapaccayā vedanā.*

31 SN III 60f.

32 MN I 259.

33 Hamilton, 1996, chapter 1, pp. 14ff.

34 *Aṭṭhasālinī*, p. 399f.

35 MN I 111.

36 *Nānattavagga* of the *Dhātu Saṃyutta*, SN II 140ff.

37 SN II 143.

38 SN II 169ff.

39 SN II 176.

40 For example, DN I 63, 70, 250; SN II 218, IV 103, 117, 194. cf. also MN I 180, 221; AN II 16, and Cousins, 1981.

41 SN IV 164.

42 DN I 70.

43 *Udāna* 2.4: *phusanti phassā upadhiṃ paṭicca, nirupadhiṃ kena phuseyyuṃ phassā?*

CHAPTER SEVEN

The Limits of Experience

"The world is everything that is the case."
Wittgenstein, Tractatus Logico-Philosophicus (1922) p. 30.

We have arrived now at the point where we can discuss more fully and specifically the nature of the world as such. Though we have seen the way the early texts suggest that the operating of our cognitive apparatus is as it were intrinsic to our experiential world, we have not so far considered what might be the implications of this for understanding the nature of that world as it were in itself.[1] It is this that I want to discuss in this chapter. To do this, I want first to draw together the various aspects of the extent to which subjectivity is correlated with objectivity. And in the light of this, I will then go on to discuss what one might broadly refer to as the ontological status of the world, how one might understand the nature of its reality, whether or not this is *all* of Reality as a whole, and the way in which, or whether, all this is accessible at an experiential level. This in turn will lead to discussion of two further aspects of the subjective-objective correlation.

First, then, we have seen the way in which early textual material clearly explains or suggests that the world of subjectivity and objectivity is dependent on the operating of cognitive apparatus. And in the last chapter, I discussed the way in which the texts indicate that the fundamental structure by which that world of experience is meaningful to us is also cognitively determined. We saw, for example, that name and form are the primary characteristics of experience for so long as consciousness operates conditioned by ignorance.[2] This was the content of the riddle to which I referred in the last chapter. At the same time I also suggested that a slightly adjusted but more illuminating way of phrasing the riddle would be: 'what is the limit of [the] name and form [structure]?'. And that the point of the answer to the riddle – in effect that the limit of the name and form structure is one's ignorance – was in accord with other passages which referred to the cessation of consciousness as the cessation of *dukkha*, experience,[3] describe liberation from rebirth as the cessation of name and form,[4] and state that the continuity tendencies which bind one to rebirth cease to function in one who is no longer in thrall to name and form.[5]

In effect what all these passages are indicating is that earthly, or worldly, existence is characterised according to the name and form structure. We have seen passages that stated that those who have achieved Enlightenment still see, know, and so on. That what is different about them is not that their cognitive apparatus no longer operates, but that they have achieved insight into what is happening, and are no longer affectively responding to their experiences in a binding way. Such statements as 'the cessation of consciousness' should, as I have already suggested, be taken metaphorically to refer to the cessation of ignorance.

According to the early texts, all worldly experience is structured according to the characteristics of name and form, then; and this of course includes both primary and secondary form as described in the last chapter. From this it is not difficult to see that what is encompassed by this is the entirety of what one might loosely and broadly refer to as objects, in all their varieties. And nor is it too conceptually difficult to see that one needs to extend the usual frame of reference of objects in this context to include abstract factors of objective experience such as ideas, thoughts, imaginings, as well as more obviously sensory but not particularly thing-like factors such as sounds, smells and so on. The point is their objective nature in relation to a subject, and their common, if infinitely variably combined, characteristics.

What is more difficult to grasp, or what is even less obvious, is that if the *structure* of the world of experience is correlated with the cognitive process, then it is not just that we name objects, concrete and abstract, and superimpose secondary characteristics according to the senses as described. It is also that *all* the structural features of the world of experience are cognitively correlated. In particular, space and time are not external to the structure but are part of it. As I have already mentioned, space (*ākāsa*) is sometimes referred to as the fifth great element of primary form. One might suggest, in fact, that all form, whatever its degree of density or subtlety, is additionally characterised by having a spacial dimension: it is spacially locatable. It is also the case that whatever is part of our experience, whether concrete or abstract, occurs temporally. Whether spacially locatable or not, all aspects of our experience are temporally locatable. Put differently, one might say that there is no such thing as experience as we know it that is not characterised by space and time.

The nature of space and time are far from explicitly dealt with in the *Sutta Piṭaka*, but it is nevertheless possible to draw together certain references to them from which their place in the cognitively dependent structure of the experiential world becomes clear.

There are very few specific references to space. The fact that space is referred to as the fifth element only occasionally perhaps suggests that the understanding of it is different from (possibly less clear than) the other four. Frequently the other four primary characteristics of the structure of experience are discussed with no mention of space. Similarly, some textual descriptions of solidity or extension, fluidity, mobility and heat have examples not just of how they relate specifically to the form-*khandha* (that is, the body) but also of their objective – that is, their non-*khandha* – application: such as floods, raging fires and monsoon winds.[6] But where space is referred to as an element, no objective application is mentioned.[7] One cannot know whether this omission is in spite of or because of the fact that there is a spacial aspect to all of the elements.

This universality of the spacial dimension of all the primary elements of form is implicit in the delineation involved in the process of making manifold as described in the last chapter, the process which conforms to the characteristics represented by the primary elements. Delineation is spacial: it is this that renders all form(s) spacially locatable. And delineation is, as we have seen, both cognitively dependent and intrinsic to the structure of the experiential world.

The only context in which space is referred to that might suggest that it is more explicitly understood as a fundamental structural characteristic of experience is in descriptions of meditation. Here what is called a 'sphere of unbounded space' is referred to as a meditative level which is achieved "by wholly transcending apperceptions or conceptions of form".[8] This treats space differently from the other elements of form, which are transcended at this meditative level, in a way that possibly suggests a recognition that it is not just a fifth element in the same sense that the others are but, rather, that all the other elements also have a spacial dimension. But the text goes on to state that it is nevertheless a level which itself has to be transcended, so it is clear that space is still within the world of experience as a whole. Put differently, what it is not stating is that space is an externally existing (that is, transcendentally real) dimension in which experience takes place. Interestingly for us, it is, indeed, explicitly described as impermanent – and therefore part of experience – because it is "constructed, part of cognitive activity".[9]

That this clearest reference to the nature of space is associated with meditation ties in with the fact that the concern of early Buddhists was subjectively focused. I referred in Chapter Four to the way the Theravāda tradition later developed a psychological cosmology. In this, levels of meditative attainment are thought to have a metaphorical correspondence with cosmological levels, which are themselves also understood spacially. As I also stated in Chapter Four, though, this correspondence was not present in the early material. Rather, the term for world, *loka*, was metaphorically used to refer to the experiential world of an individual – *one's* world. Nirvana could thus be described as the cessation of the world in that it is the occasion on which the limitations of one's world of experience cease: *dukkha-nirodha*, the cessation of experience, is thus juxtaposed in some texts with *loka-nirodha*, the cessation of the world.

In this context it is highly relevant that nirvana has no spacial reference. Attaining nirvana does not at all mean 'going somewhere else' in the sense of 'arriving in nirvana'. Rather, it refers simply to the cessation (blowing out) of the fuel of cyclical continuity. Thus the idea of the cessation of one's world of experience, which (appropriately understood) is the goal of the Buddhist path, does not carry with it any connotation of attaining a different part of a spacially characterised larger cosmos outside one's cyclical experience. The use of apparently spacial terms to refer either to nirvana or to the following of the path to it are metaphorical. Some of these I discussed in Chapter Four, but as a brief reminder examples include the notion of nirvana being a 'further shore' which is crossed to on a raft (the following of the teachings),[10] and other contexts where it is referred to as an island, cave, shelter, refuge.[11] All of these are as non-spacial in literal terms as is stating one has 'arrived at an understanding', or that one has found an 'oasis of calm' in a mentally cluttered day. This is clearly indicated in the text in that nirvana as island, cave, shelter and refuge is referred to as the goal that is the "extinction [in the sense of cessation] of desire, hatred and ignorance" – it is this cessation that is the island, cave, shelter, refuge in the storm of the desire- hatred- and ignorance-led cyclical continuity. Moreover, this is to be achieved not by travelling anywhere but by "mindfulness".[12]

It might be that because the relevance of the world was thus not considered in objectively spacial terms in the later cosmological sense, space as such was not considered as a separate topic that might need understanding. There are a vast number of references to place names, locations where events occurred or teachings were given, and so on, in a commonplace narrative sense. But there are no explicit discussions in the textual material about the nature of space in any conceptual sense. In his teaching the Buddha consistently directed the attention of his listeners to the understanding of cognitive processes. And it might be that meditative concerns were concentrated on in respect of the 'making manifold' of what is objective in the more readily graspable sense of objects, to the exclusion of discussion of less obvious structural aspects of what is objective. In any event, despite the fact that there is little overt discussion of or reference to space as part of the structure of the experiential world, our approach allows us to draw out what indications there are both to the fact that it is a structural characteristic and of its subjectively dependent nature.

There are perhaps more references to time in the *Sutta Piṭaka*, though as with space these too are far from explicit. The vast mass of references to time in the texts are in the form of narrative references to when something happened. A large number of the chapters relating to the teaching of the Buddha or his eminent followers begin with the phrase "At that time ...". Often a place name is given for what occurs next, as mentioned in the last paragraph with regard to space. But more significant for our purposes, the main context in which time is clearly relevant in the early texts is the pervading notion that the cycle of lives will continue, in the temporal sense, until nirvana is achieved. "The Pali imaginaire", as it has recently been put by Steven Collins, "is permeated with concern for temporality."[13] The concern relates to the fact that the purpose of following the Buddhist path is to achieve liberation from the cycle of lives (nirvana), which constitutes the cessation of one's experience of temporal continuity. So time is clearly associated with cyclical, pre-Enlightenment experience – the problem that needs solving. And the attaining of nirvana (more specifically one's death following nirvana) represents freedom from bondage to temporal continuity. If one brings this together with nirvana representing the cessation of (freedom from) delineation or spacial boundedness, as mentioned above, one can see that space and time are seen as restrictions, as are all the aspects of the manifold experiential world. All of the characteristics of the world of experience are restrictions in that, broadly speaking, they are part of the fundamental restriction of ignorance.

Similarly, the fundamental teaching that all the factors of cyclical experience are impermanent clearly associates all those factors with time: the concept of impermanence is temporal. More specifically in this context, what is stated is that all constructed things (*saṃkhārā*) are impermanent: this is one of the Three Characteristics of Existence. And what that constructedness refers to is making manifold as it applies to the cognitively constructed experiential world. It is the entirety of this cognitively constructed experiential world that is, in being impermanent, characterised by temporality. To relate this to nirvana again, it is significant that it is all 'constructed things' that are referred to as impermanent. Traditionally, nirvana is specifically excluded from 'constructed things' since it refers to gaining liberation *from* the 'constructed' world. So this formulaic characteristic of existence again indicates that temporality is intrinsic only to pre-Enlightenment experience.

An important reference to space and time together comes in the classical unanswered questions of Buddhism, to which I have referred in earlier chapters. These questions reflect the key concerns of the Buddha's contemporary religious seekers. In previous chapters I was referring to the questions more specifically as they related to issues concerning the self. But they also ask whether or not the world (in the cosmic sense) is eternal, and whether or not the world is finite.[14] Both of these questions (or, if one counts the 'whether or not' separately, these four questions) presuppose that space and time are transcendentally real – that is, that they operate externally to subjective cognitive processes. They seek to ascertain whether the world exists, at a transcendentally real level – that is, independently of all subjects, for ever (eternally) or only for a certain length of time, and whether it exists unboundedly (infinitely) or is finite in extent. As with the unanswered questions on the nature of the self, the formulation of these questions reflects the prevailing search at the time for permanence or immortality. If, however, as it seems to us at this stage what is stated in the early texts implies to be the case, space and time are part of the structural characteristics of the experiential world, and that that is cognitively dependent, then one can see that the presupposition of the transcendental reality of time and space is false, and that the fundamental premises on which the questions rest are therefore also false.

What this means is that though the questions are meaningful within a conceptual framework which assumes that space and time are transcendentally real, if space and time are *not* transcendentally real the questions are in effect unanswerable if one wishes to be truthful. Any formulation of a response within the same conceptual framework as the questions would not truthfully reflect a reality which does not conform to that conceptual framework. I think we come here to the crux of why the Buddha remained silent when asked these questions. According to the texts, when asked these and other similar questions he states that his reasons for not answering them are that to do so would not be conducive to attaining nirvana, and that to state that any of the possible situations is the case would constitute a view that is as wrong as any other view.[15] He states that what he, as an Enlightened man, has fully understood is the world that is experienced by all living beings. And in going on to urge the complete relinquishing of all views and opinions about beginnings and endings, the suggestion is that such matters, in not being coherent within that understanding of the true nature of the experiential world, are ultimately non-issues.[16] Put differently, the point is that the falsity of the premises of the conceptual framework within which the entirety of the experiential world operates is in fact the basis of the ignorance within which all cyclical experience continues. Not only are all metaphysical views held to within this conceptual framework false, then, but any questions asked within it cannot be answered truthfully. One might say that with insight into the nature of the experiential world comes the disappearing of all such questions. And one might further suggest that this point is implicitly made in the Buddha's doctrinal statement that all the factors of the experiential world (*saṃkhārā*) are impermanent: insight into the *nature* of that impermanence, as we can now understand it, is in fact 'seeing things as they really are'.

Elsewhere the Buddha is reported to state simply that the beginning of cyclical lives is unthinkable, that any beginning of ignorant existence is unknowable.[17] He also parodies and ridicules the cosmogonic myth of the brahmins.[18] And consistently in virtually all the contexts where such issues are referred to the point is made that the focus of attention should be to understand the Four Noble Truths, which, as we have seen, involves understanding the nature of the world of experience and how it operates – in order that one may attain liberation from continuity.

If, then, the entirety of the structure of the world as we know it is subjectively dependent, including space and time, it follows that the very *concept* of there being origins, beginnings, ends, extents, limits, boundaries, and so on, is subject dependent. The entirety of temporality and of spacial extension are concepts which do not operate independently of subjective cognitive processes. The entirety, that is to say, of dim and distant history, and of the furthest flung regions of outer space – the entirety of *whatever is knowable in temporal and spacial terms* – is not independent of subjectivity. The framework within which it is meaningful is in a very real sense a conceptual one.

Conversely, any insight gained at Enlightenment as to how reality as it were really is structured could not be conveyed accurately in conceptual terms. This reflects the point I made in Chapter Five with regard to whether nirvana was knowing whether or not one is or has a self. I stated that insight was not structured *in terms of* (conceptual categories which predicate) selfhood.

What we have arrived at here is an extension of the point made in earlier chapters that the entirety of the objective world, what one might otherwise refer to as the world of experience, and all of what is phenomenologically experienced as external to us, is correlated to subjectivity. We have earlier established the correlation between the subjective process of making manifold and the experience of the world of objective manifoldness(es). We have seen the way that objects, in other words, be they concrete or abstract as discussed, are subjectively reified: that their characteristics conform to and are correlated with the way cognitive processes operate. But what we are now seeing is that further aspects of the structural framework, as it were, of the objective world are similarly subjectively reified.

This correlation is referred to in the textual material by means of the terms internal and external. Earlier in this chapter I referred to this when I stated that the four great elements of form are said to have both internal and external application or relevance. Solidity, for example, relates both to the solid and extended parts of the human body, such as nails, teeth, bones, vital organs, and so on – and in this respect are part of the form-*khandha* as living body – and to the solid and extended parts of the world other than the body. Similarly, fluidity relates both to the fluid, liquid parts of the human body, such as blood, tears, saliva, urine, and so on, and to whatever is fluid and liquid in the external world: rains, for example, or oceans. Heat relates both to the bodily processes of maintaining temperature, digestion and decay, and also to climatic aspects of temperature and decay: the fanning of a spark to make a fire is cited by way of example. Mobility relates to the ability of the body and its parts to move around, and to distribute both blood and breath round itself, as well as, for example, to the way wind blows either gently or destructively strongly. Space, too, is said to relate as a characteristic of form both to the body-*khandha* and to whatever is external to it.[19]

What seems to be the main purpose of referring to both the internal and external aspects of the characteristics of form is that in meditation the subject is to realise that both are equally impermanent. Not only are all these aspects of the body – 'internal' form – subject to ageing, decay and eventual death and bodily dissolution, but all the external aspects are described in terms that are clearly intended to illustrate their impermanence. Solidity can be shaken up and disappear: it too is liable to destruction and decay, and it is constantly changing.[20] Rains can become floods which destroy settlements, and an ocean that is the equivalent of seven palm trees deep can dry out even to the extent that it will not come up to a single finger joint. Fire when out of control can burn up villages, whole towns, even districts and regions. But it can also be extinguished if it has no fuel. Likewise wind, when in violent mode, can destroy settlements and countryside of various kinds. But it can also fail to bring relief from heat, or stimulate the fanning of a fire.

As parts of meditative exercises, both the bodily (internal) and worldly (external) factors mentioned here are to be seen as impermanent. No matter how apparently solid and permanent they seem, however long they have been there, the nature of *all* the aspects of the experiential world is the same: constantly changing and impermanent.

That realising impermanence is the purpose of meditation is stated in other textual passages where more specific meditative exercises are described, particularly the mindfulness meditation mentioned earlier. The technique of mindfulness meditation is focused on a wide variety of objects – concrete, such as the body, and abstract, such as thoughts and teachings – in order that they should all be seen to be of like nature. Specifically, it is the generic dependently originated status of all things that the meditator should come to understand.[21] Elsewhere, a more graphic description of the body as an oozing, discharging, smelly, nine-holed object is intended to dissuade the meditator from identifying with it as his essential self by highlighting its messinesses. But notwithstanding the colourfulness of its language the point of the passage is clearly that one should realise the body is "impermanent, subject to erosion and decay, is perishable and subject to destruction".[22] As such, one is exhorted to be indifferent towards ('dis-enchanted with' has the appropriate connotations) it, as one should be towards all impermanent things.[23] The body is a commonly referred to object of meditation partly because it seems permanent, or permanent enough, to us to lend itself to being mistakenly thought of as one's 'identity', and partly because at the same time it lends itself to demonstrating impermanence and decay. In other words, the false identification with the body that one might easily have can be best overcome by meditating on its nature.

The contrast between internal and external aspects of the meditation exercises is mentioned in the descriptions of mindfulness meditation exercises. In this context the point is that one is instructed to meditate on one's own body, feelings, states of mind, and so on (whatever is the object of meditation on any given occasion), all of which are 'internal' in the sense of 'the meditator's' body, etc. And one is also to meditate on the bodies, feelings, states of mind, and so on, of other people, all of which are 'external' in the sense of being 'someone else's' body, etc.[24] Again, the point of this is to realise that impermanence is common to all.

If we return to the passage to which I was referring above, where it is the characteristics of form that are referred to as both internal and external, contrasting the form-*khandha* (one's body) with what is external in what one might call a more environmental sense, one can see that the generic impermanence of all things is more extensively suggested. And, more specifically for us here, a second purpose of this passage seems to be to suggest that the entirety of the structure of the objective characteristics of form are subjectively both correlated and reified. This is, I think, the point being made in the admittedly somewhat unclear last two pages of this chapter, following what it has to say about space.[25] In a rather roundabout way it seems to be stating that whatever the nature of the data one is conscious of experiencing, be it internal (subjective) or external (objective in the broad 'world about us' sense) (to make any sense of it, one has to assume the import of the earlier part of the chapter here), it is processed in the same way by one's cognitive apparatus (the *khandhas* and the senses are mentioned separately) according to the aforementioned structural characteristics of form (space is included here; time is implicit in the focus on impermanence). And insight into this is insight into dependent origination itself, which, it states, is the same as "seeing the *Dhamma*" – what is elsewhere referred to, as mentioned above, as 'seeing things as they really are'. This suggests to me that this is the heart of the teachings of early Buddhism: that there is a correlation between the entirety of the structure of what is experienced as the world about us – all objectivity – and the way it is subjectively processed.[26]

The issue that needs addressing at this stage, then, is: If the world of experience is entirely subjectively dependent and correlated, not only in terms of the objects that are more overtly made manifold but in terms of its entire structural characteristics, then just how real is that world? Is it the case, for example, that it is in some sense non-existent, a mere mentally constructed whim? If one's world of experience is subjectively dependent, to what extent is what one experiences the same as what someone else experiences? *Is* there anyone else? How can one know this? Is it, rather, just one person's mental construction? Is there some sort of mental 'stuff' that is manipulated by cognitive processes into 'objects'? To what extent does it make sense to think in terms of 'the natural world'? How meaningful is the work of physicists, and how might one understand it? And so on.

These questions are all to do with the ontological status of what there is, the question What is there? – a topic which has exercised a wide variety of disciplines for millennia, and a question that has been answered in a wide variety of incompatible ways by religious teachers, philosophers, scientists, and so on, in many places and at many times. It continues to fascinate. In our normal everyday perceptions, we assume that the world about us is independently real, what is called transcendentally real – that is, really existent external to and independently of us. And we assume that the separate parts of it are separately real too, what is called pluralistic realism. This is the nature of things as they really are, or Reality. Indeed, phenomenologically speaking – that is, how it seems to us – these assumptions actually characterise the way our everyday experience is structured. We feel that we are separate objects, albeit also experiencing subjects, *in* a separately existing plurally comprised world of other objects. And we take it that what we see is what there is.

In spite of these assumptions, though, we cannot actually ever get outside of ourselves to check whether this is in fact the case. However much we continue to assume transcendental realism, it can only ever be an act of faith. One cannot, in fact, even know for sure whether anyone else exists at all; they may *seem* to, but one cannot get outside of oneself to check that they really do. Everything operates fine if one assumes that they do, but if one really wants to know for sure one cannot do so. This is fascinating to some, and subversively traumatising to others.

In the West in fact we collectively tend to regard all of what I have said in the last paragraph as highfalutin nonsense (why on *earth* would one question if an apple is really an apple? is how a friend dismissively, but I think representatively, put it). As well as the three main religious traditions of Judaism, Christianity and Islam assenting to transcendental realism, we also tend to take it that our collective secular act of faith in transcendental realism is justified because of the way we understand our advanced scientific knowledge: that scientists have told us so much about the cells, waves, particles, and so on, of our world, that they have established for us the transcendental reality of that world; that if we know so much of the way it is comprised, to question its ontological status is absurd. So ingrained is this view that we happily ignore the irony that what we know from recent advanced science in fact makes our act of faith virtually certain to be a mistaken one, highly likely to be highfalutin nonsense itself.

By contrast, the Indian worldview differs radically in that there the assumption is that while the world might *appear* transcendentally real, in fact that appearance does not correspond to transcendental Reality. Though Indians like all other people experience the phenomenon of pluralistic realism, their underlying assumption tends to be that whatever Reality is outside of ourselves, it is not how it appears to us. It is true that in more recent decades, more Indians are being seduced (if I may dare so to put it) by the increasingly hegemonic 'scientific' view of the West. And there have always been Indian materialists who are exceptions to the generally accepted worldview, and one of the six so-called classical Indian worldviews, Nyāya-Vaiśeṣika, is usually cited as an example of pluralistic realism in India.[27] But such views have not been the norm. The realism of Nyāya-Vaiśeṣika, moreover, includes human souls – whose existence they maintain can be established by means of their particular formulation of logic. They use their logic (the system's method is what lends it to being studied in Western philosophy departments) to establish their realistic ontology. And the ultimate purpose of doing this (which is usually ignored in Western philosophy departments) is, as with virtually all Indian worldviews, soteriological. That the six classical systems are referred to as worldviews and not philosophies reflects this: their aim is to gain a view of – that is, to know in the experiential sense explained earlier – Reality, because such a view is believed to be significant soteriologically.

In spite of the fact that the view that what we see is not what there really is is common in India, there have been several suggestions as to what Reality actually is. Though the claims are variously arrived at, each worldview system giving a different order of priority to the epistemological validity of its sources, it is also the case that no one account of Reality is logically entailed in the appearance premise. Thus Sāṃkhya, for example, another of the classical Indian worldviews, is ontologically dualistic. Sāṃkhya states that Reality is – to put it in Western terminology – comprised of souls (numerically plural but ontologically identical) and matter (the plurality of which is only phenomenological). It is the proximity (which itself is unexplained) of souls to matter that causes matter to manifest as the phenomenological world. The problem for us as subjects is that in our ignorance what we mistakenly identify with (for each of us, our 'I') is in fact matter. Because of this we continue to suffer all the vicissitudes of rebirth. It is only when we see what we are doing, and perceive that in Reality each soul is transcendent of our thinking 'I', that the experience of rebirth ceases. Moreover, it is only at the level of the phenomenological 'I' – that is, matter – that rebirth is experienced: souls are in Reality unchanging and unaffected by rebirth.

Another of the classical worldviews of the Indian tradition is Śaṅkara's Advaita Vedānta, based on the *Upaniṣads*. Here, too, one's ignorance leads one to identify erroneously with a notion of

'I' in the sense of being a separate part of a plurally real world. Again it is this ignorance that leads to rebirth: in effect, one might say, for so long as one thinks one is part of such a world, one *is* part of it. Reality, though, is monistic – in this system, following the *Upaniṣads*, referred to as Brahman: whatever there is is Brahman. Moreover, Brahman is radically One, completely inactive and unchanging: our experience of plurality is entirely appearance, a level of reality founded solely on one's ignorance. The famous analogy given by Śaṅkara to illustrate the nature of reality based on ignorance is that of mistaking a rope for a snake. It is not that the snake one experiences is entirely non-existent, in the way that the son of a barren woman is: perceiving the snake induces all kinds of emotional, psychological and behavioural responses. But in fact there is really only a rope that has itself remained unchanging. Realising that the perspective of the world of plurality is a similar misinterpretation of Brahman, and that one's identity is in fact none other than Brahman (this is where the ontological formula *ātman*/self is Brahman comes in), constitutes liberation from rebirth. The name of this system reflects both its stance and its source: Vedānta means the end of the Veda in the sense of the last portion of the texts knows collectively as the *Veda*, which is what the *Upaniṣads* are, and Advaita means non-dual. For Śaṅkara what is stated in the *Upaniṣads* has absolute epistemological validity: he regards himself as an exegete. So this system is a non-dual interpretation of the *Upaniṣads*, formulated as a 'way of appearance', *vivartavāda*.

A different formulation of non-dualism within the Vedānta (that is, *Upaniṣadic* exegesis) tradition is the system propounded by Rāmānuja known as Viśiṣṭādvaita Vedānta. As its name states, this teaches qualified (*viśiṣṭa*) non-dualism (*advaita*). For Rāmānuja, while everything is Brahman, the experience of multiplicity is not *merely* an appearance. Rather, Brahman itself becomes – changes into – the manifest world: this is non-dualism formulated as a 'way of transformation', *pariṇāmavāda*. The relationship between Brahman and plurality (souls and the world), Rāmānuja states, is similar to that between a rose and its redness. The point of this for Rāmānuja (and one has to accept this on his terms in order to understand him) is that one cannot have a rose that is not of some colour: roseness and colour are in fact inseparable aspects of one thing, he says, but because they can be referred to separately one can properly think of the oneness as qualified. The actively changing nature of Brahman is crucial for Rāmānuja because though ontologically *ātman* is identical to Brahman in this qualified way, Rāmānuja believes that one is saved through the activity of grace that is also part of the nature of the oneness. Humans suffer both bondage to rebirth and ignorance of the nature of Reality (Brahman), and they have to seek to know the truth about Reality because this is what the *Upaniṣads* state they should do, but in this case, unusually in the classical Indian worldview systems, salvation is through grace. In fact it is certain that Rāmānuja was a sectarian theist first, and an *Upaniṣadic* exegete second, and that the point of his proceeding with the latter was to gain orthodox status for the former. His system nevertheless demonstrates a different Indian way of understanding Reality in the context of the prevailing view that things are not what they seem.

These and other Indian worldviews virtually all have, as I have stated, soteriological purposes. To ignore this point is in my opinion to do violence to them as systems of thought: it is not, that is to say, properly to empathise with their context, where they are coming from, what they are trying to do, the way one should interpret their premises, and so on. One can certainly extract sections of their writings for interest, and study them with no consideration of their context, and as intellectual exercises of a variety of kinds such an approach can be stimulating. But one does not arrive at an understanding of the worldview itself.

What can be helpful, however, in attempting to understand any of these worldviews is to use an ontological model in the purely philosophical sense as a way in, as a framework, so to speak. Particularly as in many of the systems of thought, their ontological stance is intrinsically relevant to their soteriological method. When faced, for example, with attempting to understand Śaṅkara, a Westerner might find it helpful to use the structure of absolute idealism as a model. I emphasise that I mean the *structure* of absolute idealism here, and not any detailed partisan kind of absolute idealism as propounded by A rather than B. The structure gives one the key factors of impersonal monism, and a phenomenological world of appearances. And one can then adapt this to reflect exactly how Śaṅkara understands it. Similarly, Sāṃkhya can be understood within the general framework of ontological dualism, one part of which is numerically plural. As well as adapting the models and filling in details, one naturally has to take into account key aspects of the relevant conceptual framework, in the Indian context almost always including the points I discussed in Chapter Two. Though helpful, then, it is crucial that one makes use of an appropriate ontological model loosely, at all times directing one's empathy towards the material one is working on rather than towards the model itself.

Even if others would prefer a different approach, with regard to any of the so-called classical Hindu worldviews, or the worldview of Jainism, there would, I think, be no reason to object to this suggestion on principle. As I said in the last paragraph, understanding their ontologies is a major factor in understanding the systems as a whole. So in using an ontological framework as a model one would not be in danger of distorting the material. But this is not the case with Buddhism, particularly the early Buddhism with which we are concerned here. The Buddha was consistent in maintaining his silence when asked ontological questions of a wide variety of kinds, formulated principally around the nature of the existence of the self and the world. Furthermore, not only is his teaching stated to be the Middle Way between *all* such views, in effect dismissing any possible permutation of them at a single sweep, but the mere holding to a view is considered to be one of the most binding of the continuity tendencies, one of the final four so-called *āsavas* that need to be 'rooted out'. We read in several contexts comments such as that it is considered 'nonsense-talk' to talk about whether there are things or nothing;[28] whether everything exists or nothing exists;[29] and that the very notions of both existence and non-existence and any combination of them, positive or negative, are 'just views';[30] and so on. No matter if this is incomprehensible and bewildering.[31]

Notwithstanding this, I think we are now in a situation both to see clearly why such an apparently non-ontological stance was so consistently maintained, and also of being able to suggest what one might loosely call an ontological model by means of which the nature of Reality might be understood in early Buddhism.

As I said above, the problem with expressing views, ontological or in fact otherwise too, is that they can only *be* expressed within a conceptual framework. And the only conceptual framework with which we are familiar, that has any meaningful reference for us, that is, indeed, conceptual as we mean that term, is one which is appropriate only from the standpoint of ignorance as to the nature of Reality. Specifically, talking in terms of things and nothing, existence and non-existence, is within the conceptual framework of manifoldness and permanence. What is more, when associated with the nature of Reality, it is talk that in fact assumes transcendental realism: that the structural framework of the experiential world is external to and independent of us. But in fact its meaningfulness is wholly limited to the world of experience understood not as it really is but as it seems to us in our ignorance to be. The Buddha having gained insight into how things really are, into the nature of Reality as it really is, knew that none of such questions could be truthfully answered.

This is precisely why understanding dependent origination, in the sense that subjectivity and objectivity are mutually dependently originated, means *one will no longer ask* questions about existence, past, future, or present, such as, 'is it/am I?' or 'is it/am I not?', 'what is it/am I?', 'why is it/am I?', 'this "thing" that it is/I am, where has it/have I come from, where will it/I go?'.[32]

In other words, the problem with the ontological questions the Buddha was asked was that they were formulated in too limited a way. If, then, one is to have any understanding of what the Buddha is said to have described as "deep, difficult to see and understand ... hard if one is of another view",[33] one has clearly got to be ready to relinquish one's 'either/or', 'is/is not' way of thinking. In short, one has to be ready to attempt to accept the unthinkable.

Before discussing the structure within which I suggest one might do this, though, I need to explain why I do not consider certain other structures to be more appropriate. In particular, some of the questions I raised above in introducing the issue of the reality of the world, such as Is there anyone else? How can one know this? Is it, rather, just one person's mental construction? imply the possibility that the early Buddhist material suggests solipsism. This needs to be discussed not only because solipsism might be thought to be compatible with the mutually dependent subjective/objective world of experience as I have described it, but also because in fact it is logically irrefutable. There actually is no way I can check for myself that there is anyone else: the nature of experience precludes my getting outside of myself in order to do this.

There are, however, several reasons why I think solipsism is not what the Buddhist material is suggesting. First and in fact in any case, I think it can be rejected on the grounds that "As a serious conviction ... [solipsism] could be found only in a madhouse; as such it would then need not so much a refutation as a cure."[34] It seems to me that from a sane point of view, it is simply inconceivable that I alone have experienced, not to mention created, every tiny aspect of the entire course of human history, even insofar as I know it. Aside from this, it also seems to me that the Buddhist texts themselves affirm that this is not their view. They are replete with references to a multitude of different people, of many different occupations and statuses, who express a wide variety of views. Not only are such references to be found as it were randomly throughout the early texts, narratives and discourses frequently referring to whoever is listening to, or arguing with, the teacher, and so on, but there are also numerous specific references to a multi-populated world. Perhaps the most relevant is the second of the Buddha's insights at Enlightenment – that he saw other beings being born and reborn according to their previous actions. It would be utterly bizarre to suggest that this might be compatible with a teaching of solipsism. I have also referred several times to the classic passages in which other 'views' are mentioned, for example. And comparable passages refer to 'types' of people according to whether they are Enlightened, ignorant, average, virtuous, or characterised by any number of other qualities.[35] One might even suggest that in many respects the multiplicity of people and views are crucial to the way the teachings are recorded. The Buddha is described as one man among many who were engaged in a spiritual quest. His teachings are given in the context of their difference from and superiority to those of others. Points are made and issues are clarified by virtue of comparing them with what others think. All of this is intended to encourage others to practise his teachings themselves. This ties in with the rationale for giving the teachings at all, which is so that others might attain the Enlightenment experience that the Buddha claimed he had. It was to this end, from the first sermon onwards, that the intention was to spread the word of the Buddha to as many others as possible. There is absolutely no evidence that the Buddha claimed to be anything but an exemplar for others, and beyond claims that his teachings were right and those of others misleading or pointless, there is certainly no evidence that he might have been an egoist of the monumental and peculiar kind that claims to solipsism suggest. In short, even if one were to choose to argue the case that the Buddhist teachings suggest solipsism, in my view this would be to distort what one finds in the canonical material so grossly that the argument would be unsupportable.

Aside from possible solipsism, other questions I proposed above, such as Is it the case that the world is in some sense non-existent, a mere mentally constructed whim? and Is there some sort of mental 'stuff' that is manipulated by cognitive processes into 'objects'? suggest that one also needs to consider the possibility of what is called idealism as the most appropriate model for the ontological structure underpinning the Buddhist material. Idealism might loosely be described as the theory that 'all there *is* is the mind', in the sense of 'there is no external world, there is *only* mind-stuff: this is what the world *is*.' This is how some have interpreted certain later, Mahāyāna, forms of Buddhism, notably the 'Mind Only' (*citta-mātra*) school of Yogācāra Buddhism. There has been disagreement as to whether the name of this school of Buddhism is representative of its idealism in the ontological sense, or whether it refers to the fact that the focus of the practice of yoga ('practice of yoga' is what *yogācāra* means) is only the workings of the mind.[36] The latter would give priority to the method for attaining liberating insight and leave aside the issue of any underlying ontology, and the former would take it that this form of Buddhism teaches that 'all there is is the mind', in the way I have just described.

With regard to early Pali Buddhism, the general view among scholars and Buddhists alike has tended to be a practical acceptance of Theravāda Buddhism's cosmological schema. That is to say, what one might call a working realism is understood, usually as tangential to the theme of a work which itself is not concerned with the issue of ontology. Even works whose aim is to draw out the extensive use of imagery and metaphor in the early texts have not tended to question the underlying ontology.[37] This has been partly because the focus of the Buddha's teachings is generally regarded as being 'not about ontology', both because he refrained from answering a multitude of questions regarding the ontological status of self and world, and because holding to any ontological position is considered to be holding to an erroneous 'view'. Thus the adoption of what I have called a working realism has largely been for pragmatic reasons rather than to make any ontological point. It has also perhaps partly been because it is not generally recognised that Theravāda Buddhism came to adopt the multilevelled cosmological schema in a real and spacial sense only relatively late in the development of the tradition. The evidence in the earliest texts, the *Sutta Piṭaka* on which I am drawing, suggests that originally cosmological references were focused on the world as metaphor for the life of the individual as I outlined in Chapter Four. There was simply no interest shown in the spacial cosmos in an ontological sense. Later texts developed the imagery into the psychological cosmology I have previously referred to.[38] It was only recently, however, that it has been pointed out that it was not until later stages of the tradition that Theravāda textual exegetes took the metaphorical structure literally. They "lost the original metaphorical structure ... [and] reified the ethical teaching into a hierarchic cosmology."[39] Thus the prevailing understanding of Theravāda Buddhism has resulted in a situation in which anyone not specifically concerned to investigate ontological issues has gone along with what is in fact a late development in the tradition without realising it.

Notwithstanding this general situation, there have also been suggestions, albeit largely implicit or tangential to the main theme of the respective works, that one should understand the early Buddhist material with which I am now concerned in the idealist sense explained above. Some have implied this in the way they have translated ambiguous passages from the Pali into English,[40] or have brought the implication into what they have called the psychology of Buddhism.[41] Others have concentrated on the fact that Buddhist meditation is intended to 'de-construct the phenomenal world', or have arrived at interpreting the early Buddhist teachings in terms of a 'phenomenology' not incompatible with idealism.[42]

It is certainly also the case that the material as we have come to understand it does in several respects lend itself to an idealistic interpretation. The way in which the manifoldness of the world of experience is dependent on cognition is a key feature of idealism. And there are many references in the texts to the effect that the cessation of the world (*loka-nirodha*) is linked to the cessation of experience (*dukkha-nirodha*), as cited in Chapter Four. Even more explicitly the world is also referred to as 'empty', or 'void' (*suñña*), because all the objects of which it is comprised are impermanent because they are sensorily dependent.[43] For this reason the world 'disintegrates' with the disintegrating of the sensory process. Its very status as world is based on this.[44]

Prima facie, then, from the generality of the evidence one might readily argue that there is a strong suggestion of idealism in the early Buddhist material. And based on this, one might conclude that the reality of the world is 'mental' in some way, whether imaginary or in terms of mentally constructed 'mind-stuff'. As it were outside of this, it has no reality: this is, as it were, the limit of its reality.

I think, however, that the argument for idealism understood in this way would overlook several of the more particular features of the evidence, and would rely on a misinterpretation of the various passages cited above. Taken together, I suggest that a more appropriate model for our purposes would be that of what is called transcendental idealism. Before elaborating, in the light of the multitude of problems associated with taking any such 'view' as discussed above, I would first reiterate that one needs to approach the using of this model with caution. It is extremely unlikely that an ontology that might be compatible with what the Buddha taught would have been expressed, or even endorsed, by him in terms of a specific philosophical theory. Pinned down in such a way it would undoubtedly have been rejected along with other 'views'. And it is also the case that none of the various ontological views of the time was expressed as a systematic philosophy. Even the views of those that were systematised during following centuries, such as those described earlier in this chapter, were not presented by their proponents in terms of packages whose ontological stance could be indicated by a philosophical label. Useful as I believe it can be, this is an approach that is very much associated with twentieth century academic study of the Indian tradition as a whole. In using the model I am not, therefore, suggesting that the Buddha did or necessarily would have put it this way, and the model itself needs to be loosely understood and loosely applied: not, that is, along with any of the specific minor characteristics attributed to it by anyone with whom the model is associated in the Western philosophical tradition.

Transcendental idealism is the philosophical theory that what we take to be the 'external' world (in the cosmic sense) about us, with us 'in' it, only appears to us like that because that is the way our cognitive apparatus presents it to us, not because Reality is in itself really like that. We are unable to see Reality as it is in itself because we cannot transcend our cognitive apparatus. But we only experience the world *at all* because Reality is actually there: what we are experiencing is our *interpretation of* a transcendentally existent Reality. Put differently, one might say that our worldly experience and the transcendentally existent are twin aspects of Reality as a whole. But apart from its existence, nothing at all, of any nature whatsoever, can be known about the transcendental aspect because, *in being* transcendent, it is beyond any of our cognitive conceptual categories. In fact, being transcendent of the entire framework of our conceptual categories, Reality itself can properly be indicated only apophatically – even the notion of 'existence' being problematic in this respect in that the properties so predicated are meaningful only within our conceptual framework. Though in the West – through its association with Kant, who first formulated this theory – transcendental idealism can be and is sometimes associated with God, in fact the philosophical theory stands on its own. And it is strictly in this as it were God-less sense that I am using it as a model.

What I am suggesting now, then, is that though the world of experience is, as I have been suggesting above, cognitively dependent – that subjectivity and objectivity are correlated in the way we have discussed, the material also implies that there is in fact a further dimension to Reality as a whole. First and most importantly, I think this is implicit in the dependent nature of the world of experience. If objectivity – what we think of as experienced – is 'only' dependent on subjectivity, the implications of this lead one inexorably to one of two possibilities. One is some form of solipsism, my reasons for rejecting which I have given above. The other is idealism and the fundamental unReality of the world, as some form of figment of a collective imagination. And, as I have also stated above, my reasons for rejecting this are that it overlooks the relevant factors I shall be bringing into the discussion below. It further and significantly seems to me that if dependence were 'limited' in this way, it would not have been necessary for the Buddha to have been so careful to remain silent when asked questions about the world's finitude and eternality.

Rather, I think the material suggests that the experiential world as a whole, in which all subjectivities and the whole of objectivity are as it were parts of what is dependently originated, is dependent – period. And it follows from this that there *must* be something else. If there were not, the empirical world – this world of experience taken as a whole – would have to be autonomous. And this would directly compromise, both explicitly and implicitly, the Buddha's teaching on dependent origination. There must, therefore, be a Reality which is transcendent of experience on which the experiential world is dependent. And it is, I suggest, the common human experience *of* transcendent Reality (whatever 'it' is – once again constraints of language preclude any less singularising alternative – in *itself*, whatever its nature, it is clearly not, and *cannot* be, part of experience) that constitutes the empirical world.

It is in order to draw out the complementarity between the empirical world of shared human experience and whatever it is that that experiential world is dependent on that the model of transcendental idealism is useful. And the sense in which it is crucially different from idealism as it is usually understood lies in this transcendental dimension. Idealism as it is usually understood posits that all there *is* is mind, or mental constructions; in that respect it can be stated that nothing is as it were Really real. Transcendental idealism, rather, states that while the world of experience is subjectively conditioned and what there Really is is transcendent of what can be experienced, we can *have* the experience that we do only *because* the transcendentally Real is there.

I have come to think this is precisely the meaning of the famous (and famously ambiguous) passage which states:

> "There is an unborn, an unbecome, an unconstructed, an unconditioned, without which the resultant born, become, constructed, conditioned could not be known [experienced]. But because there is an unborn, an unbecome, an unconstructed, an unconditioned, the resultant born, become, constructed, conditioned can be known [experienced]."[45]

And it is striking that the meaningfulness of this statement does not lie in its positing of entities, things, the 'what'-ness of the world. Rather, it lies in its indicating the significance of the relatedness of transcendent Reality (the unborn), and the empirical world (the born), and experience. And I think the negatives – unborn, unbecome, and so on – should be understood only in the sense that they serve to highlight the contrast between transcendent Reality and the experiential world, which is described in Buddhism as conditioned and therefore 'born', 'become' (not independent is the point).

Perhaps less substantially, another point in favour of transcendental idealism in the context of the early Buddhist material is the extent of the Buddha's concern with the human lot. Acquaintance with the material leaves one in little doubt of the genuineness of his concern at an existential level, the reality of which is such as to present the problem that is the *raison d'être* of all of his teachings.

There is not even the merest suggestion of 'never mind, it is all ultimately unreal anyway'. On the contrary, when questioned the Buddha insists that *dukkha*, experience, exists. It is this that he knows and sees.[46] Nor is there any suggestion that, in Reality, nothing exists. Again, quite the reverse. Though questions as to the actual nature of the world remain unanswered, we read in several passages to which I have previously referred that talking about what there is in terms of non-existence is *as wrong* as predicating its [permanent] existence. We also read that having the view that nothing exists "smells of something not cooked properly (raw)".[47] The expression has the sense of dismissal of an infantile or absurd view: raw or undigested as in un-thought[-through]. And in the context of the passage as a whole, it further suggests that such a view is highly disadvantageous to making progress along the path, reflecting an impure state of mind. In short, it is plain ignorance.[48]

The voidness or emptiness of the world, expressions to which I have referred earlier in this chapter, are properly understood in the sense of void or empty of permanence, of the independence we erroneously assume it to have. The Pali texts refer to this in terms of self-hood, and its meaning, corresponding to the Mahāyāna use of the expression as discussed in earlier chapters, is revealed in that in relating this to the sensory process as it does, the point is not that something does not exist, but that the notion of its independence is a product of the subjectively dependent cognitive structuring of the world.[49] Similarly, the associating of the disintegrating of the world with the way the sensory process 'disintegrates' as it is ever changing, refers to the way the features of the world are discerned, and their nature as it were interpreted or imposed by us, rather than to their unreality.[50] One needs to grasp that the point being made is about the process, not the object. This corresponds to the need to understand references to the cessation of the world, the end of the world, and so on, as metaphors, as I have suggested. They refer to the cessation of ignorance.

The real point here is that such passages are not questioning the fact of what there is. The focus of the teachings as a whole is experience. As the subject of the first Noble Truth, this could not be clearer. And far from denying its reality in any respect, the teachings are about what is happening in order that *that* is what we experience. They are not stating that all there *is* is what we experience, and that there is Really nothing. In relating the structure of that empirical world to the structure of the cognitive processes, they are explaining the manner in which we experience the empirical world.

This is the focus of transcendental idealism too. Rather than denying the reality of the experiential world, experiential reality is what it seeks to explain. The subject/object structure of the empirical world, characterised as it is according to space and time and various primary and secondary characteristics, can be understood on the one hand, as is usually the case, as the natural world, the world that is the arena of concepts and language and science. On the other hand, it can also be understood in terms of the way cognitive processes operate in relation to a transcendent Reality. In both cases the reality of experience is affirmed. In the second case, the epistemological mechanics of experience are also explained.

The correlation of the structure of the empirical world with subjective cognitive processes informs us that the limits of the empirical world *as we know it* are associated with the limits of cognition *as we know it*. And in the context of the Buddhist teachings as a whole, what this is establishing is that the limit of the world of (pre-Enlightenment) experience as a whole is correlated to the limit of ignorance. The limit of this correlation is also the limit of the problem the Buddha set out to solve. But none of this is stating that that is all there *is*.

Rather, it is explaining that it is false either to assert that the world of experience, and/or any of what we take to be its components, Really exist, or that it and/or they Really do not exist, because both such terms predicate characteristics of independence which do not apply to it/them. Put differently, one might say that it is not that all of the characteristics which underpin the structure of the experiential world, and all of its conceptual categories, are either real or unreal, existent or non-existent, right or wrong. They are simply experiential. Furthermore, while Reality encompasses this, and indeed is a necessary condition for this, it, too, cannot be described in such terms because *the terms* are experiential. All such terms, predicating as they do external and independent existence in a way that is congruent only with subjective and ultimately inappropriate criteria, are applicable *neither* to the world of experience *nor* to ultimate Reality. As the texts put it, one who sees the world as it really is does not talk about existence or non-existence.[51] And one can say of the holding of all and any views predicated in such a way, that they are inappropriate, misleading, to be relinquished. Thus it is that the rooting out of all views is one of the binding continuity tendencies, and the Buddha's teachings are intended to bring one to realising this.

Though nothing can be said about the nature of the transcendentally existent aspect of Reality, one can at this stage draw out one or two further points about what can be known of the nature of experience. I stated above that the limit of the (pre-Enlightenment) experiential world is correlated to the limit of ignorance. This is, I think, a different way of putting the same point that is being made when the world is used as a metaphor for an individual life. In Chapter Four I cited passages which stated, for example, that an Enlightened person "is said to have come to the end of the world, he lives at the end of the world, he has overcome attachment to the world."[52] And that the Buddha stated: "I declare that the end of the world is not to be learned, seen, or attained by going to the end of the world. Nor do I declare that the end of experience can be made without attaining the end of the world."[53] Several points follow from this. The first is that in gaining insight, the cessation of ignorance, one gains insight into the nature of both oneself *and* of the world, a point I made in Chapter Five. Though the Buddha consistently draws attention away from externals to internals, so to speak, it is by means of focussing on cognitive processes that experience as a whole, the subjective/objective correlation, is understood. This is what experience is: neither the world nor 'I' in it are *other than* experience. In focussing on the understanding of the *khandhas*, in fact what one ends up with is an understanding of a breathtaking – certainly inconceivable, and one might in all seriousness say mind-blowing – profundity.

Second, and leading on from this, from what we are happy to accept about the nature of objectivity, one can draw out profound implications for the nature of subjectivity. Though I have discussed in this and earlier chapters the way subjectivity and objectivity are correlated, the discussions have been what one might call subject-focused. That is to say, I have pointed out the ways in which the structure and characteristics of objectivity are referred to in the early texts in terms of subjective processes. But what one can extrapolate from the correlation must surely also work the other way. If a certain characteristic is a factor of objectivity, it must correlate with a corresponding subjective process. And looking at the correlation as it were this way round, from the objective to the subjective, suggests a subjective complexity far beyond the basic structural characteristics of what we associate with so-called normal perception. We readily acknowledge, for example, that there are vast areas of *worldly* complexity about which we are at present ignorant *even as to their nature*. If, as is suggested by the Buddha's teachings, these are subjectively correlated, then it is highly likely that there are corresponding complexities in our cognitive faculties about which we are also at present ignorant in like manner. Furthermore, from twentieth century discoveries in the world of physics, some of which seem literally incredible, we know that there are activities and behaviours of parts of the objective world that are both unobservable *and unimaginable*. This suggests that any attempt to understand subjectivity in intellectualisably limited terms might be seriously reductionist.

It follows from this that the limits of what is knowable, the limits of the world of experience, might be very considerably beyond what we might at first think they are. It is possible, that is to say, not only that what we do not (yet) know about ourselves and our world might be open to us in a way we do not tend to think it is, but also that the *way* that we know it might not be limited to the extent that we tend to think it is. Put differently, if our subjective processes might be able to work in ways of which we are not yet aware, we might eventually be able to know a great deal about what we currently think simply cannot be known.

This suggestion would of course come as no surprise to a Buddhist. But that it can be made in terms of an implication that can be drawn from material contained in the texts, as I have, might surprise. Buddhists usually accept the possibility of the transformation of the cognitive faculties in effect as an act of faith.

The correlation between subjectivity and objectivity, and the way this is described in the texts, has one further implication to be drawn out here. A slightly different way of referring to all of the features of objectivity would be in terms of a spectrum of density.[54] The characteristics of what is collectively referred to in terms of form are structured in this way: density and extension, liquidity or fluidity, mobility and temperature, all combine in varying degrees of density, from a diamond to imperceptible vapour. In addition there is all of what collectively can be referred to only in terms of name, also referred to in the texts as formless (*arūpa*). These are all correlated subjectively: one's body, the form-*khandha*, comprised according to the same characteristics as objective form, from teeth and bones to breath and bodily cavities, and one's ability to think abstractly corresponding to whatever is name. The entire range of density and subtlety corresponds to the entire range of whatever is concrete and abstract both subjectively and objectively.

What one might generally call the form aspects of all this are relatively simple to understand. The way one's bodily characteristics as it were mirror similar characteristics of the objective world is not too conceptually, or even phenomenologically, problematic. But the correlation of what is name is less straightforward, and certainly the implications of it are less obvious. This is particularly the case if one considers the nature of abstractness. Though I have in earlier chapters referred to whatever is name in terms of its object status, this has tended to overlook the significance of its abstract status. The latter is suggested if one looks at descriptions of stages of meditation.[55] These explain that meditative exercises result in levels of experience that are characterised by progressively less form-bound features. The very first level involves the early stages of relinquishing sensory attachment and states of mind that detract from making progress.[56] At successive levels, boundaries are gradually seen for what they are (that is, subjectively imposed: "constructed and cognition dependent" is what the text states[57]) by means of progressively extending one's empathy in various ways. The teaching is that by using feelings such as friendliness, compassion, sympathetic joy, and non-partiality one understands that boundaries are as it were self-imposed.[58] In also being part of what is constructed and cognition dependent, even these states need to be understood as impermanent. But each level nevertheless confers a degree of 'freedom of mind' (*cetovimutti*): freedom from being grounded in the lower, more concrete levels of experience. Eventually, so-called formless levels described as the complete "transcending of apperceptions or conceptions of form", "unbounded [that is, un-boundaried] awareness", and "the plane of no-thing-ness [that is, non-manifoldness]" are experienced.[59] Having experienced these levels, and realised the role of cognition dependent construction, one sees 'the way things really are' and is able to uproot the binding continuity tendencies.

What this suggests is that there is a correlation between what is objectively most dense with ignorance (which is but an extension of a common metaphor in our own culture) and between what is most subtle and rarefied with subjective insight (we tend to refer, in this respect, to brightness). The more abstract the experience, that is to say, the less it is grounded in concrete boundaried-ness, and the more conducive it is to seeing the nature of constructedness.

Increasing abstraction eventually involves transcending (as it were) even the formless level of name alone: non-manifoldness is neither form *nor* name. I referred to this point in Chapter Five, where I cited a reference which states that in deep meditation what is experienced at a level that is beyond differentiating criteria leaves an 'abstract impression'.[60] What is experienced – that is, what leaves the impression – even at such rarefied levels, is objective. Subjectively, one is aware in a correspondingly entirely non-manifold way. One of the points I made in Chapter Five in this context was that such trans-manifold experiences *can* be interpreted according to manifold criteria, cognitively processed in the way that all other experiential data are. But the point of following the Buddha's teachings is that eventually one acquires the ability to understand the implications of what one is doing, that cognitively processing it transforms according to name-and-form criteria what is *not* manifold. And also, the material further implies, one becomes able to understand it *without* processing it. And in not processing it, as it were, both the subjective and objective aspects of such rarefied experience remain, again as it were, rarefied: one's construction of subjectivity is as correspondingly abstract as one's construction of objectivity.

This correlation between increasing abstractness or subtlety and spiritual progress (which is what we are talking about here in the Buddhist context) is also to be seen in references in the texts to subtle modes of existence, to which I have already briefly referred. We read that with greater insight one also gains the ability to effect a subtle mode of being, referred to as a mind-made body.[61] And some beings exist 'only' abstractly or conceptually.[62] Any of such beings are able to behave in a manner which is not restricted to the normal boundaries of other objective forms. Examples given in the texts include having a body which extends over two or three villages, but which is harmless to others;[63] and, more frequently, the ability to fragment and subsequently re-unify oneself, to be visible or invisible, to pass through solid objects or the ground on which one is walking, to walk on water without sinking, and to fly through the air.[64] Such abilities can also be utilised by those who, in gaining insight into how their cognitive apparatus works and having understood the creative power of that process, have gained the ability to use that apparatus to different effect. This is referred to in terms of the supernormal powers (*iddhis*) that are acquired at advanced stages of the path, and in effect one can make oneself into anything one wishes. The analogy given in the text is of a skilled potter or his apprentice being able to make or create out of well prepared clay any shape of bowl he likes.[65] Occasional references are also made to occasions when the Buddha disappears from one place and instantaneously reappears elsewhere, for example from one side of a river in spate to the other.[66]

In other words, increasingly abstract experiences can be understood as corresponding to increasingly less dense bodily, or even conceptual, existence, and/or being subject to increasingly fewer of the restrictions associated with density. Though the texts actually describe such modes of existence, the point here seems to be to emphasise that one's 'normal' experiential existence is correlated with one's state of mind in the sense that ignorance 'creates' one's dense physical body. This is stated in a passage I have referred to before: "Volitional activities volitionally construct the conditioned phenomenon that is the body ...".[67] One might say that one's conscious identification with one's separate manifoldness, which in Buddhist terms corresponds to the density of ignorance, is correlated with the continuity of a correspondingly dense physical body. And that increasing insight brings with it freedom from the restrictions associated with that body. As one's mind 'becomes great' (*mahaggata*), in the sense of becoming unrestricted by the boundaries of manifoldness, one sees that *all* manifoldness, including the grossest density of form, is correlated with ignorance.[68] And one is able thereby to release, so to speak, one's dense body from its restrictions.

Such possibilities are not uncommon within the broad range of Indian religious teachings. There, the acceptance of the practice of yoga – meditative disciplines which radically affect the way the mental faculties operate – has resulted in, or rather included, the acceptance of correlated possibilities with regard to one's body. So widely and for so long have they been accepted, that the concern there is usually not to make claims for their possibility but to guard against their abuse – either for material gain or for seeking spiritual status. The latter was such a concern of the Buddha's that such abuse became one of only four so-called forbidden acts for members of the monastic order, bringing with it self-expulsion from the community.

In the West such possibilities are considered as absurd as the possibility of radically altering one's cognitive apparatus. But anyone who is inclined to accept the correlation between subjectivity and objectivity as feasible, however notionally, must surely consider the need for a greater degree of open-mindedness – quite literally, one might say – as to the nature at least of subjective cognitive processes, if he is to avoid being forced to ignore what we already know to be the case with objective processes.

It is worth noting here, too, that the unknown extent of what is involved in the correlation between subjectivity and objectivity as I have discussed indicates that there is a great deal of room for aspects of what in Buddhism is generally referred to as *saṃsāra*, the cycle of lives, to occur in ways of which we are not aware. *All* of what occurs to any being prior to Enlightenment is within this experiential, here Buddhists would say conditioned, arena. It is not, that is to say, that rebirth involves sorties into and out of the conditioned arena from the arena of transcendent Reality. It is not until he gains Enlightenment that the Buddha says he has achieved liberation from *saṃsāra* as a whole. Rather, what is suggested is an area of the experiential realm of which we are normally simply unaware.

The status of the world, then, is in every sense not one that is understandable in any terms which relate to existence or non-existence. Rather, it is dependently originated. One can say that it is not non-existent because it *is* dependently originated. But because it is dependently originated it is not in itself – that is, *in*dependently – existent. It is not meaningful, though, to state that it is both existent and non-existent, nor that it is neither existent nor non-existent. The point, to put it differently, is that the reality of experience is experiential. And the reality of Reality is unknowable in (normal) experiential terms. The aim for the Buddhist is to understand the nature and limits of experience by means of understanding the nature and extent of one's subjective cognitive apparatus. As the text states, in understanding experience one also understands the world.[69] In Buddhist terms, this subjectively and objectively correlated insight is knowing and seeing how things really are.

Notes

1 Some of what is contained in this chapter was first given in a lecture at London University's School of Oriental and African Studies in November 1995, subsequently re-written for publication as "The 'External' World: its Status and Relevance in the Pali Nikayas" (Hamilton, 1999).

2 DN I 223; SN I 15, and see also *Sutta Nipāta* 1036–7.

3 *Sutta Nipāta* 734: *viññāṇassa nirodhena n'atthi dukkhassa sambhavo.*

4 SN I 13, 35.

5 *Sutta Nipāta* 1100.

6 MN I 185ff.

7 MN I 423, III 241; DN III 247; AN I 176.

8 MN I 352: *rūpasaññānaṃ samatikkamā* ... *ākāsānañcāyatanaṃ.*

9 *Abhisaṃkhatā abhisañcetayitā.*

10 SN IV 174f; MN I 135, 260.

11 SN IV 372. Masefield (1983, p. 81) draws on such terms to illustrate that nirvana "is spoken of as a place as often as it is a state of mind" and to suggest "There is ... no reason why we should not take such expressions quite [spacially] literally." As is obvious from my discussion here and elsewhere, I disagree with this.

12 SN IV 373. *Kāyagatā sati*, mindfulness of the body, is given. I think the use of the body in such contexts is pragmatic, in that it most readily presents itself as a meditation object for understanding impermanence. All dependently originated things are impermanent, and the purpose of meditating on any/all such things is to understand their generic nature.

13 Collins, 1998, p. 240. Part I of Collins' book is entitled "Nirvana in and out of time" and deals with many aspects of time in Theravāda Buddhist sources as a whole. His discussion is, however, concerned with different issues from those with which I am dealing in this book.

14 See, for example, MN I 428ff.

15 The fullest discussions are found in the *Pāsādika Suttanta*, DN III 134ff, and the *Brahmajāla Sutta*, DN I 12ff, but more concise references to the unanswered questions are also found at MN I 428ff; SN II 223, V 418.

16 DN III 135ff.

17 *Nānattavagga* of the *Dhātu Saṃyutta*, SN II 140ff. See also SN II 178f, 187ff; III 149ff; V226, 441. I do not think it is correct to state that the early texts regard cosmic time to be infinite since the universe has neither beginning nor end (Gombrich, 1996, p. 87). The point is the inconceivability of a beginning: this is why questions regarding the finitude or otherwise of the universe were not answered by the Buddha.

18 This has been extensively discussed by Gombrich (1992b and 1996). See also Gethin, 1997.

19 All these examples are found in MN I 184ff. See also MN I 421ff., AN II 164. The Pali terms for internal and external are *ajjhataṃ* and *bahiddhā.*

20 Again, this and the following examples are found in MN I 184ff. Rather quaintly, the only reading for *pakuppati*, the term I have rendered as 'be shaken up', given in the Pali-English Dictionary (p. 380) is 'to be angry'.

21 The key texts on mindfulness meditation, *sati*, are at MN I, *sutta* 1 and DN II, *sutta* 22. See also Lang, 1994, who cites (p. 150) *Sutta Nipāta* 487: "The Tathāgata ... perceives with insight [the nature of] all phenomena".

22 AN IV 386.

23 The term I have translated as exhorting indifference or dis-enchantment is *nibbindathā*. For reasons why I do not think it should be understood, as it sometimes has been, to mean 'be disgusted' see Hamilton, 1996, chapter 8. The body is referred to as impermanent in the same way as a wide variety of other things at MN I 500.

24 This is the traditional interpretation of 'internal' and 'external' in these contexts, possibly because this is how the commentarial tradition has interpreted them: at MA I 249 and DA III 765 *ajjhattaṃ* is taken as *attano* – of oneself – and *bahiddhā* as *parassa* – of another.

25 MN I 190f.

26 I am not aware of any other interpretation of this passage, and given the content of the earlier part of the chapter it seems to me highly likely that this is the point of it.

27 The views of Nyāya–Vaiśeṣika have been made accessible to Westerners in recent years mainly by the late Bimal Matilal: see in particular his *Perception.*

28 SN V 419: *tiracchānakathaṃ*, literally 'animal-talk', perhaps our colloquial 'gobbledegook' would come closest to it. The Pali for talking about things or nothing is *itibhavābhavakathaṃ*.

29 SN II 76, 77: *sabbaṃ atthīti ... sabbaṃ natthīti.*

30 In particular see the *Aggi-Vacchagotta Sutta*, MN I 483ff.

31 ibid, p. 487.

32 SN II 27.

33 MN I 487.

34 Schopenhauer in his *The World as Will and Representation*, i.104, quoted in Magee, 1997, p. 122. I am indebted to Bryan Magee's book *The Philosophy of Schopenhauer* for stimulating my interest in the parallels between what is suggested in the early Buddhist texts and the thinking of Kant and Schopenhauer.

35 Interesting examples are found at SN II 152ff.

36 Different views are given in, for example, Paul Williams, 1989; Thomas Kochumuttom, 1982; and Ian Harris, 1991.

37 I think Steven Collins was the first to write in some detail on the imagery in the Pali material in his *Selfless Persons* (1982). Richard Gombrich has also written widely on the Buddha's use of metaphor and allegory. An example is his "The Buddha's Book of Genesis" (1992b).

38 See Chapter Four, notes 13 and 14.

39 Gombrich, 1996b, p. 85. The reference to ethical teaching reflects the fact that the original metaphorical structure related to the spiritual path, progress along which has a strong ethical dimension.

40 For example, Johansson, 1979: see p. 83.

41 Ibid, *passim*, and Reat, 1990.

42 For example, Lang, 1994, and Kalupahana, 1975. Harvey (1995a) gives an interesting and useful critical discussion of certain aspects of Kalupahana's and others' work.

43 SN IV 54.

44 *Lujjati ... tasmā lokoti vuccatīti*: SN IV 52.

45 *Udāna 80f: atthi bhikkhave ajātaṃ abhūtaṃ akataṃ asaṃkhataṃ, no ce taṃ bhikkhave abhavissa ajātaṃ abhūtaṃ akataṃ asaṃkhataṃ, na yidha jātassa bhūtassa katassa saṃkhatassa nissaraṇaṃ paññāyetha. Yasmā ca kho bhikkhave atthi ajātaṃ abhūtaṃ akataṃ asaṃkhataṃ, tasmā jātassa bhūtassa katassa saṃkhatassa nissaraṇaṃ paññāyati 'ti.* My phrasing does not overlook the genitives – which I take in the sense of 'the issuing of what is born, become ...': it merely makes more sense of the passage in English. In order to support his spacial understanding of nirvana, Masefield (1983, p. 83) translates

these genitives as ablatives: that one 'escapes from' the born 'to' (spacially) the unborn.

46 SN IV 20: *na kho natthi dukkhaṃ; atthi kho dukkhaṃ ... jānāmi dukkham passāmi dukkhaṃ.*

47 *Sutta Nipāta* 43: *natthikadiṭṭhi ... esāmagandho.* 'Tainted fare' is K.R. Norman's PTS translation of this expression.

48 MN I 401ff refers to 'a world beyond' (*para loka*). In the context, though, I think it refers to rebirth, using the term world as metaphor for an individual's experiential 'world'.

49 SN IV 54.

50 SN IV 52.

51 SN II 15f.

52 AN IV 431f.

53 SN IV 93.

54 This expression is borrowed from Johansson (1979).

55 See, for example, the *Aṭṭhakanāgara Sutta*, at MN I 349ff. See also AN I 342ff.

56 *Vivicca kāmahi vivicca akusalehi dhammehi.*

57 *Abhisaṃkhatam abhisañcetayitaṃ.*

58 *Upekhā* is usually translated as equanimity, but I think non-partiality better conveys the point of non-attachment, which arises through perceiving the like nature of all things.

59 MN I 352: *Rūpasaññānaṃ samatikkamā ... anantaṃ viññāṇaṃ ... ākiñcaññāyatanaṃ.* My interpretations of these terms are intended to draw out the point(s) they are making.

60 *Mahāniddesa*, Vol I, p. 222; and cf. Chapter Five, n.15.

61 *Manomāya.*

62 MN I 410 describes *devā arūpino*, formless (that is, abstract) beings, as *saññāmayā* (conceptually created).

63 AN III 122.

64 DN I 78.

65 Ibid.

66 DN II 89.

67 SN III 87.

68 MN I 59. Since Aldous Huxley's book *The Doors of Perception* in 1954, and more prolifically in the sixties, we have been familiar with the idea of 'mind-expanding' drugs that break down the barriers of normal perception. And though, like the Buddha two and a half thousand years ago, most contemporary Indian religious teachers have taken pains to reject the efficacy of the use of *any* drugs for spiritual purposes, there are nevertheless some parallels to the point being made.

69 SN IV 93.

CHAPTER EIGHT

A World of Metaphor: Continuity, Death and Ethics

"For whatever a man sows, that will he also reap."
Galatians 6, v.7.

In earlier chapters of this book, I have in many contexts referred to the way certain of the teachings found in the early texts can be, and in some cases are best, understood in terms of metaphor. Some have been new or extended suggestions made by me, and some that I have included by way of illustration or comparability have been previously suggested by others and subsequently widely recognised. The question that arises from all such suggestions is whether or not the Buddha, or the compilers of the texts, intended these teachings to be interpreted metaphorically. To what extent, in other words, is one introducing a new way of interpreting the material that might in fact distort the way they were originally intended to be understood? In this chapter, I want to suggest that in fact the use of metaphor was an accepted didactic device from the beginning of the tradition. Further, I will also suggest that losing sight of this style of teaching has contributed to the way certain of the teachings came to be understood as they have over time. In the light of this, and of the metaphorical framework I have established, I will discuss references to Māra, variously a tempter figure, the supervisor of hellish realms, and a representative of death (*māra* means death), and the way these relate to ignorance. And I will go on to discuss the way one might understand certain issues that relate to continuity – that is, how one might understand dependent origination and karma (that actions have consequences) – not in terms of causation but of choice. In tandem with this I will consider the Buddha's concept of personal responsibility, the promise of being able to change and improve one's experience, and the possibility of freedom from rebirth.

First, then, to what extent were the early teachings intended to be interpreted in terms of metaphor? Of course, in real terms one cannot know the answer to this, as Richard Gombrich has pointed out.[1] We cannot actually determine the intentions of the Buddha himself, other early preachers and preservers of the teachings, or the compilers of the texts. But I think one can suggest from the evidence contained in the texts with which I am concerned in this book, and the way slightly later Buddhists themselves referred to them, that metaphor was widely used, not just as an occasional illustrative device but because it best served the conveying of the metaphysics underlying the teachings. I think the extent of the use of expressions that make little sense *unless* taken as metaphors in itself suggests that their use cannot have been either accidental or confined only to one or two specific aspects of the teachings. Relevant here is the point I mentioned in a slightly different context in the Introduction, that the Theravāda Buddhist *Abhidhamma* scholars pronounced the style of *all* of the early *Sutta Piṭaka* material to be figurative, just 'a way of putting things' (*pariyāya*). The reason for this, according to the Abhidhammikas, was that in the early stages of the tradition didactic devices were of prime importance. Neither the Buddha nor his immediate followers, the earliest entourage of peripatetic teachers, saw their role in terms of recording 'the Buddhist teachings' in the sense of 'a system of thought'. Rather, their aim was to convey to their audience of the moment something that audience could understand and that would contribute to their gaining Enlightenment. Here lies the origin of the traditionally accepted point that on hearing or coming across the teachings of Buddhism one should understand them not according to a teacher's rules or any intrinsic doctrinal criteria but according to one's own abilities. Because needs and abilities varied from audience to audience, so the teachings were not always given in precisely the same way. But, as any teacher knows, whatever the specific needs of an audience the use of analogy and metaphor, and figurative ways of putting things in general, provide one with powerful didactic devices for the communicating of points that are unfamiliar, elusive, complex, counter-intuitive, and so on. It was on the grounds that this is what the early teachers did that the later Abhidhammikas were able to claim that what they were doing was interpreting and explaining the earlier figurative and *ad hominem* teachings in non-figurative, 'definitively put' terms (*nippariyāyena*) in their own texts. Unlike the earlier teachers, they were looking at the material as a whole in the sense of 'a system of thought'.

The most common and consistently used metaphors in the early texts are those I discussed in Chapter Four. The idea that one's continuity in the cycle of rebirth is fuelled by the fact that one is 'on fire', an idea that is itself then expressed in a variety of ways in different contexts, powerfully illustrates the way one's ignorance and appetitive intentions need to be understood. The metaphor conveys not just the fuelling of continuity but its power, volatility, the need to keep it under control, and, because the fire is destructive of one's best interests, that the aim is to put it out. It is infinitely more illustrative of the point being made, for example, than are the statements that 'cravings bring about *dukkha*' (which is the second Noble Truth) and that 'karma is intention', which not only relate to the same point but are also generally and interchangeably taken as the correct doctrinal way of making the point.

Similarly, the metaphor of the stream, current, whirlpool of life after life, clearly conveys the relentlessness of continuity if great effort is not expended on doing something about escaping from its bondage. And the notion that gaining insight involves going *against* the stream or current indicates the radical nature of what is involved, and that achieving it will be no small or simple task. The aim, though, is the peace of freeing oneself from the flow of the current in which one is caught, of gaining the further shore that is nirvana.

No-one would take such metaphors literally. We know we are not in the literal sense either on fire or in a current of water. Furthermore, no-one is confused by the use of both the metaphors: one has no difficulty grasping the point being made by each and how they relate. This is the case even though if taken literally the metaphors are incompatible, since the water would extinguish the fire. Rather, one understands that the notion of the peaceful shore is analogous to the notion of the cool that comes with the cessation of the fire, and that both are used as further metaphors for nirvana.

Situations where the metaphor is less obvious are more problematic, however, particularly if the juxtaposition of two or more terms is involved in a single metaphor. I discussed earlier the way *dukkha*, the *khandhas* and *loka* (the world) are juxtaposed in certain contexts, for example. I was in fact suggesting that the way to understand the equating of the *khandhas* with *dukkha*, as in the first Noble Truth and elsewhere, is in the light of the way *dukkha* is sometimes juxtaposed with the term for world, and in the further light of understanding that the world is a metaphor for the life of the individual. That is, that all three terms refer in effect to the way one's experience (*dukkha*), the apparatus of which is one's *khandhas*, is one's world (*loka*). And that as the teachings are designed to enable one to understand one's world of experience by means of understanding the operating of one's *khandhas*, and so bring about the ability to achieve liberation from rebirth, the attaining of that understanding, Enlightenment, can be indicated by expressions such as "the ceasing of all the *khandhas* that are *dukkha*",[2] becoming a "world-ender",[3] and the "attaining of the end of the world".[4] These expressions, however, refer to the cessation of ignorance, because it is that that is the primary condition for continuity. It is because one is ignorant that one is on fire, or caught in the current. Enlightenment is insight into how continuity works, which enables one to effect the ceasing of this fundamental fuel of continuity. So though the point is that one will no longer experience rebirth, because one's *khandhas* are no longer operating ignorantly and one has overcome the limitations of the experiential world in the way described in the last chapter, it is *not* the case that all experience, cognitive processing and worldly life are instantaneously extinguished. The Buddha continued to live an apparently normal life for forty-five years after his own Enlightenment.

Unlike teachings where the terminology used is obviously meant to be understood metaphorically, such as those involving fire and current, the *dukkha*/*khandha*/world teachings have not previously been recognised as collectively and interrelatedly relating to the metaphor of an individual's pre-Enlightenment life. Though the metaphorical nature of references to the world have begun to be pointed out in recent years,[5] failure to recognise it in the early stages of the tradition no doubt contributed to the development of the complex cosmology of later Theravāda Buddhism, which to all intents and purposes is understood realistically.

One might suggest in this instance that provided the metaphor is given due consideration there is no reason why it should not stand alongside such a cosmology. That is to say, why should one not see the metaphor of the individual's world, which is the focus of his meditative practices on the path to his Enlightenment, fitting in to the overall picture of the world in the realistic cosmological sense?

In some respects, there is no reason why one should not see it like this. The Buddha himself is reported to have referred to one's being "a phenomenon which is a world in the world".[6] And there is absolutely no suggestion, as I discussed in the last chapter, of the reality of the world of experience being denied. But though the individual's world as the focus of his problem is recognised here, this as it were 'double picture' understanding of the world overlooks the significance of the connection of the world metaphor with *dukkha* and the *khandhas*. It furthers the false notion of the individual me in the external world, rather than drawing out the way the individual's world of experience is not other than the world as such. In short, it overlooks the metaphysics of the situation as a whole.

In my opinion it is the long term and persisting failure to recognise the extent of the *dukkha*/*khandha*/world metaphor that has contributed to the failure to understand what the metaphysics of the situation is. Indeed, it is only if one relates the subjective and objective aspects of experience by means of these three aspects of the metaphor that the metaphysical implications are suggested. And this is important because the significance of understanding the point of this complex metaphor is not just of theoretical interest. It is intimately and crucially intrinsic to what the following of Buddhist teachings is about, what is involved, and the extent and profundity of what one is aiming to gain insight into. This extent and profundity are particularly important for early Buddhism because later Buddhists pointed all sorts of critical fingers at early Buddhists for their insularity, narrowness and self-centred understanding of the teachings. That is to say, the accusations focused on what was claimed to be the selfish aim for nirvana on the part of early Buddhists, to the exclusion of compassion for the welfare of others, and their failure to understand the generic nature of dependent origination. I shall be returning to the issue of compassion below, but it is already more than clear that the criticism of early Buddhist teachings with regard to their limited application of dependent origination was not justified, at least in principle. It is nevertheless possible that by the second or third generation of early Buddhists they themselves did not realise the full import of their teachings if they failed to grasp this specific use of metaphor. And if this was the case, their mis-grasping of the teachings may have been compounded in other ways that collectively opened them to justified criticism.

The use of the *dukkha/khandha/*world metaphor to indicate the way the teachings are focused on their implied metaphysics, insight into which is accessible subjectively, is in my opinion not just the utilisation of a didactic device as in other contexts. Because the ontological status both of what is dependently originated – that is, the experiential world – and of whatever else there is – that is, what the experiential world is dependent on – cannot be stated in terms of any of the usual categories of existence, non-existence and so on, the metaphor serves to point to the focus of the teachings without being ontologically misleading. Because it is a metaphor, whatever it predicates is automatically accompanied by a qualifying 'as it were'. It is not, that is to say, putting forward any specific, and therefore intrinsically misleading, 'view'. Quite apart from the obvious and widespread use in the early material of metaphors, analogies, allegories, and so on, only some of which have I related in this book, which together compellingly suggest that such devices were consciously utilised in the giving of teachings of a variety of kinds, it is in my opinion highly likely that the metaphor associated with the world in the broadest sense, and its association with *dukkha* and the *khandhas*, was also used consciously.

Another term I think was consciously used metaphorically is Māra. Māra appears in the texts in various guises as the personification of death. As such, he became a pan-Buddhist phenomenon, represented as the Lord of the cycle of life (that is, being subject to repeated death and subsequent rebirth), pictured in Tibetan representations of the wheel of life, for example, as the horrific and monstrous overseer of the cyclical process, devourer of liberating knowledge. Personified, he tries to tempt people from following the right path, from attaining liberation, and so on. He is said to be the supervisor of the hellish realms where people will go if they follow him. According to the early tradition, shortly after the Buddha attained Enlightenment, Māra appeared before him and tried to tempt the Buddha away from helping others to gain Enlightenment by offering him a retinue of nymphs who would for incalculable aeons provide a wide variety of services for his sensory delight. Naturally the Buddha resisted this temptation, and went instead to teach the Four Noble Truths in his first sermon, and then to spend the rest of his life spreading his teachings. This particular story is part of a general Theravāda Buddhist life of the Buddha myth which is intended both to indicate his extraordinary greatness and to highlight certain factors involved in attempting to tread a similar path for oneself. That is to say, the myth is both hagiographic and didactic, but not historical. Some aspects of the myth are also intended to indicate the erroneous strictures of other religious teachers. The account of the Buddha's leaving of his wife and son in order to seek Enlightenment, for example, has no historical foundation. Rather, it makes the point that in the following of a spiritual path it is not necessary to follow the Brahmanical injunctions to the householder life.

Outside this traditional myth, Māra appears in several contexts in the early *Sutta Piṭaka* material, the most concentrated references being found in the *Māra Saṃyutta*.[7] Here are recounted numerous occasions on which the Buddha is visited by Māra for the purpose of distracting him from his certainty that he will no longer be reborn, of causing the Buddha to feel fear and anxiety, of asserting that there is no point in others following the Buddha's teachings, of discouraging people from expending effort to achieve liberation from rebirth, of asserting that rebirth is something to be desired rather than overcome, of the Buddha's incompetence to teach others, even of accusing the Buddha of unjustifiably taking time off the task in hand. The Buddha is able to see and resist or overcome all such so-called visitations from Māra. Māra also takes on other shapes in order to provide a distraction at a key moment in the Buddha's delivering of a sermon so that the audience will miss the point of it. In one case, for example, Māra becomes a bullock whose wandering through the audience threatens to cause breakage to a nearby pile of pottery bowls. In another he creates the sound of an earthquake. In both cases, the Buddha recognises the distraction for what it is and is able to explain to his audience that it is essential that they do not allow their attention to be diverted and so fail to understand the teaching he is giving them.[8]

The point of Māra being the personification of death is indicated in that the cycle of lives is referred to as the 'stream of Māra', and when one achieves liberation one has 'cut across the stream'.[9] Put differently, Māra represents the almost infinitely wide variety of un-Enlightened states of mind, all of which in turn can be understood as aspects of ignorance, as opposed to liberating insight. In the Buddhist scheme of things, each individual's primary existential problem is his ignorance, and the rationale of the teachings is that each individual has the potential to solve his problem by gaining insight. The reason ignorance is of primary concern is that it is the conditioning factor of all consequential actions. In particular, it is because of ignorance as to the nature of Reality that one persists in having desires and cravings, not realising that they are the fuel of continuity in the cycle of rebirth. Conversely, Enlightenment, which is the cessation of ignorance, brings with it the cessation of all continuity-producing negative states of mind, of whatever kind or degree.

Māra, then, can be seen as a metaphor not just for death but for all negative states of mind – or, more generically, for ignorance. As such, one can see that what is being suggested in the passages cited above is the way one's own negative states of mind threaten to distract one's concentration, to subvert one's purpose, to dislodge one's achievements. The examples indicate that even in moments of certainty, one can be assailed by the fear which doubt brings if one is not resolute. Similarly, however much one is intent on understanding something, one can be distracted at a crucial moment if one's guard is down. And however much one has achieved, one can throw it all away in a single instance of failure to understand that the maintaining of the achievement is incompatible with thoughtless self-indulgence. And so on. Moreover, they indicate the way we usually see distraction of whatever kind as something that happens *to* us. Something outside of us is the tempter, the diversion, the exploiter, the frightener, or the confuser. Each and any of these we see, to put it in Buddhist terms, as Māra intent on doing us ill. But what is being suggested by the way the metaphor relates to one's own state of mind is that it is in fact in our own control. It is entirely up to us to resist fear, ignore the distraction, refuse to be diverted, be steadfast at all costs.

Later in the *Māra Saṃyutta* this point is made specifically with regard to sexual indulgence in the story of how Māra's daughters set out to seduce the Buddha, specifically in order to cause great disturbance in his mind. Perennially, finding someone distractingly sexually attractive is seen in this format: that it is they (almost invariably female) who set out to seduce, and the seduced is in effect their defenceless victim. But here it is the daughters' names, Craving, Discontent and Passion, that draw attention to the fact that they themselves are not to be seen as the tempters, but that what they represent is oneself seeking the indulgence of desires.[10] In another text, we read the Buddha describing sense pleasures, discontent, hunger and thirst, craving, laziness, fear, doubt, hypocrisy, obstinacy, self-congratulation, and so on, in terms of 'the armies of Māra', who is the 'kinsman of the negligent'. The only way the armies can be overcome is through insight. But once insight has been achieved, and such states of mind have been understood as they really are, one is able to resist them however much they arise (the armies are said to have accompanied the Buddha step by step, in vain, for seven years) to the point that they disappear. Even those on the path to insight can, with vigilance, make progress in spite of the attacking armies of such negative states of mind.[11]

Each of us, then, is Māra to ourselves. If we are negligent, we allow armies of negative states of mind successfully to overwhelm us. And, since insight is the only efficacious weapon that can repel such armies, our negligence, and their success, are dependent on whatever is our state and degree of ignorance. And for so long as we retain any state and degree of ignorance, it is in this way that we fuel our continuity and condition the circumstances of future lives. In this sense, Māra is indeed the supervisor of hellish realms, in that the more gross the self-indulgence or the more negative the states of mind, the more unfavourable will be the circumstances of a future life or lives. Following the metaphor, the hellish realm is not so much a spacial location as a distinctly undesirable – hellish – set of circumstances. One might suggest that Māra is not just a metaphor for death rather than liberation, but also for the psychological and cognitive 'living death' one can bring upon oneself if one ends up in appalling conditions. Examples given in the texts for such conditions are graphically horrendous, both in physical and in psychological terms.[12]

From this can be seen the intimate, indeed intrinsic, association of insight and behaviour. Another way of putting this would be in terms of the profoundly ethical implications of the metaphysics of dependent origination, referred to earlier. Ignorance consists primarily of our failure to understand we are not in fact separately independent in the way that we think we are. And it is this failure that leads us to behave as desirers, craving things we also mistakenly perceive separately, and having all manner of self-centred aspirations and responses, and self-absorbed, narrowly subjectively focused states of mind. All these activities and their consequences constitute the operation of karma as taught by the Buddha, explained in the second Noble Truth as the way one's experience (*dukkha*) is fuelled.[13]

The way to overcome this, then, is to see the way one's self-centredness is entirely detrimental for one's well-being in the long run, however much one might feel self-indulgently, even self-righteously, fulfilled in the short term. And in the long-term process, one gains insight into the way one is responsible not just for present states of mind and actions, but for one's present and future circumstances also. Future beneficial circumstances, and indeed spiritual progress on the path to Enlightenment, are dependently originated in present vigilance against the armies of Māra. This metaphor ties in with the metaphor of needing to guard the sense-doors, referred to earlier. Neither is about not literally allowing something to invade; rather, each refers to how one responds and behaves in any given circumstance – to controlling oneself, not to controlling something else.

Initially, according to Buddhist teachings, one needs to expend considerable effort on the setting out on and following of the path: right effort is one of the eight aspects of the Noble Eightfold Path itself. But at the heart of the metaphysics of dependent origination lies the paradox that if the manner in which human beings exist is not independent then there is no place for any notion, let alone any possibility of the experience, of individual liberation in the self-gratifying or self-congratulatory sense. This point is implicit in references in the texts to the way insight and ethical behaviour interact in a mutually 'cleansing' way, and their presence in an individual is mutually correlated.[14] The point of the reference to cleansing is to the overcoming of negative states of mind, and the correlation relates both cognitive and affective aspects of one's mind in the broadest sense. Progress on the Buddhist path is clearly understood to result in progressively less self-centred outlook and behaviour. This is classically expressed in Buddhism as having compassion at the same time as gaining wisdom.

Compassion is more overtly associated with later, Mahāyāna, forms of Buddhism than with early Buddhism. Or, rather, Mahāyāna Buddhism makes greater claims to practising it in that they claim the superiority of their path on the grounds not just of the absence of a proper understanding of dependent origination in early Buddhism, as described above, but also of a lack of proper compassion for others. Whatever was the state of Buddhism at the time of such claims, which may or may not have justified them, in early Buddhism the notion of compassion is both implicitly and explicitly central to the following of the path.

In the first instance, the giving of the teachings by the Buddha is said to be out of compassion for others. And he subsequently exhorted others to spread the teachings for the same reason. The giving of the teachings is, indeed, said to be the greatest gift one can give to another person, because it enables them to make progress on their own path to achieving the cessation of *dukkha*. As well as this, in his first sermon the Buddha taught the Noble Eightfold Path, with its profoundly ethical suggestions in terms of practising right thought, speech, action, livelihood, and so on. There are also passages, classically the *Sīgalovāda Sutta*,[15] in which the way one's relationships, with one's spouse, family members, friends, strangers, and others, are encouraged to be based on respect, kindness, consideration, sympathy, courtesy, and so on. And there are numerous references, some of which I have mentioned, to the need to overcome the broad spectrum of negative states of mind that are summed up as greed (that is, whatever is self-interested) and hatred (that is, whatever is against the interests of others). As well as this, key meditation practices involve the extending of loving kindness, sympathetic joy for others, compassion and impartiality as previously explained; and selfless love is said to be a vehicle for achieving mental freedom.[16] If one were to achieve the putting into practice of all these qualities, one would, I think, be as near to living altruistically as it would be possible to live. In other words, no overt claims to a teaching of compassion seem necessary here.[17]

What is not found in the early texts is anything more specifically exhortatory or even advisory about exactly how to put compassion into practice. This would directly contravene the whole point of accepting personal responsibility that is so fundamentally a part of the Buddha's teachings, in contrast to the Brahmanical religion of his time. According to the Buddha, it is up to each person to act compassionately in their own way. Similarly, because of the centrality of accepting personal responsibility, which is correlated to understanding that what is consequential are one's intentions, what is also not found is any associating of compassion with helping others in the sense of enabling them to bypass their own responsibilities. Compassion is often understood in the sense of an altruistic willingness to do something *for* someone. And conversely, if one does not do so, one can be thought of as lacking compassion. This is a topical issue today as many peoples and societies, small and large, local and even international, struggle to decide whether it is as compassionate, in every sense, or more, or less so, to help people to help themselves rather than to do something on their behalf so they need not do it at all. I suspect that much of the contemporary dilemma originates in the extent to which the structure of the great theistic religions of the West has permeated the worldview of the developed world. In the overall context of spiritual progress as presented in the early Buddhist material, however, it is clear that making progress cannot be achieved by anyone except oneself. Compassion lies in seeing and effecting what will best help someone to help themselves; and this is in fact the most profoundly constructive thing one can do for another person.[18]

That this sometimes involves choosing the lesser of two evils, in the sense that helping someone to help themselves might involve hurting them in order to assist them in avoiding a greater pain in progress terms, is made explicitly clear. The Buddha explains this with the analogy of helping a baby who has something stuck in his throat: getting it out might involve drawing blood. In such situations, it is the assisted person's long-term good that is of central concern, though it is also essential that in such circumstances one's actions are motivated by love.[19]

I think all of the teachings with regard to accepting personal responsibility need to be understood in this context of love, or compassion. The aim to achieve un-self-ishness comes about through insight into inter-connectedness. And what one is connected with is, or gradually becomes, of as central a concern to one's actions as is one's own well-being. Thus love, or compassion, is inseparable from the efficacy of one's actions. The point is to act harmlessly, and it would be grossly to distort the message of the Buddha's teachings to omit this from the picture of accepting personal responsibility. While there may not be any detailed ethical injunctions as such in the teachings, and while one might therefore suggest that ethical issues are to a large extent open to interpretation according to circumstances, the accepting of personal responsibility in making decisions and choices is properly understood only in the context of aiming for harmlessness in the sense of having the interests of others, rather than oneself, genuinely at heart.

The importance of understanding the complex *dukkha*/*khandha*/world metaphor is also relevant here in that the wider metaphysics it alludes to indicates the extent and profundity of the effect of one's actions, conditioned as they are by one's state of mind, not just on one's subjective continuity but also on the entirety of its objective correlate. What it implies is that one's personal responsibility is not just linear; that is to say, it is not just one's own continuity for which one is responsible. Rather, whatever state one is in subjectively is correlated objectively. Thus one is responsible not just for the neutrally cognitive structural aspects of objectivity, but also for its qualitative aspects. Indeed *whatever* is part of objectivity is subjectively dependent, even if it be hurricane, desertification or famine. To a certain extent it is not difficult to see that this is demonstrably the case. But what the Buddhist teachings suggest is that the correlation is connected primarily through the matrix of subjective states of mind, what today would be called attitude. For example, it is not simply that one physically cuts down rainforests, but that one should *want* to, that is the origin both of the climate in which such exploitation can flourish and of the subsequent physical devastation. In this respect, responsibility has a collective and far reaching dimension in the Buddhist schema. Many of the appalling conditions in which people find themselves are the result not just of their own actions but of all of our actions.[20]

Though the Buddha's teachings clearly indicate the need to understand this 'as you sow, so shall you reap' mechanics of one's circumstances, one of the ways in which dependent origination is explained is in my view somewhat misleading unless other aspects of the teachings are taken into consideration when interpreting it. A formula is given for dependent origination as follows:

> When this is, that is;
> This occurring, that occurs;
> When this is not, that is not;
> This ceasing, that ceases.[21]

The way this is worded suggests that dependent origination is a system of causation in the a causes b pattern. But I think that in order to understand it accurately, one has to see it not in terms of causation but of origination. What I mean is that dependent origination is not stating that a will cause b, but that b occurs because there was a. Further, to grasp the mechanics better one needs to see it in the even looser sense that if there is a b, then there must have been an a.

The significance of my point lies in connecting the mechanics of dependent origination with the ethical dimension of the teachings, and the fact that the accepting of personal responsibility is so cardinal to what the Buddha taught. What is crucial about the adjustment I am suggesting is that it highlights the possibility of freedom of choice that is essential if any notion of being personally responsible for one's behaviour, and making moral decisions, is to have any credibility. Though wherever one is is conditioned by previous actions in their broadest sense, one is not bound to proceed in a narrowly specific way. One can make a wide range of choices, conditioned only by the specifics of one's situation at any given time. Though one cannot, that is to say, choose to scuba dive if one is in the Highlands of Scotland, one *can* choose better or worse courses of action or response in any given set of circumstances. One is free to follow one's conscience or not at any given time. One is free to do what one knows is right however difficult it may be to do so.

Indeed, as I said in Chapter Three, this is a profoundly demanding ethical path to follow. One cannot deny that one is free to choose a difficult path just because it is difficult. Nor can one claim that the armies of Māra are outside one. Both would be ways of devolving responsibility.[22] Furthermore, in the Buddhist worldview one's responsibility has ramifications over many life-times. One cannot claim one is not responsible for where one starts in any given life because all aspects of this would be conditioned in previous aspects of one's continuity. Added to this are the implications for each person of the inseparability of all aspects of the experiential world. This is highlighted by the nature of the metaphors that are extensively used in the early material. Fire, stream, forest, house, village and town, indeed all aspects of the world as we know it, stand as objective correlates to their subjective counterparts in one's metaphorically indicated subjective world.

Freedom of choice of action is what makes it possible for the Buddha to state that one is able to improve and change one's experience. His teachings advocate coming to terms with wherever one is, understanding the history of all of the factors involved in that situation, and accepting that any improvement is entirely in one's own hands. They indicate how one can come to understand the mechanics both of one's past and also of one's future. However much some might associate a metaphysics of impermanence with imperfection, unreliability, uncertainty, unpredictability, and so on, in fact what impermanence allows is change in the positive sense of growth, progress, improvement, achievement. This is why Buddhists regard the teachings as offering an opportunity to achieve the highest goal open to human beings: seeing how things really are.

Notes

1 Chapter 3, 'Metaphor, Allegory, Satire', in Richard Gombrich's *How Buddhism Began*, to which I have referred before, is a highly relevant discussion of these issues in the early stages of Buddhism.

2 Found frequently throughout the *Nidāna Saṃyutta*.

3 AN II 6, IV 432.

4 SN IV 93.

5 See, for example, Harvey (1995b), chapter 5. Harvey discusses the metaphor alongside a distinction between self and Self, which I think is unnecessary.

6 SN III 139.

7 SN I 103ff. See also Gombrich, 1996, chapter 3, for other references and a discussion of Māra.

8 All these examples are in the *Māra Saṃyutta*.

9 MN I 225f. cf. also *Sutta Nipāta* 715, 948.

10 SN I 124f. Liz Wilson (1996) interestingly discusses the negative female imagery found in Pali material from a feminist point of view. But in my opinion this is to overlook that much of it is to be understood in the metaphorical way I am suggesting here.

11 This story is the subject of chapter III.2 of the *Sutta Nipāta*.

12 See in particular the *Devadūta Sutta*, MN III 178ff, for the physical horrors, and SN IV 126 for the psychological horror of regarding every aspect of one's experience in repellently ugly and repulsive terms.

13 The *Nidāna Saṃyutta*, the key text on dependent origination, discusses dependent origination almost interchangeably with karma (SN, Vol II). Many examples of how a range of behaviours result in a corresponding range of rebirths are given in the *Cūḷakammavibhaṅga Sutta*, MN III 202ff.

14 DN I 124.

15 DN III 180ff.

16 SN II 264ff.

17 See Gombrich, 1998, for a discussion along these lines.

18 MN I 392ff.

19 Ibid, p. 395, and AN III 6.

20 The way the actions of others affect us is referred to at SN II 38. That the origin of one's circumstances is more complex than simply one's own previous actions is mentioned in several other contexts, for example SN IV 210f, 230f; AN II 87. These do not specifically make the collective point, however; this is implicit in the metaphysics.

21 For example, at MN III 63; SN II 28, 95.

22 I see strong parallels between the Buddhist view of freedom of action and responsibility and some of Isaiah Berlin's comments in his essay 'Historical Inevitability', most recently published in *The Proper Study of Mankind*, Farrar, Straus and Giroux, 1998. cf. also Gombrich, 1992a, p. 249.

POSTSCRIPT

On What is a human being?

Much is written on this subject, from Locke to modern animalist approaches. As I write, biologists vie with psychologists, philosophers with clerics, and all with each other, about what we are. Such is the interest, that a significant number of books on the subject have become highly debated and sometimes influential bestsellers. Given that the focus of the Buddhist teachings is the human being, one or two comments regarding some contemporary concerns are apposite.

Whatever the discipline, current questions often focus on questions such as What if your cerebrum is transplanted into another body: have you lost your cerebrum or gained a body? The point of such speculation is to be able adequately to define what a 'person' is. Some of this is important for legislative purposes, particularly for the establishing of ethical standards in relevant areas. But to submit the Buddhist understanding of the person, such as it is ascertainable, to any such speculation is in my view unhelpful and anachronistic. The Buddha's teachings were about and for healthily normal human beings, in the sense of those who are capable of freely choosing to follow them, at a time when any such gross tampering with living beings was simply, and in my view mercifully, unimaginable. The Buddha and his disciples knew perfectly well who the subjects of the teachings were, and the very idea of a 'definition' as such would have seemed bizarre. As my description of the operating of the *khandhas* has shown, there is no idea of one being a body with a detachable psychological appendage: the body is intrinsic to the operating of the cognitive apparatus as a whole, which includes the complexities of one's emotional, appetitive, intellectual, psychological, aesthetic – and so on – make-up. The whole package, *including* one's body, has been fuelled by previous volitional activities, as is graphically illustrated in the textual passage I have referred to more than once which states that one's volitional activities volitionally construct the conditioned body, sensations, apperceptions, volitional activities and consciousness.

Furthermore, it seems to me that the whole notion of identity in the sense of What am I? is only meaningful if associated with the notion of self-consciousness. Dogs do not think 'I am a dog; What is a dog?', and non sentient things are simply objects which human beings have given names to. We may ask rhetorically What is it that makes this a book? But in fact it is a book because human beings have decided to call what it is a book. And we all know what dogs are: a definition is wholly superfluous. Any suggestion that it might be problematic that human beings are both animals and persons seems to me to be perverse. Why cannot we share certain biological characteristics with other animals and at the same time not share other characteristics? The Buddhist teachings are clearly focused in this way in that while the sentience of all sorts of beings is recognised, the teachings themselves are for humans – that is, for sentient beings who know what self-consciousness is.

In Buddhism, the cardinal starting point is in any case existential and not theoretical, with one's own experience of subjectivity. Aspects of this experience vary from person to person in a wide variety of ways. This much is evidenced nowadays by the plethora of contemporary material describing the nature of the person with which one is either hard put to find any common experiential criteria whatsoever, or about which one is left incredulous that so much of importance can have been omitted. And variety is readily acknowledged in the early Buddhist texts. But that we are self conscious experiencing subjects is generic to all people. However much we differ from each other in the character of our emotional, appetitive, intellectual, psychological, aesthetic – and so on – make-up, Buddhist teachings focus on our generically common experiencing apparatus, in whatever state it happens to be right now. It is this that makes Buddhism of relevance to anyone anywhere at any time.

Bibliography

I have used the Pali Text Society editions of all Pali texts and quote from them by permission of the Pali Text Society which owns the copyright to the works. Where references are given to published translations of Pali Texts these are also to Pali Text Society editions, but all translations given in the book are my own unless otherwise stated.

Adikaram, E.H. *Early History of Buddhism in Ceylon.* Colombo: M.D. Gunasena, (repr.) 1953.

Ahmad, Aijaz. *In Theory.* London: Verso, 1992.

Aramaki, Noritoshi. "A Text-strata-analytical Interpretation of the Concept *pañcaskandhas*" in *The Humanities*, Vol. XXVI, Kyoto University, 1980.

——. "The Fundamental Truth of Buddhism: Pratītyasamutpāda" in *Machikaneyama-Ronso*, No. 22, Faculty of Letters, Osaka University, 1988.

Basham, A.L. *The History and Doctrine of the Ājīvikas.* Delhi: Motilal Banarsidass, 1951.

Bastow, David. "Levels of self-awareness in Pali Buddhism" in *Scottish Journal of Religious Studies*, Spring, 1994, pp. 5–20.

——. "Debates on Time in the *Kathāvatthu*" in *Buddhist Studies Review*, 13, 2, 1996, pp. 109–32.

Bechert, Heinz. "Theravāda Buddhist Sangha: Some General Observations on Historical and Political Factors in its Development" in *Journal of Asian Studies*, 29, 1970, pp. 761–78.

Bechert, Heinz and Gombrich, Richard (eds) *The World of Buddhism.* London: Thames and Hudson, 1984.

Bodhi, Bhikkhu. "*Khandha* and *Upādānakkhandha*" in *Pali Buddhist Review*, Vol. I, No. 1, 1976, pp. 91–102.

Boisvert, Mathieu. *The Five Aggregates: Understanding Theravāda Psychology and Soteriology.* Canada: Wilfrid Laurier University Press, 1995.

Brereton, Joel. *The Rigvedic Adityas.* New Haven: American Oriental Society, 1981.

Bronkhorst, Johannes. *Two Traditions of Meditation in Ancient India.* Delhi: Motilal Banarsidass, (repr.) 1998.

Boyd, James. "Symbols of Evil in Buddhism" in *Journal of Asian Studies*, 31, 1971, pp. 63–75.

Carter, J.R. *Dhamma: A Study of a Religious Concept*. Tokyo: Hokuseido Press, 1978.

Carus, Paul. *Nirvana: A story of Buddhist Psychology*. New Delhi: Asian Educational Services, (repr.) 1997.

Collins, Steven. *Selfless Persons*. Cambridge: Cambridge University Press, 1982.

——. "On the Very Idea of the Pali Canon" in *The Journal of the Pali Text Society*, 15, 1990, pp. 89–126.

——. "Notes on some oral aspects of Pali literature" in *Indo-Iranian Journal*, 35, 1992, pp. 121–35.

——. "What are Buddhists *Doing* When They Deny the Self?" in Frank E. Reynolds and David Tracy (eds) *Religion and Practical Reason*. New York: State University of New York Press, 1994, pp. 59–85.

——. "A Buddhist Debate about the Self; and remarks on Buddhism in the work of Derek Parfit and Galen Strawson". Unpublished paper.

——. *Nirvana and other Buddhist felicities*. Cambridge: Cambridge University Press, 1998.

Copleston, F.C. *Aquinas*. London: Penguin, 1955.

Cousins, L.S. "The *Paṭṭhāna* and the Development of the *Theravādin Abhidhamma*" in *Journal of the Pali Text Society* Centenary Volume, 1981, pp. 22–45.

——. "Pali Oral Literature" in Denwood, P. and Piatigorsky, A. (eds) *Buddhist Studies: Ancient and Modern*. London: Curzon, 1983, pp. 1–11.

——."The 'Five Points' and the Origins of the Buddhist Schools" in Skorupski, T. (ed.) *The Buddhist Forum* Vol. II. London: SOAS, 1991, pp. 27–60.

——. "Persons and Self", a paper given at the Dhammakāya Foundation's First International Conference 'Buddhism into the Year 2000', and published as an offprint by the Dhammakāya Foundation, Bangkok, 1994.

——. "Good or Skilful? *Kusala* in Canon and Commentary" in *Journal of Buddhist Ethics*, Vol. 3, 1996, pp. 136–64.

Frauwallner, E. *The Earliest Vinaya and the Beginnings of Buddhist Literature*. Rome: Serie Orientale Roma VIII, 1956.

Freeman, J.M. *Untouchable: An Indian Life History*. London: George Allen and Unwin, 1979.

Gethin, R.M.L. "The Five *Khandhas*: their treatment in the *Nikāyas* and early Buddhism" in *Journal of Indian Philosophy*, 14, 1986, pp. 35–53.

——. *The Path to Awakening: A Study of the Thirty-Seven Bodhipakkhiyā Dhammā in the Nikāyas and Abhidhamma*. Leiden: Brill, 1992.

——. "Cosmology and Meditation: From the Aggañña-Sutta to the Mahāyāna" in *History of Religions*, Vol. 36, No. 3, 1997, pp. 183–217.

Gombrich, Richard. "Ancient Indian Cosmology" in Carmen Blacker and Michael Loewe (eds) *Ancient Cosmologies*. London: George Allen & Unwin, 1975, pp. 110–42.

——. "Notes on the Brahmanical Background to Buddhist Ethics" in Dhammapala, G. (et al) (eds) *Buddhist Studies in Honour of Hammalava Saddhātissa*. Sri Lanka: Buddhist Research Library Trust, 1984.

——. *Theravāda Buddhism*. London: Routledge and Kegan Paul, 1988.

——. "Recovering the Buddha's Message" in T. Skorupski (ed.) *The Buddhist Forum: Seminar Papers 1987–1988*. London: SOAS, 1990.

——. "Can we Know or Control our Futures?" in P. Thera, L. Perera and K. Goonesera (eds) *Buddhist Essays: A Miscellany*. London: Sri Saddhatissa International Buddhist Centre, 1992a, pp. 240–52.

——. "The Buddha's Book of Genesis" in *Indo-Iranian Journal*, 35, 1992b, pp. 159–78.

——. "Buddhist prediction: how open is the future?" in Leo Howe and Alan Wain (eds) *Predicting the Future*. Cambridge: Cambridge University Press, 1993, pp. 144–68.

——. "Selfless Buddhists: ethics without metaphysics?" Wolfson College Lecture Series *From Soul to Self*, 1996a. Publication forthcoming.

——. *How Buddhism Began: The Conditioned Genesis of the Early Teachings*. (The Louis H. Jordan Lectures, 1994) London: Athlone Press, 1996b.

——. "Kindness and Compassion as Means to Nirvana", the 1997 Gonda Lecture. Published as a paper by the Royal Netherlands Academy of Arts and Sciences, 1998.

Gonda, J. *Loka: World and Heaven in the Veda*. Amsterdam: N.V. Noord Hollandsche Uitgevers Maatschappij, 1966.

Gorak, Jan. *The Making of the Modern Canon*. London: Athlone Press, 1991.

Griffiths, Paul J. "Pure Consciousness and Indian Buddhism" in Robert K.C. Forman (ed.) *The Problem of Pure Consciousness*, Oxford: Oxford University Press, 1990, pp. 71–97.

Hallisey, Charles. "Ethical Particularism in Theravāda Buddhism" in *Journal of Buddhist Ethics*, Vol. 3, 1996, pp. 32–43.

Hamilton, Sue. "Anattā: A Different Approach" in *The Middle Way*, Vol. 70, May 1995, pp. 47–60.

——. *Identity and Experience: the Constitution of the Human Being according to Early Buddhism*. London: Luzac Oriental, 1996a.

——. "Buddhism: the Doctrinal Case for Feminism" in *Feminist Theology*, No. 12, May 1996b, pp. 91–104.

——. "Passionlessness in Buddhism" in *The Scottish Journal of Religious Studies*, Vol. XVIII, No. 1, 1997, pp. 3–23.

——. "The Centrality of Experience in the Teachings of Early Buddhism". A paper given at the British Association for the Study of Religions Conference at Manchester College, Oxford, in September 1997: publication forthcoming.

——. "The External World: its Status and Relevance in the Pali Nikayas" in *Religion*, 29, 1999, pp. 73–90.

Harris, Ian. *The Continuity of Madkyamaka and Yogācāra in Indian Mahāyāna Buddhism*. Leiden: Brill, 1991.

Harvey, Peter. *An Introduction to Buddhism*. Cambridge: Cambridge University Press, 1990.

——. "The Mind-body Relationship in Pāli Buddhism – a Philosophical Investigation" in *Asian Philosophy*, Vol. 3, No. 1, 1993, pp. 29–41.

——. "Contemporary Characterisations of the 'Philosophy' of Nikāyan Buddhism" in *Buddhist Studies Review*, Vol. 12, 2, 1995a, pp. 109–33.

——. *The Selfless Mind: Personality, Consciousness and Nirvana in Early Buddhism*. Richmond: Curzon Press, 1995b.

Hoffman, Frank J. "The Buddhist Empiricism Thesis", in *Religious Studies*, Vol. 18, 1982, pp. 151–8.

——. *Rationality and Mind in Early Buddhism*. Delhi: Motilal Banarsidass, 1987.

——. "'Orientalism' in Buddhology" in Frank J. Hoffman and Deegalle Mahinda (eds) *Pāli Buddhism*. Richmond: Curzon Press, 1996, pp. 207–66.

Husserl, E. *Ideas: General Introduction to Pure Phenomenology*. (trans. W.R. Boyce-Gibson) London: George Allen & Unwin, 1931.

Inada, K.K. *Nāgārjuna, A Translation of His Mūlamadhyamaka-kārikā with an Introductory Essay*. Tokyo: Hokuseido Publishing, 1970.

Jayatilleke, K.N. *Early Buddhist Theory of Knowledge*. Delhi: Motilal Banarsidass, (repr.) 1980.

Johansson, R.E.A. "*Citta, mano, viññāṇa* – a Psychosemantic Investigation" in *University of Ceylon Review* Vol. 23, Nos 1 & 2, 1965, pp. 165–215.

——. *The Psychology of Nirvana*. London: George Allen & Unwin, 1969.

——. *The Dynamic Psychology of Early Buddhism*. Oxford: Curzon Press, 1979.

Kalupahana, David J. Causality: *The Central Philosophy of Buddhism*. Honolulu: University of Hawaii Press, 1975.

——. *Buddhist Philosophy – A Historical Analysis*. Honolulu: University of Hawaii Press, 1976.

Karunadasa, Y. *The Buddhist Analysis of Matter*. Sri Lanka: Colombo Department of Cultural Affairs, 1967.

——. "The Buddhist Doctrine of Non-Self and the Problem of the Over-Self" in *The Middle Way*, Vol. 69, No. 2, August 1994, pp. 107–18.

Keown, Damien. *The Nature of Buddhist Ethics*. London: Macmillan, 1992.

——. *Buddhism and Bioethics*. London: Macmillan, 1995.

——. *Buddhism and Abortion*. London: Macmillan, 1998.

Keown, Damien (et al) (eds). *Buddhism and Human Rights*. London: Curzon Press, 1998.

Kloetzli, R. *Buddhist Cosmology: From Single World System to Pure Land*. Delhi: Motilal Banarsidass, 1983.

Kochumuttom, Thomas. *A Buddhist Doctrine of Experience*. Delhi: Motilal Banarsidass, 1982.

Kumar, Bimlendra. *Theory of Relations in Buddhist Philosophy*. Delhi: Eastern Book Linkers, 1988.

Lamotte, Étienne. *History of Indian Buddhism*. (translated by Sara Webb-Boin) Lourain: Institute Orientaliste, 1988 (original French edition 1958).

——. "Passions and Impregnations of the Passions in Buddhism" in L. Cousins (et al) (eds) *Buddhist Studies in Honour of I.B. Horner*. Dordrecht-Holland: D. Reidel Publishing Company, 1974.

Lang, Karen. "Meditation as a Tool for Deconstructing the Phenomenal World" in T. Skorupski (ed.) *The Buddhist Forum* Vol. III. London: SOAS, 1994, pp. 143–59.

Limaye, V.P. and Vadekar, R.D. (eds) *Eighteen Principal Upaniṣads*, Vol. I. Poona: Vaidika Saṃśokhana Maṇala, 1958.

Magee, Bryan. *Popper*. London: Fontana Paperbacks, (repr.) 1982.

——. *The Philosophy of Schopenhauer*. (2nd ed.) Oxford: Clarendon Press, 1997.

——. "Misunderstanding Schopenhauer", The 1989 Bithell Memorial Lecture. Institute of Germanic Studies, University of London, 1990.

Magee, Bryan and Milligan, Martin. *On Blindness*. Oxford: Oxford University Press, 1995.

Magee, Bryan (ed.) *Modern British Philosophy*. London: Secker & Warburg, 1971.

Masefield, Peter "Mind/Cosmos Maps in the Pāli Nikāyas" in Nathan Katz (ed.) *Buddhist and Western Psychology*. Boulder: Prajñā Press, 1983, pp. 69–93.

McDermott, J. "Scripture as Word of the Buddha" in *Numen*, Vol. 31 No. 1, 1984, pp. 22–39.

MacQueen, G. "Inspired Speech in Early Mahāyāna" in *Religion*, Vol. 11, 1981, pp. 303–19 and Vol. 12, 1982, pp. 49–65.

Monier-Williams, M. A *Sanskrit-English Dictionary*. Delhi: Motilal Banarsidass, (repr.) 1986.

Ñāṇajivako, Bhikkhu. *Schopenhauer and Buddhism*. Kandy: Buddhist Publication Society, 1970.

Ñāṇavīra Thera. *Clearing the Path*. Colombo: Path Press, 1987.

Ñāṇananda, Bhikkhu. *Concept and Reality in Early Buddhist Thought*. Sri Lanka: Buddhist Publication Society, (repr.) 1986.

Nyāṇatiloka (Fourth Revised Edition ed. by Nyanaponika) *Buddhist Dictionary: Manual of Buddhist Terms and Doctrines*. Kandy: Buddhist Publication Society, 1980.

Norman, K.R. *Pāli Literature*. Wiesbaden: Harrassowitz, 1983.

——. "A note on attā in the Alagaddūpama-Sutta" in K.R. Norman *Collected Papers*, Vol. II. Oxford: Pali Text Society, 1991, pp. 200–10.

Olendski, Andrew. "A Proposed Model of Early Buddhist Liberation" in Frank J. Hoffman and Deegalle Mahinda (eds) *Pāli Buddhism*. Richmond: Curzon Press, 1996, pp. 43–56.

Pérez-Remón, J. *Self and Non-Self in Early Buddhism*. The Hague: Mouton Publishers, 1980.

Popper, Karl R. "Philosopher of the Enlightenment: Immanuel Kant" in *The Listener*, London, February 18, 1954, pp. 291–2 & 303.

——. *The Poverty of Historicism*. London: Ark Paperbacks, (repr.) 1961.

——. *The Open Society and its Enemies*. (5th ed.) London: Routledge & Kegan Paul, (repr.) 1966.

Puligandla, Ramakrishna. "What is the Status of the Doctrine of Dependent Origination?" in Frank J. Hoffman and Deegale Mahinda (eds) *Pāli Buddhism*. Richmond: Curzon Press, 1996, pp. 175–83.

Radhakrishnan, S. (trans.) *The Principal Upaniṣads*. London: George Allen & Unwin, 1953.

Rahula, Walpola. "Wrong notions of *dhammatā*" in L.S. Cousins (et al) (eds) *Buddhist Studies in Honour of I.B. Horner*. Dordrecht-Holland: D. Reidel Publishing Company, 1974.

——. *What the Buddha Taught*. (2nd ed.) London: Gordon Fraser, (repr.) 1985.

Reat, N.Ross. "Some Fundamental Concepts of Buddhist Psychology" in *Religion* 17, 1987, pp. 15–28.

——. *Origins of Indian Psychology*. California: Asian Humanities Press, 1990.

Rhys Davids, C.A.F. *Buddhist Psychology*. London: G. Bell & Son, 1914.

Rhys Davids, T.W. and Stede, W. (eds) *Pali English Dictionary*. London: Pali Text Society, (repr.) 1986.

Röer, E. (ed.) *Bṛhadāraṇyaka Upaniṣad with the Commentary of Śaṅkara Ācārya and the gloss of Ānanda Giri*. Calcutta: Asiatic Society of Bengal, 1849.

——. *Chāndogya Upaniṣad with the Commentary of Śaṅkara Ācārya*. Calcutta: Asiatic Society of Bengal, 1850.

Ruegg, David Seyfort. *Buddha Nature, Mind and the Problem of Gradualism in a Comparative Perspective: On the Transmission and Reception of Buddhism in India and Tibet*. London: Athlone Press, 1989.

Russell, Bertrand. *A History of Western Philosophy*. (2nd ed.) London: Unwin, (repr.) 1985.

Sadakata, Akira. *Buddhist Cosmology: Philosophy and Origins*. Tokyo: Koosei Publishing Co, 1997.

Said, Edward W. *Orientalism*. New York: Vintage Books, 1979.

Skilling, Peter "On the Five Aggregates of Attachment" in *Buddha Dhyāna Dāna Review*, Vol. XXXII, No. 2, April–June 1995, pp. 39–55.

Smart, Ninian. "Theravāda and Processes: *Nirvāṇa* as a Meta-process" in Frank J. Hoffman and Deegale Mahinda (eds) *Pāli Buddhism*. Richmond: Curzon Press, 1996, pp. 196–205.

Stiver, Dan R. *The Philosophy of Religious Language: Sign, Symbol and Story*. Cambridge, MA: Blackwell Publishers, 1996.

Thomas, E.J. *The History of Buddhist Thought*. London: Routledge & Kegan Paul, 1972.

——. *The Dhammapada*. Madras: Oxford University Press, (repr.) 1988.

Upreti, G.B. *The Early Buddhist World Outlook in Historical Perspective*. New Delhi: Manohar, 1997.

Watson, Gay. "The Consciousness that Views: Some Ideas on the Self". Unpublished seminar paper given at the Buddhist Forum, SOAS, London University, March 1996.

Wells, H.G. "The Country of the Blind" in *Complete Short Stories*. London: A & C Black, (repr.) 1987.

Wijayaratne, M. *Buddhist Monastic Life*. (translated by C. Grangier and S. Collins) Cambridge: Cambridge University Press, 1990.

Williams, Paul. *Mahāyāna Buddhism: The Doctrinal Foundations*. London: Routledge and Kegan Paul, 1989.

Liz Wilson. *Charming Cadavers: Horrific Figurations of the Feminine in Indian Buddhist Hagiographic Literature*. Chicago: University of Chicago Press, 1996.

Zürcher, E. *Buddhism: its Origin and Spread in Words, Maps and Pictures*. London: Routledge & Kegan Paul, 1962.

Index